LA FONTAINE AND HIS FRIENDS

A Biography

By the same author

THE UNIVERSAL SELF
A STUDY OF PAUL VALÉRY

La Fontaine and His Friends

A BIOGRAPHY

by

Agnes Ethel Mackay

George Braziller
New York

Published in the United States of America in 1973
by George Braziller, Inc.

Copyright © 1972 by Agnes Ethel Mackay
Originally published in England by Garnstone Press, Ltd.

Standard Book Number: 0-8076-0694-4
Library of Congress Catalog Card Number: 73-79049

Printed in the United States of America

CONTENTS

74916

LIST OF ILLUSTRATIONS

LA FONTAINE AND HIS FRIENDS

A Biography

I

THE BACKGROUND

To enjoy the full significance of any particular poet, we should choose the line of approach most likely to bring us closest to him. To do this we must accept the limitations as well as the possibilities offered by the civilisation to which he belongs. Each individual poet has a limited creative range, conditioned and defined by the actual circumstances of his life. Poems spring from the sensitive response of the individual who desires to create something in a particular medium, they are not written by influences or movements: all the same we should be alive to the climate and tendencies of the time, so as to recover more fully the personal element in the poet's point of view, which is the soul of biography.

Therefore without claiming to make an academic study, I beg my readers, before they meet the poet, to consider the following brief summary of the historical and literary background of La Fontaine's genius.

Let us first consider the general literary conceptions of the poets of the early seventeenth century directly preceding La Fontaine. In the last years of the reign of Henri IV – who died in 1610 – a new social relationship between aristocrats and poets was organised, following the example of the Italian Courts. This fresh alliance between refinement and intellect owed a great deal to d'Urfé's novel *Astrée* which was the immediate source of the ideals of politeness and gallantry of the *société précieuse*. The Court learnt from the poets, and the poets for their part learnt to please the Court by giving them what they wanted; a position that led to certain serious limitations. Henceforth the cultured and spontaneous lyrics of the post-Renaissance were replaced by a school of poetry of a highly artificial and complicated kind, laborious in conception but technically negligible. Even the finest poets of the time fell under the spell of fashionable preciosity, and in the bulk of minor verse the wit of courtiers mingled with the fantasy of professional rhymers.

This trend in poetry originated in Italy in the works of Marino, and was known as Marinism; in Spain it first appeared in the verses of Gongora, who also founded a school. These two influences were merged in France, constituting Baroque poetry. '*Le chevalier Marin*,' as the French called him, was typically Italian. He has been underrated because of his often tortuous style, his far-fetched comparisons and wildly mixed metaphors. Yet at times he achieves a purity of conception, raising organic matter to a sort of spiritual substance, as in the suggestive description of a fountain. Here, fascinated by the resemblance between the infinitely vast and the infinitely small, seeing in each crystal drop the counterfeit image of the Universe, he seems to point the way to a greater sense of the universal element in poetry – a promise which however was not fulfilled in the mass of his long smooth verses so replete with fantastic analogies, in which nature, man's artifices, senses, and all kinds of phenomena, are intermingled, conveying in the most fanciful language the most trivial thoughts.

Marino's followers in France developed the movement he had set in motion, according to their capacities, from the maximum to the minimum of accomplishment; leaping from the natural to the artificial, from the pure to the precious, from the picturesque to the grotesque, often all in the same verse if not in the same breath, without any sure method or guiding principle beyond that of dazzling and intriguing their readers by effrontery and affectation.

Yet though sense was too often reduced to absurdity in their verses, many of the Baroque or Précieux poets were sensitive and impressionist. Had they not fallen victims to fashion, replacing power by rhetoric, grace by affectation, posterity would have treated them with more respect. As it is, a careful selection of their works would reveal much of real poetic value. There was Théophile de Viaud, spontaneous and charming, opposing with his brilliant fantasies the pompous reality of Malherbe's eloquence; Tristan l'Hermite, who at his best expressed a gentle melancholy in light and graceful verse; Saint-Amant the poet of Gothic solitudes, master of the grotesque, who had a tremendous sense of rhythm; François Maynard, who wrote many fine lines and certainly had a high idea of his art. These poets had personality and imagination and they all wrote some good poetry. But their general output was somehow unconvincing and flat. They had in fact neglected almost everything that the generation of poets of 1660 was to consider as essential to art; a complete reaction was inevitable against lack of technique, extravagances, prosaic negligence and above all an affected attitude towards nature, often dangerously near to burlesque. Boileau was the first to demolish the whole movement, in any case moribund and out of date. Evidently a return to technique therefore to classical models, a renewal of natural conceptions and a logical social attitude, were clearly indicated, and were characteristic of the new age.

Nevertheless before dismissing the Baroque poets, a word should be said for the group of wits and authors who frequented Mme de Rambouillet's salon in the early years of the century. Their desire was to create a more flexible and elegant language and they had a considerable cultural significance, in so far as their purpose was to discuss style in writing and to acquire elegance in conversation. They gave great importance to the meaning and value of words to express ideas, more particularly in the realm of sentiment. On the one hand they gave language greater freedom in developing the finer shades of meaning; and on the other hand by condemning many words as vulgar, and at the same time introducing an element of fastidious euphuism often reducing sense to absurdity, they paralysed the natural growth of expression. The two laureates of this movement, Voiture and Benserade, produced little except affected and often futile verses in which gallantry took the place of passion, and the great number of madrigals, written by their followers, who had learnt the trick, were merely sentimental exercises and were immensely fashionable.

This insistence on refined and extravagant language was admirably satirised by Molière in his *Précieuses Ridicules*. Possessing the same powerful gift of satire as the Greek comedian Aristophanes, Molière was the first of his generation to repudiate the artificial, hackneyed theatre which he effectively revolutionised with his earliest comedies. By this he delighted La Fontaine; both poets insisted on a return to nature, and by nature they meant a natural simplicity of direct statement expressing the truth as they saw it. Boileau had also reacted against his immediate predecessors, urging his contemporaries to return to classical models, and denouncing the Baroque poets, the burlesques of Scarron, the dull imitations of Honoré d'Urfé's pastoral *Astrée*, together with the long-winded novels of the Scudérys (brother and sister), Gauthier de la Calprenède and a host of lesser authors whose works were the common fare of the common reader.

The generation of poets to which La Fontaine, Molière, Racine and Boileau belonged, corresponds to the epoch of 1660 when the young king Louis XIV took the affairs of state into his own hands. Henceforth, thanks to the organisation imposed by Colbert, the chief activities of the kingdom were under the direct authority of the crown. The particular unity implied in this conception of government gave certain advantages to artists and writers: art became official; Molière was the King's comedian and used all the means at his disposal, showing his genius as a man of the theatre in combining his comedies with Beauchamp's choreographies, Le Nôtre's magnificent *décor*, and Lulli's music, all contributing to the glory of the Roi Soleil. Racine's exalted tragedies also shed reflected lustre on the majestic scene of the court.

It was not surprising that the younger poets accepted the opportunities offered them by this acknowledged state of society, for it provided an appropriate setting for the intellectual values they had inherited, combining a new unity in a unique centralisation. The civilisation they had been born into had acquired a collection of general ideas difficult to refute or surpass, deeply rooted in the foundations of culture and offering immense possibilities for comedy, tragedy and satire. Society, free at last from civil wars, wished to be amused, people enjoyed laughing or weeping at the spectacle of the world they knew, as offered by the contemporary stage. Undoubtedly the theatre was the dominating and all-absorbing art of the age – an art that had grown rapidly to maturity. Thus every poet of consequence aspired to be a playwright; La Fontaine repeatedly attempted to write for the stage and justified his fables in saying that they were *'une ample comédie en cent actes divers'*.

It is true that poetry tended to be *une poésie d'esprit*, governed by formal conceptions, with leanings towards grandeur; its greatest possibilities lay in the direction of drama; the Alexandrine verse-form lent itself admirably to tragedy, to the portrayal of passions and noble sentiments. This was particularly the case in the theatre of Racine, all his characters are swept onward in the pure flow of language, and the inexorable action of destiny is shown through language alone, owing nothing to stage craft. In this dramatic art there is no place for general reflections or meditative soliloquy, nor for anything but the main issue. Although the whole scene vibrates with the stress of intellectual and emotional reactions, all is clarity and precision. Nor is life imitated, passions and the calamities caused by them are the sole concern of the dramatic poet. This abstract objectivity is a striking feature of the new age. It was considered imperative that a dramatic author should reveal as little as possible of his own intimate feelings. The self should appear before the public fully dressed, or at least partially draped, but never completely nude. Good manners and wigs were the fashion. Even in conversation, objective topics and gossip about other people were in general more interesting than reflections about the state of one's soul, and the self was still a soul and a body rather than an integral entity. Thus the soul was the concern of priests and the guidance they offered, but the body was fully occupied intellectually and physically with living; art was a form of social intercourse, its main object was to please, and its aim was to do so through perfection of expression.

Technique was therefore of the utmost significance, and of absorbing interest to this group of classical poets: it was the evidence and proof of the poetic art, the *sine qua non* of the poets' vocation, they discussed it and corresponded about it. In this preoccupation, and this high conception of art, poetry tended to become musically pure and solidly constructed, with the greatest economy of means and the most irreproachable language inspired by a passion for perfection.

All this was far removed from the subjectivity that has ruled later periods analysing subconscious states of mind. The poets of 1660 sought to treat a theme and not to exploit their own feelings, but to show emotions evoked in given circumstances; their art tended to be abstract and formal. Molière's comedies were reasonable and satirical, profound yet gay; Racine's tragedies were intellectual and passionate; La Fontaine's fables were imaginative and realistic. No sentimentality blurred Molière's penetrating vision; no linguistic fireworks dimmed the skies of Racine's supreme poetry; no preaching weighed down La Fontaine's stories. In these authors language triumphed, becoming one substance with thought that shone unobscured by the trivial ornament that had been so characteristic of the preceding age. Poetry was more positive and more self-contained than it had been since antiquity, beautifully remaining in its own sphere.

The rich endowment of classical mythology, having been laid aside for some time, now presented fresh opportunities in the wide experience it summarised, and provided a recognised background, holding a prominent place in education and adult culture. Indeed, since childhood the individual had constant intercourse with gods and heroes of antiquity whom he found in poetry and on the contemporary stage, as well as in classical texts which were freely read. Many young men of good education might have said with La Fontaine:

> Térence est dans mes mains; je m'instruis dans Horace
> Homère et son rival sont mes dieux du Parnasse.[1] *

Classical myths had to some extent remained since the Renaissance, replacing in contemporary imagination the religious background of the Middle Ages, and classical deities still peopled the poet's solitude filling his mind with dramatic images; a pleasant chorus of nymphs, dryads and satyrs continued to inhabit the rivers, forests and mountains, and were readily evoked by poets and scholars who strolled in the seclusion of parks and gardens.

A century later, with the growth of that worship of beauty which we consider as the Romantic movement, poetic reveries found continuous nourishment in the expanding universe of contemporary thought, in the exploration of poetic destinies and the renewed contemplation of the beauties of nature. But in the classic period La Fontaine's meditations, and those of his contemporaries, were largely sustained by the works of Greek and Latin authors. The names of the ancient gods, together with the magic that a word or phrase may convey, were still capable of stirring a deep emotional response in the receptive minds of the late seventeenth century. Nor was it only the lucid order of words, but also the density in the quality of their meaning that fascinated poets: a single Greek or Latin adjective often has the force to stir such complex vibrations, that to translate it adequately we would be obliged to employ more than one word in order to convey the full significance of the original text. If the nearest single equivalent word is not sufficient to translate the full sense, the result is that the classical work, when rendered in modern language, appears terse and severe: consequently classical poetry is frequently judged exclusively from the point of view of the perfection of its external form – its unity, pattern and style, while the greatest of all aesthetic qualities, that intense inner harmony of thought which is the secret of all great art, generally passes unperceived. This is a point I wish to stress, for the pleasure that a line of Greek or Latin verse may give to privileged readers has become almost unknown under the sway of a quite different approach to poetry. Since the days of La Fontaine this source of imaginative delight has dried up for most of us, and we have lost the significance of these themes which arose from

* Translations of French quotations will be found at the end of each chapter.

the glory of Apollo and the depth of the Orphic night: as a very old man under the burden of his own sufferings shrinks into a shell of forgetfulness of all he used to feel and know, so old age overcomes the imaginative perception of nations. But La Fontaine and his friends could still delight in the works of antiquity; it was not till a generation later that neo-classical and formal expression lacked all real inspiration and became lifeless and dull.

It would therefore be a mistake to consider as unpoetical this age permeated by Greek and Latin culture, in which language was submitted to rigorous grammatical rules and verse was governed by strict laws of prosody. The poetry of this period was a mature art conscious of its own merits, having reached its zenith. Between the lyrical dawn of Ronsard's time, and the neo-classical evening of the eighteenth century, there was this bright noon of imperious and vital expression, developed and organised to convey to the public all that the author wished to say.

Although the spirit of the Renaissance, that had so brilliantly animated the sixteenth century, had passed into the French language, it is interesting to note that the poets of the *Pléiade* and those of the Middle Ages were strangely neglected in the reign of Louis XIV. Nor was Montaigne's assertion of the individual's isolation given much importance in this social and objective age. In fact it has been said that the critical literary consciousness of the generation of 1660 passed directly from the Augustan age to their own time. Yet it was Montaigne's good sense and his vigorous prose that prepared the way for the perfect and rhythmical periods with which Descartes expressed his positivism; and the philosopher's style was to illuminate the works of the prose writers who came immediately after him, such as Pascal, Bossuet, La Bruyère and Fénelon in his *Lettres Spirituelles*.

Descartes' theories –

> Une certaine philosophie
> Subtile, engageante et hardie,
> Qu'on appelle nouvelle,[2]

new in opposition to the philosophy of the Scholastics – had set the authority of rationalism on the literature of the age. The immediate effects had first appeared in the dramas of Corneille, he was thirty-three years older than Racine who became his rival. The new philosophy shone like a beacon through the whole of Corneille's theatre. He adopted the theories of love and will-power, expressed in Descartes' *Traité des passions*, which marvellously enhanced the heroic aspect of tragedy. Thus many of Corneille's principal characters act according to the dictates of reason, and the triumph of their will-power is one of the chief traits of both heroes and heroines:

> Je suis maître de moi-même comme de l'univers
> Je le suis, je veux l'être . . .[3]

cries Auguste in *Cinna*, and the strong-minded Pauline, for her part declares:

> Oui, je veux de nouveau dompter mes sentiments
> Et sur mes passions ma raison souveraine
> Eut blamé mes soupirs et dissipé ma haine.[4]

Undoubtedly this fixity of purpose and grandeur of sentiment, insisted on throughout the plays, tended to falsify the psychological aspect of the drama through a too logical sequence of behaviour, and Racine severely criticised Corneille's conventional heroes, in whom too much sublimity overrides the human interest. Nevertheless, Corneille had greatly enlarged the scope of psychology in the French theatre, which from Hardy to Garnier had been almost exclusively inspired by the plays of Seneca, till the gradual rise of Spanish influence which the author of the *Cid* had fully adopted, thus preparing the way for Racine's tragedies.

Having briefly indicated the position of poets in the seventeenth century, I should like to consider the fundamental principle that under-lies the intuitive, sensual and personal response of the poet to his art. And I propose to make a fresh approach and divide major poetry into two main groups or categories, the 'Universal' and the 'Social'. For in accepting these two psychological sources, we may bypass the dilemma of classic-romantic tradition, without entering into complicated and paradoxical aesthetics, yet adding to the range of our critical enquiries. All definitions are, and can only be, partial and limited when used in discussing a living art, for points of view change, ideas grow, their garment of words becomes outworn, and though accepted terms have their value, a fresh aspect renews our interest and should bring us closer to the sources of the artist's innate reactions to what most moves him.

For this purpose the term 'Social' indicates poetry that has its foundations in human associations whether its form be classical or romantic; it is primarily concerned with interpretations of the intercourse, the actions and reactions between individuals or communities, and the passions, the thoughts, the feelings, involved in the conflicts of these entities, arising in some or other organised environment as seen and felt by the poet. The classical and neo-classical concepts are eminently social, and Social poetry reaches its highest point in the reign of Louis XIV.

In contrast to Social poetry we may use the term 'Universal' to indicate poetry that springs from the poet's awareness and ardent participation in a wider sphere than that of human society; and this other world includes a vaster conception of nature, implying an intellectually universal art, and may be symbolised in images having for readers the value of Constants, as in the poetry of Paul Valéry. The Universal poet contemplates, and communicates with, the whole of life around him beyond that of his fellow men. Everything speaks to him

Ayant l'expansion des choses infinies.[5]

Though Universal poetry has not as yet been codified, we find it existing through the ages: its most remarkable modern development is found in the magnificent Odes of the lyrical English poets Keats and Shelley, and throughout the poetry of the European romantic movement; and among the post-romantics the most universal poet and innovator was Mallarmé. Major poets are generally both universal and social; Shakespeare is a typical example, and many others belong to both categories. But no poet can be universal all the time.

In the established sphere of Social poetry we should doubtless include most religious poems, for in religion man tends to consider himself as the central and even unique being beloved or chastised by his God – a God who perpetuates a soul in human beings exclusively, and distinct from the creation of other forms of life. This is certainly a social and carefully cultivated notion; a lamp within a closed temple, a valued belief that for centuries controlled powerful moral responses in the realm of faith. Yet the purest aspirations of religion may assume universal attributes: Buddhism is the result of a supreme effort to escape from the Social to the Universal; and much Oriental religion may certainly claim to fill the *Néant* of man's mind with a universal *élan*. So that we may say that religion like poetry can rise to universal conceptions.

Although Social poetry may assume all the classical conventions, it is not always of classical origin. It is often found in a period of minor poetry after the fall of Icarian imagination when the means are no longer adequate to support a flight towards universal heights. The poet, in a romantic or neo-romantic age, tends to descend into prosaic realism: as in nature the Ant drops his wings after the nuptial flight into the air, and returns to the crowded paths and caves of his race, ignoring all the phenomena of heavy-treading signs and portents that surround his world; so too the poet walks in the paper-strewn slums of circumstance, assuming the roll of political socialist.

Like his confrères La Fontaine was eminently a Social poet, perhaps even in his solitude, in the sense that when alone and preoccupied by dreams, he frequently dreamt of Nymphs of varied status, those unaccountable creatures whom he classed as 'Clymènes' and 'Jeannetons'. Yet he sometimes escaped into the peace of pure consciousness, if even for a brief moment. He also belonged very much to his time in his appreciation of classical authors, though showing his preferences among the French poets who had immediately preceded him, whose influence he acknowledged, and to whom I shall return. All through his life he was the poet of the opposition. His patrons and protectors were Fouquet, the duchesse de Bouillon, the Grand Condé, the Contis and the Vendômes; many of his friends were the libertines and intellectuals who frequented Mme de La Sablière's salon before her conversion. All those who had been or would have liked to be *frondeurs* were sympathetic to him. The originality of his genius placed him apart from his contemporaries, and though he looked back to the classics, he also led the vanguard of future developments, not only by the liberty he took with his technique of which he had supreme mastery but through his power to enlarge the range of human sympathies, and, *le cœur féru d'amour*, to create a greater understanding of the world of nature in general. He had the gift of being confidential, personal and completely natural in his finest poetry, at a time when it was not at all fashionable to be so. This partly explains why Louis XIV did not appreciate his work. Also his particular love of solitude and his understanding of animals were beyond the comprehension of the monarch, who looked with indifference at the paintings of Louis Le Nain, and disliked anything that might lessen the *status quo* and dignity of Kings.

La Fontaine often praised and flattered the King, but did not hesitate to criticise and even censure his actions when the occasion arose, and while accepting kingship as a necessary feature of society, he knew that it lent itself to all possible injustice.

So greatly have values changed since La Fontaine's day, that it is difficult to appreciate fully the originality of his art. Considerations which were of the greatest importance four centuries ago have lost for us their full significance, while other conceptions that did not exist in the past have imposed hypotheses expressed through psychological approaches, which would have been totally alien to authors of former ages. Doubtless human nature does not change much in four hundred years, yet in every generation the individual cannot but react to the conditions of existence, which impose either revolt or acceptance on his intelligence and sensibility; as the beliefs that govern contemporary actions must necessarily affect his imaginative response to life. Education, class-relationship, politics and religion, all play a part in the formation of poets as of other men. Certain characters become typical of their time. In the telling phrase of E. M. Forster, the light changes, and (to continue this symbolism) the arc lights of our time throw a strange hypnotic glare on the architecture of past centuries, replacing the deep-shadowed flame of torches and the flower of candle light, while the music of lute and theorbo has faded away before the hollow shout of loudspeakers.

Although similarities remain, the spiritual as well as the physical universe has changed. An immense transformation has taken place in our conception of time and space, as in religious ideas. Thus the threat of the Day of Judgement, that grandiose and terrifying concept of the *Dies Irae* which so deeply affected La Fontaine in his old age, has become a definite menace to both saint and sinner alike; in so much as humanity has acquired the means of total self-destruction both spiritual and material, for both friend and foe, by the actual abuse and misuse of material forces, to destroy, by a never-free will, the creation as we know it. So that we are now at the last act of the intellectual tragedy played out on the thin crust of our planet.

Yet human nature remains; love and hate, desire and abhorrence – and all that these signify – still govern the world as they did in the life and social poetry of La Fontaine.

TRANSLATIONS

[1]Terence is in my hands, I learn from Horace / Homer and his rival are my gods of Parnassus.

[2]A certain philosophy / Subtle, engaging: audacious, / That is said to be new.

[3]I am master of myself as of the universe / This I am, and this I wish to be.

[4]Yes, I wish to control my feelings anew / For my supreme reason, ruling my passions, / Would have blamed my sighs and dispelled my hatred.

[5]Having the expansion of infinite things.

II

CHILDHOOD AND EARLY LIFE AT
CHATEÂU-THIERRY

1. Childhood

Jean de La Fontaine was born in 1621, at Château-Thierry on the borders of Champagne and the Ile-de-France. His father, Charles de La Fontaine, was *conseiller du roi et maître des eaux et forêts* of the duchy of Château-Thierry known then as Chaûry, and his grandfather Jehan de La Fontaine had been first a merchant, and later *maître des eaux et forêts* in the same region. The family belonged to the prosperous middle class that was coming up in the world, a class of functionaries or administrators called officers, forming small administrative groups. They acquired a certain importance as royal rather than seignorial executives, and were responsible to the king, who now controlled the financial benefits. Some of the most talented men of the reign of Louis XIV came from the same province in the north of France and among them were Corneille, whose father was *maître des eaux et forêts* of the vicomte de Rouen, and Racine, born in 1639 at La Ferté-Milon, where his father was controller of the *grenier à sel*.

Jean de La Fontaine's mother was Françoise Pidoux, born in 1582. She belonged to a well-to-do Poitevin family, the Pidoux of Poitiers, renowned for their long noses and long lives. Her father had been doctor to Henri III and Henri IV, and one of her relatives had been mayor of Poitiers; her first husband was Louis de Jouy, a rich merchant from Coulommiers, by whom she had a daughter, Anne de Jouy, who came with her to Château-Thierry and in 1627 married Philippe de Prast of that town; Anne made a second marriage with Henri de Villemontée also of Château-Thierry. Françoise Pidoux had married Charles de La Fontaine, the poet's father, in 1617; she was then thirty-seven, and her husband was probably about the same age. This was considered a good match for Charles; evidently Françoise Pidoux brought with her a considerable dowry. Though little is known about her, we may assume that Jean inherited something of his intellectual qualities from his mother's side. Unfortunately an obscure law-suit between the poet's father and the Pidoux made a breach between the two families when Jean was very young, and it was not until his journey to Limoges twenty years later that he had the pleasant surprise of meeting one of his mother's relations.

Jean's father seems to have been a kind, hardworking man, though he had not much idea of organisation, and in his latter years, perhaps from the time of his wife's death, he let himself be imposed upon, and incurred debts that he was unable to meet. Jean was the first-born of the marriage, he was baptised by the curé on July 8th 1621 in the parish church of Saint-Crépin, which still stands with its tall square tower outside the ramparts of the town. Two years later the second child, Claude, was baptised in the same church. The date of Françoise Pidoux's death is unknown; her signature – Françoise de La Fontaine – appears for the last time in the year 1634 as witness in the Register of baptisms in the parish church; she must have died sometime between that date and the year of Jean's marriage with Marie Héricart at La Ferté-Milon in 1647, for he received as part of his marriage portion *biens à lui appartenant par le décès de sa mère*. He had therefore lost his mother when he was between the ages of fifteen and twenty-six; he never alluded to her personally in his poems but he said of mothers in general:

> A ses enfants mère ne sait que faire
> Pour leur montrer l'amour qu'elle a pour eux . . .[1]

which may indicate memories of his mother's tenderness. But in general at that time parents were not very sentimental about young children, who so frequently died in the cradle.

The town of Château-Thierry was built round the spur of a hill, from whose height the spacious walled precincts of the fortified castle dominated the wide expanse of wooded country, through which the winding Marne took its slow or rapid way according to the season. The castle was a massive structure, intended to give shelter to the inhabitants of the town in this perpetually invaded country. At the east end still stands the solid vaulted *salle de garde* with its imposing portcullised gateway. Within the walls rose the ancient square keep, the tall-spired chapel; and west of these stood the residential château with its courts and gardens, of which not a stone remains. The town was approached by a bridge of nine arches over the Marne, leading to the principal gateway whose towers rose above the turreted ramparts. To the west beyond the walls, the church of Saint-Crépin, repaired after it had been destroyed by the English in 1421, has since then withstood all the wars that devastated much of the town. Towards 1659 La Fontaine wrote a 'Ballade' begging for funds to restore the bridge – severely damaged by a series of floods:

> Depuis dix ans, nous ne savons comment
> La Marne fait des siennes tellement
> Que c'est pitié de la voir en colère
> Pour s'opposer à son débordement
> L'argent sur tout est chose nécessaire . . .[2]

This particular bridge was finally destroyed in the war of 1940.

The handsome three-storied house in which Jean de La Fontaine was born belonged to his father; situated in the steep winding rue des Cordeliers leading past the Convent of that name, it stood behind its own solid gateway below the castle hill. The façade, pleasantly decorated with fleur-de-lis and interwoven crescents on the sculptured pillars, faced south-east and suggested security and comfort. The garden and orchard behind the house stretched as far as the immense wall that encircled the town. The stables and outbuildings, dove-cots, poultry-yard, courtyard and well, were enclosed at the lower end of the premises. In front of the house a perron with a wrought-iron balustrade led from a sunny court to the main door. A large vaulted cellar added to the advantages of the property. The house was built, or repaired, in 1558, but the date at which La Fontaine's family acquired it is unknown.

It was here that Jean spent the greater part of his first thirty years. Very little is known of his childhood; he seems to have been good-humoured and studious, taking easily to learning, though he had not a high opinion of schoolmasters. The school he attended was in the rue du Château quite close to his home, it had a reputation for good teaching and boys were sent there from other towns: François de Maucroix and his elder brother Louis came from Noyon in the Ile-de-France to start their education. La Fontaine is said to have followed the school course only as far as the third class, that is for the first four years, leaving two years to finish, perhaps in Paris, for Antoine Furetière said in 1652 that he had known Jean de La Fontaine for sixteen years having been at school with him, but we have no further evidence of his going to Paris at that time. An interesting relic of his schooldays at Château-Thierry was a note written on the flyleaf of a book of Latin translations, a selection from the Dialogues of Lucian, published at Poitiers in 1621 for the use of the Jesuit college in that town. In this volume, which unfortunately is now lost, the name of Ludovicus Maucroix was crossed out and the words *De La Fontaine, bon garçon, fort sage, fort modeste* were inscribed. Scholars who have studied the question consider this document to have been authentic, it disappeared from Château-Thierry some time in the nineteenth century. The writing was probably that of the elder Maucroix, being in a round childish hand. We may accept it as a pleasing summing up of the poet's school-days, for although we know little about his early years, we do know that he had congenial companions in the Maucroix brothers and in Antoine Furetière with whom he remained on friendly terms, the younger Maucroix became his life-long friend. Other companions at Château-Thierry were the brothers Vitard, the Petits, Jean Josse – whose wife was god-mother to the poet's son in 1653, the Pintrels who were related to him by marriage, and Charles de La Haye who became *prévôt* to the duc de Bouillon. With these companions the time passed pleasantly enough.

Jean's father had a great respect for learning and considered the writing of verse as a desirable and elegant accomplishment. He encouraged his sons in their love of books. So when Jean, who already showed a studious disposition, expressed his desire to go through a noviciate at the Oratoire, there was no question of opposition; nor had Jean any definite idea of entering the church as a vocation.

Perhaps an instinctive need for imaginative development may have been the subconscious motive, or it may have been the influence of certain pious books lent to him by a canon from Soissons, that set Jean on this venture. It is possible that the death of his mother woke in him a new curiosity about religion with its promise of eternal life. His brother Claude also joined the Oratorians some time later and became a priest.

At this epoch few young men gave themselves entirely to religion, but few completely left it. For the well brought up religion was a sacred obligation, a necessary bond, which they might neglect but must not entirely renounce. *Faire son salut* – to save one's soul – was considered as the fundamental purpose in life, though many people put off this duty till towards the end of their days. In general youth was considered as the time of lovemaking and old age the time for religion. Thus La Fontaine's last years were given up to the most sincere piety.

Yet his retreat to the seminary at the age of twenty was quite in the accepted custom of the time, merely showing that he wished to devote himself to the culture of letters, for he always said that theology bored him: '*ce n'est pas mon fait de raisonner sur des matières spirituelles*,' he declared, '*j'y ai eu mauvaise grâce toute ma vie*'.

The Congrégation de l'Oratoire had been founded in Rome in 1564 by Saint Philippe de Neri and was introduced into France by the Cardinal de Bérulle in 1611. Their main function was to train priests with the idea of raising the cultural standard of the clergy. Their church was built in 1621, in the rue Saint-Honoré, where it still stands; in 1811 it became a Protestant church. The brethren of the Oratory were known as *les prêtres des beaux chants*, their music was of a high quality. They founded their rule entirely on a spiritual basis; that is to say that their members were not tied down to concrete regulations or manifestations of piety, such as are exacted in religious orders. At the Oratory life was peacefully calm and gentle, the principal tenet was the adoration of the birth, life and death of Jesus and the Virgin Mary. One of the most influential authorities in this community was a certain visionary priest, Father Condren, who had retired from the directorship a short time before La Fontaine went there. In the doctrines of this recluse the ideal became real, and the relationship of Divine Nature with human nature was proclaimed as evident and perceptible, excluding all the material obligations that imprisoned worldly individuals. Perhaps the greatest merit of the Brotherhood was that it gave to its members the means of peaceful meditation and in doing so encouraged their intellectual life, while sheltering them from the grosser preoccupations of the world.

Many years later La Fontaine referred to the months spent at the Oratory in his *Poème de la captivité de Saint Malc*, in the following lines:

> Je vous ai fait récit quelquefois de ces heures
> Qu'en des lieux séparés de tout profane abord
> Je passais à louer l'arbitre de mon sort.
> Alors j'avais pitié des heureux de ce monde.
> Maintenant j'ai perdu cette paix si profonde
> Mon cœur est agité . . .[3]

This is doubtless an idealised picture of his state of mind at that time, but it shows that he was sensitive to an atmosphere of spiritual peace even though the impression did not last long, and offers us a sympathetic aspect, too often overlooked, of his life at the Oratory.

Undoubtedly the religious aspirations and doctrines of the Oratorians must have been in perfect agreement with his fundamental love of dreamful ease. This atmosphere perfectly fitted a certain psychological aspect of his nature, encouraging him in his withdrawal from the ordinary obligations of a bourgeois existence. He was also much attracted by the poetic mysticism suggested by the visions of a contemporary saint, Marie de Valence, who died in 1648, for whom the priests of the Oratory had a particular cult; and the influence of her writings may be traced in the poet's description of the tapestries in his *Songe de Vaux*, and in his *Psyché*.

It is recorded that Jean de La Fontaine went in the summer of 1641 to the country residence at Juilly where the novices were sent *se nourrir de silence et de recueillement* ;[4] from there he passed on to Saint-Magloire in the rue d'Enfer (now the actual site of the Institut des Sourds-Muets) where he was received by the reverend fathers, *pour y étudier la théologie, à quoi il doit être convié et pressé* – urged and incited to work – may we not detect in this advice the chief reason for Jean's failure to please his superiors? For our dreamer, quickly bored by pedants and uninterested in theology, had no intention of working on anything that did not awaken his imagination.

On his arrival he gave a pleasant impression of devout youthfulness with his trim collar, his cardinal's cap, and a book under his arm. From his room on the second floor whose window overlooked the *basse-cour*, he amused himself by filling his biretta with bread crumbs and letting it down on a string, while he laughed at the gluttony of the quarrelsome cocks and hens. The book he had brought with him was his beloved *Astreé* by Honoré d'Urfé, a diffuse pastoral novel in which the ideas of gallantry and politeness are presented in the story of the love of Celadon for the shepherdess Astrée. The scene is placed in the seventh century on the banks of the Lignon, a little river in Forez (Lyonnais). Though mannered and sometimes artificial, the romance has a psychological side, and is to some extent a fore-runner of the *Princess de Clèves*. The observations are subtle and give distinction to the story, which had been a veritable bible for the *société précieuse*, and the main source of gallant literature and of dozens of forgotten novels and pastorals of that time. La Fontaine said of it:

> Non que monsieur d'Urfé n'ait fait une oeuvre exquise :
> Etant petit garçon je lisais son roman,
> Et je le lis encore ayant la barbe grise . . .

Et soutins haut et clair qu'Urfé, par-ci par-là
De préceptes moraux nous instruit à sa guise . . .[5]

He re-read and cherished this book throughout his life.

Now for the first time La Fontaine entered into contact with a different world from that of Château-Thierry, and emerging from the mists of a provincial childhood, installed himself tranquilly on the margins of this cultivated community of divine adoration. But this innocent beginning was destined to be cut short, for after he had been at the Oratory for eighteen months, it was decided that he should return to the world. It was evident that he did not want to study theology and that his capacity for dreaming could not be taken for a religious vocation. Left to himself he became more interested in profane poets than in religious authors. Moreover, his natural diversity asserted itself and he showed his desire for a change of scene by making fun of the more devout Brethren. His spiritual director was Desmares, the Jansenist theologian who later became a celebrated preacher, who was said to have made such an *affreuse retraite* while at the Oratory that his contemporaries did not realise his true worth; but we must not take *affreuse* to mean anything very deadly when used in this connection. When La Fontaine was asked many years later how he had spent his time there, he replied: *Desmares voulait m'enseigner la théologie, ils crurent qu'il ne pourrait me l'enseigner, ni moi que je pourrais l'apprendre. Ainsi Desmares s'amusait à lire son Saint Augustin et moi mon Astrée.'*[6]

Yet the benefit that La Fontaine received from his eighteen months of retreat was considerable. His contact with the more intellectual of the priests had stimulated him to read, and had developed his imagination, inspiring him with a taste for good music and also giving a deeper significance to his faculty of dreaming. But now his easy acceptance of circumstances, his naiveté and his changeable mood, led him to take the easiest way out of a situation that had become boring, and this road led him back to Château-Thierry and a secular life.

On Jean's return home, his cousin Antoine Pintrel who made excellent translations, urged him to read Horace, Virgil and Terence, and from this time he began to take seriously his taste for writing verse and to develop his innate love of telling a story. He now spent much of his time reading Latin and French authors. His first master was undoubtedly Horace whose good-natured and materialistic Epicureanism is easy of approach. Horace is the poet of every-man; his clear common sense, the force and simplicity of his *Satires*, influenced La Fontaine at an impressionable age, and we find these qualities in the *Fables*. In *Clymène*, one of his earliest and slightest comedies, La Fontaine says:

> Horace en a de tous (les tons)
> J'aime fort les auteurs qui sur lui conduisent.
> Voilà les gens qu'il faut à present imiter . . .[7]

and many years later he wrote:

> Térence est dans mes mains; je m'instruis dans Horace.

As for his French models, he owed much to Rabelais, whose free, forcible language and picturesque names delighted him. At the age of twenty-two he came under the spell of Malherbe's eloquence, and was greatly impressed when he heard an officer at Château-Thierry recite the Ode *Que direz-vous races futures*, and for a time he set himself to imitate, and to learn all he could from this robust and formal master. But he had more in common with Malherbe's pupil, the gentle, absent-minded, disillusioned Honorat de Bueil marquis de Racan, whom he called the inheritor of Horace's lyre – though Racan is said to have known no Latin. In speaking of the fable *Le meunier et son fils*, La Fontaine tells us:

> Autrefois à Racan Malherbe l'a conté,
> Ces deux rivaux d'Horace, héritiers de sa lyre,
> Disciples d'Apollon, nos maîtres pour mieux dire . . .[8]

Vincent Voiture, another pupil of Malherbe, had also a certain influence on La Fontaine:

> . . . maître Vincent, qui même aurait loué
> Proserpine et Pluton en un style enjoué . . .

In speaking of early favourites he placed Voiture with Clément Marot:

> J'ai profité dans Voiture
> Et Marot pas sa lecture
> M'a fort aidé, j'en conviens.[9]

Marot's wit and good humour were expressed in a very personal and colloquial style to which La Fontaine owed a considerable debt. There is a Marot in La Fontaine just as there is a Jodelle in Racine, though these fore-runners are almost forgotten today.

2. The Provincial Bourgeois

The life of provincial bourgeois society at Château-Thierry was easy-going and more or less prosperous. The most privileged of the middle class to which La Fontaine belonged, enjoyed comfortable houses, possessing well-stocked cellars and agreeable gardens. They were simple, uninhibited and complaisant. They knew that pleasures were fleeting, and that life was uncertain, for at any moment political events might rudely interrupt their lives; so after the horrors and deprivations of civil war, and in spite of constant invasions, they set out to enjoy themselves in the most simple manner. Food was given great importance, they ate enormously, and drank generously. When they invited their friends, broad stories and much laughter accompanied their feasting, and the meal was completed by the ritual of dessert and song. They were fond of music, played cards for comparatively high stakes, and greatly enjoyed mascarades and carnivals when these were provided for them. On the other hand they were constantly pre-occupied by the vagaries of the ruling class, which they considered unjust particularly when taxes or fines were imposed. Such was the social background of the time; medical science was dangerously primitive and death an ever-present threat. Yet in their homes there was a certain security for which they had worked. Hunting and love-making were the chief pastimes of the younger men.

La Fontaine accepted the life that such conditions offered. His family was well off and held an honourable position in the town, and after leaving the Oratory he enjoyed the freedom of living at home with his father with whom he was on excellent terms. He was now twenty-two, good-natured, ready to be amused and fond of reading. Of the two demons, love and ambition, which were, as he said, to share his life, so far it was only love that raised its hitherto sleeping head:

> Deux démons à leur gré partagent notre vie,
> Et de son patrimoine ont chassé la raison,
> Je ne vois point de cœur qui ne leur sacrifie.
> Si vous me demandez leur état et leur nom,
> J'appelle l'un Amour, et l'autre Ambition.
> Cette dernière étend le plus loin son empire
> Car même elle entre dans l'amour.[10]

But this was the mature opinion of later years, and certainly his was no old head on young shoulders. His sentiments towards women were neither passionate nor idealised, neither his heart nor his head was ever broken in his amorous adventures. Light come and light go, he loved all pretty women without much preference. He had a sort of gay and natural sensuality which sometimes led him into embarrassing situations, saved by his gracious manners and his simplicity. Tallemant des Réaux in the *Historiettes*, described La Fontaine as '*un garçon de belles lettres et qui fait des vers*,'[11] attributing to him various scandalous adventures, one of which seems to belong to this period. It refers to an intrigue with no less a person than the wife of the Lieutenant-General of Château-Thierry, and tells how during a night of hard frost, La Fontaine, wearing long white boots and carrying a dark-lantern, set off to walk a good league to the lady's house. Another time he kidnapped her little dog, because it was too good a watch-dog; and when the master of the house was absent, the poet used to hide under a table in the lady's bedroom, under a dust-sheet. This is perhaps the adventure he refers to in his *Élégie première* when he speaks of Amarille:

> La nuit que j'attendis tendit enfin ses voiles,
> Et me déroba même aux yeux de ses étoiles:
> Ni joueur, ni filou, ni chien, ne me troubla.
> J'approchai du logis: on vint, on me parla;
> Ma fortune, ce coup, me semblait assurée.
> 'Venez demain, dit-on, la clef s'est égarée'
> Le lendemain l'époux se trouva de retour . . .[12]

The 'Four Elegies', though written at a later date, and not published till 1671, evidently refer to this period. The first of these begins with an early adventure, probably with some servant girl whom he calls Chloris, when he was too young to appreciate her advances; and he compares this episode with his unrequited love for Amarille, while complaining that love will not leave him in peace, and that he has only known its pains:

> Car, quant à ces plaisirs, on ne m'a jusqu' içi
> Fait connaître que ceux qui sont peines aussi.
> J'aimai, je fus heureux: tu me fus favorable
> En un âge où j'étais de tes dons incapable;
> Chloris vint une nuit: je crus qu'elle avait peur.
> Innocent! Ah! pourquoi hâtait-on mon bonheur?
> Chloris se pressa trop; au contraire, Amarille
> Attendit trop longtemps à se rendre facile . . .[13]

But if the first Elegy is founded on actual experience, the other three seem to me to be romantic rather than realistic. Who is the mysterious Clymène to whom they are addressed, and for whom he sheds so many tears and makes such ardent vows? It has been suggested that she was the young duchesse de Bouillon, but the easy, friendly yet respectful tone of La Fontaine's letters to her, does not seem to bear this out. It is, I think, possible that the dramatic history of his friend Maucroix may have inspired La ontaine, for they were in close touch with each other at this time, and he knew all the circumstances of Maucroix's troubles.

If La Fontaine's love affairs were disreputable, his friendships were loyal and lasting. All through his life circumstances led to a divergence between friendship and love. He had many friends among cultivated women who were his patrons, or whom he met in society, and to whom he showed the most sincere and delicate devotion; while on a lower level he was ready to make love to any wench who came his way if only she was good-looking. He was perhaps incapable of any lasting passion, and although he would torment himself about some girl or other who had taken his fancy, his enthusiasm soon fell into a reverie and lost itself in the details of some story. These two aspects of his character – his intellectual friendships with distinguished men and women, and his free and easy love affairs – are exemplified in the two categories into which his chief works may be divided: the *Fables* representing a pure art, and the *Contes* with their free manner and matter and what Paul Valéry called '*leur fausse volupté*'.

It was in the nature of things that Jean should follow in his father's footsteps and succeed to the office of *maître des eaux et forêts*, and for this the study of law was necessary. Accordingly in the year 1645, in company with Maucroix who had frequented the Parisian law courts since 1640, La Fontaine went to Paris to study law for two years. These years in Paris had a significant bearing on his future; for now he had free intercourse with men whose literary tastes he shared. Here he met Olivier Patru, an advocate, regarded by students as an oracle on all matters of erudition. Another acquaintance of consequence was Antoine de La Sablière, a clever composer of madrigals, who ten years later married Marguerite Hessein – one of the fixed stars of La Fontaine's destiny. Antoine de La Sablière was the brother-in-law of Tallemant des Réaux whose *Historiettes*, witty and vivid, recount the scandalous behaviour of many of his contemporaries, somewhat in the tone of a gossip column of the less discreet modern weeklies.

La Fontaine now became a member of a literary academy, *les Paladins*, a new Round Table. They met in the house of Paul Pellisson, later the business agent of Fouquet whose disgrace he shared, suffering imprisonment in the Bastille for five years. He nevertheless finally became historiographer to Louis XIV, and wrote a history of the Académie Française. At the period of the *Table-ronde* he was very popular with young writers. La Fontaine referred to him as *le notaire du Parnasse*. Other members of this literary confraternity were Maucroix, Carpentier and Furetière – whom we shall meet again. An amusing incident was recorded in verse by Maucroix, when La Fontaine left Paris without bidding farewell to the noble knights of the Round Table:

> Épitre, va chanter injure,
> Mais grosse injure, à ce parjure
> Qui, par un étrange ourvari,
> S'en est fui dans Château-Thierry.
> Que la belle fièvre quartaine
> Vous sangle, sieur de La Fontaine,
> Qui si vite quittez ce lieu,
> Sans avoir daigné dire adieu
> Vraiment la troupe fait un livre
> Qui va bien vous apprendre à vivre . . .[14]

Thus Damoiselle Courtoisie scolds him, but is persuaded to forgive him:

> Mais Damoiselle Courtoisie
> N'en soyez pas si fort saisie,
> La Fontaine est un bon garçon
> Qui n'y fait point tant de façon;
> Il ne l'a point fait par malice
> Belle paresse est tout son vice,
> Et peut-être quand il partit,
> A peine était-il hors du lit . . .[15]

When La Fontaine returned to Château-Thierry in 1647, he had passed his law examinations successfully and was described as *avocat en la cour de Paris*. He was now sufficiently qualified for the career of *maître des eaux et forêts* when a post should become vacant. Personally he was in no hurry to settle down to any fixed employment, and the best of his time was spent in reading and writing verse, he also made frequent flights to Paris, or on horseback galloping across the fields to

Portrait of Jean de La Fontaine, by his friend Rigaud

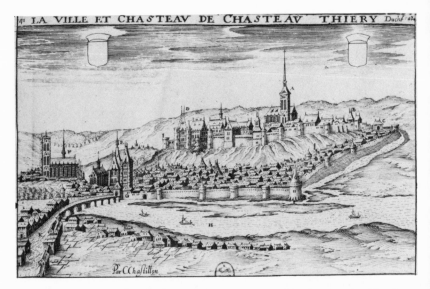

The town and castle of Château-Thierry, topographic drawing by Claude Chastillon. (p. 22)

Birthplace of Jean de La Fontaine (interior court in 1838) (p. 23)

Rheims, where he enjoyed with Maucroix *vin et gentilles gauloises friandes assez pour la bouche d'un roi*.[16]

François de Maucroix was an interesting and paradoxical character. He is remembered for his friendship with La Fontaine whom in many ways he resembled, and also for his translations which were free and general rather than exact, and sometimes missed the authors' finer shades of meaning. Boileau described him as '*agréable et fin*' and called him '*un berger en soutane*'.[17] He was born at Noyon and was the son of a *procureur* or *avoué*; he himself was a poet and wrote admirable prose and sensitive verses with a Virgilian naturalism and classical form. He adored Horace and Virgil and said of the latter: '*Virgile est ma folie, et je soustiendrai jusqu'à la mort, que ses Géorgiques sont le plus bel ouvrage qui soit jamais sorti de la main des Muses*'.[18] His own poems have a certain charm, for instance in the following lines which might be taken for a portrait of La Fontaine or possibly of himself:

> Heureux qui sans souci d'augmenter son domaine
> Erre, sans y penser, où son désir le mène
> Loin des lieux fréquentés!
> Il marche par les champs, par les vertes prairies,
> Et de si doux pensers nourrit ses rêveries,
> Que pour lui les soleils sont toujours trop hâtés.
>
> Et couché mollement sous son feuillage sombre,
> Quelque fois sous un arbre il se repose à l'ombre,
> L'esprit libre de soin;
> Il jouit des beautés dont la terre est parée;
> Il admire des cieux la campagne azurée
> Et son bonheur secret n'a que lui de témoin . . .
>
> Il rit de ces prudents qui par trop de sagesse,
> S'en vont dans l'avenir chercher de la tristesse
> Et des soucis cuisants:
> Le futur incertain jamais ne l'inquiète,
> Et son esprit content, toujours en même assiette,
> Ne peut être ébranlé, même des maux présents . . .[19]

Maucroix was capable, at least once in his life, of an ideal and pure passion such as La Fontaine described in the second, third and fourth Elegies. This unique love raised him above commonplace adventures: he adored and idealised the daughter of Monsieur de Joyeuse, Lieutenant du Roi, to whom he acted as secretary at Rheims. Tallemant des

Réaux has recounted at some length the story of how Maucroix, knowing that Mlle de Joyeuse was socially above him, loved her secretly and when she was betrothed to the marquis de Lenoncourt wrote verses for the marquis to send to her when he was absent with the army. Lenoncourt was killed at the siege of Thionville and Mlle de Joyeuse was married to the marquis de Brosses. But the marriage was not a happy one, and she finally retired to Rheims where Maucroix and his brother looked after her till her death. François de Maucroix has himself described in verse the gentleness and sensibility of his deep affection for her:

> Que la terre à mes pieds s'ouvre pour m'abimer,
> Si je cherche en l'aimant que le bien de l'aimer,
> C'est là tout mon désir; car enfin si j'aime,
> C'est seulement pour elle, et non pas pour moi-même.
>
> Jaloux, de mon bonheur si bien persuadés,
> Voyez si vos soupçons ne sont pas mal fondés,
> Si l'on peut m'accuser de la moindre licence,
> Et si jamais Amour fut si plein d'innocence . . .[20]

It was after this lady's first betrothal that Maucroix decided to change his lay career for a religious one, and bought a vacant prebend which entitled him to become a canon of Rheims cathedral. In this step some of his biographers have seen an act of sacrifice and a retreat caused by despair. But his deepest disappointment was after the death of her first fiancé, and the jealousy he felt for her mourning – which seemed to exclude him from her friendship – is vividly described by La Fontaine in the fourth Elegy. It is probable that in taking orders Maucroix was looking for a comfortable and protected life in circumstances that lent themselves to his natural propensity for an easy and civilised way of living, where he might enjoy 'a green thought in a green shade' when he felt inclined to do so. However, this lover of quiet leisure did not escape from missions and the honours they brought with them, nor from the responsibilities they involved. Thus at the time of the last fête at Vaux in 1661, he was in Rome on a mission on behalf of his patron Fouquet – for which he had to answer before the court of Justice at the superintendant's trial. In 1682 he became secretary-general of *l'Assemblée du Clergé* in which he played an important part. He left a volume of Memoirs which are disappointing, being merely concerned with ecclesiastical disputes about the privileges of the

Chapter, visits of the Cardinal to Rheims and *faits divers* to do with church etiquette and other episcopal matters, closely resembling hundreds of similar records.

Maucroix was by no means a model churchman, nor with one exception a faithful lover, yet his faults, like those of La Fontaine, were natural and accepted in his epoch; and in his self-indulgence he always remained elegant in the contemporary sense of the word. Late in life, in a letter to an intelligent woman friend, when speaking of a new liaison he said '*voyez-vous, le corps est si près de l'esprit, on ne saurait quasi les séparer*'.[21]

3. La Fontaine's Marriage

Charles de La Fontaine, although an indulgent father, was troubled by his elder son's preoccupation with women and his apparent idleness, and decided that it was time for Jean to marry and settle down. Marriage was considered an essential part of the social system, its function being to maintain the institution of family life, and as such it rested on a financial basis implying solid foundations and security. Love was not considered necessary, suitability of class and adequate means were the chief factors in the making of a successful future. It is probable that Jean would have preferred to remain a bachelor, for he had no respect for marriage nor had he any desire to be tied to a wife; freedom to come and go without responsibility was almost a necessity to him. However, to please his father he consented. '*Son père l'a marié, et lui l'a fait par complaisance*,' said Tallemant. The wife his father chose for him was Marie Héricart, daughter, of the civil lieutenant of La Ferté-Milon. Her family were in an honorable position, and were allied to Racine who came from the same town. She brought a dowry of 30,000 *livres* to their marriage settlement, which was considerable for that time, and Jean de La Fontaine brought 15,000 *livres* as his part, so they were very comfortably off. The marriage contract was signed in the presence of Thierry François, notary at La Ferté-Milon, on November 10th 1647.

Marie Héricart was pleased at the prospect of her marriage, and for a time was amused and happy. She was only fifteen and her husband was twenty-six. She was lively and loved reading novels, and in marrying a young man already known locally as a poet – who with his embroidered boots and gay clothes cut quite a figure, she saw herself taking a leading part in the literary life at Château-Thierry. She did in fact very soon become an assiduous member of the *Académie des beaux-esprits*, known as the *Rieurs du Beau-Richard*, who met on the green of that name at the cross-roads of the town; her husband belonged to this group and wrote a ballet for them. Some years later, in a letter to La Fontaine, Racine asked him to show a poem '*les bains de Vénus*', to 'your academy at Château-Thierry, and also to your wife Mlle de La Fontaine, I don't ask her to be gracious towards my works but to treat them severely.' This indicates that Racine respected her judgement, though it does not go so far as to prove that she founded a literary salon, as critics have sometimes assumed.

When we look at Marie's portrait, attributed to Pierre Mignard, we see a simpering face with pronounced features framed by dark curling hair; the forehead is high and narrow, the nose rather large over a long upper lip, and our first impression is of a mouth suggesting affectation or perhaps merely a desire to take a dignified pose – her air of self-importance is accentuated by her reproachful dark eyes that look on the world with disdain. Yet it is the mouth that dominates the portrait and in spite of a very well developed chin leaves us with an impression of silliness. Here there is none of that benevolence and sentiment such as we find in the portrait of Mme de La Sablière by the same artist.

Yet although Marie does not appear to have been particularly amiable, and was described by her husband as lazy and frivolous, she had neither the dullness of Dante's Gemma, nor the ferocity of a Xanthippe; she may have been the kind of woman that a man finds easy to leave, for although she bored her husband she does not appear to have bullied him and he was not afraid of her. Like most sensualists La Fontaine was very weak where women were concerned; had his wife possessed a more energetic or violent nature she might have kept him to some extent under her influence, not that he would ever have been faithful for long. As it was, both husband and wife had the same short-comings: both were extravagant, careless and incapable of supervising their household which after all should have been the wife's province. But Marie seemed quite indifferent to such matters. Jean had the right to expect that his wife would interest herself in the general comfort and economy of their everyday life, was that not one of the reasons why he married? But he was too lazy or too preoccupied to take the trouble of telling her so. As it was she was the worst possible wife for the poet, and he was the most impossible husband for her.

Nevertheless they had tastes in common, for they both loved reading novels and romances, though it is doubtful whether Marie ever read anything but the *romans de la Table ronde*, unless we associate her with Cloris in the Ballade '*Je me plais aux livres d'amour*' written some ten years after their marriage.

Many anecdotes are told about the first years of La Fontaine's married life. Tallemant has quite a lot to say and tells us: 'His wife says that La Fontaine dreams so much that sometimes for as long as three weeks he forgets that he is married. She is a coquette who lately has not behaved herself very well; but he does not mind in the least. When any one says to him, so-and-so is flirting with your wife he replies, "upon my word, he can if he likes. I do not care in the least, he will soon be tired of her as I am." This indifference enrages the lady, she wastes away with vexation, and he makes love where he can.'

A scandalous episode, also reported by Tallemant, concerns *une grande dame religieuse, peu farouche*,[22] of whom he says: 'an abbess, having taken refuge in the town of Château-Thierry in the autumn of 1657, was lodged by La Fontaine, and one day his wife surprised them together. La Fontaine not in the least disconcerted, drew back bowing and retired.' The lady was Mme de Coucy, Abbess of the Benedictine convent of Sainte Marie-de-Mouzon in the Ardennes. The story is remembered because of the remarkable poem 'Lettre à M.D.C.A.D.M.' that La Fontaine addressed to her, which begins thus:

> Très-révérente Mère en Dieu,
> Qui révérente n'êtes guère,
> Et qui moins encore êtes mère
> On vous adore en certain lieu . . .[23]

And he says that if he fell into the hands of bandits or Spaniards when going from Château-Thierry to Mouzon, he would explain to them:

> Je suis un homme de Champagne,
> Qui n'en veux point au roi d'Espagne
> Cupidon seul me fait marcher . . .[24]

Legend says that as the result of an intrigue between Marie and Antoine Poignac, *ancien capitaine de Dragons* – who came from La Ferté-Milon and was a cousin of Racine – La Fontaine, pressed by his friends, challenged Poignac to a duel; and when they had gone out beyond the town said to him, 'I want to fight with you for I have been

told to do so.' Then having explained the matter La Fontaine took up
his sword, at which Poignac drew out his and with one stroke sent his
adversary's weapon flying. After which they went home reconciled
and breakfasted together. This Poignac later ran a tavern in Paris where
La Fontaine and Racine sometimes met.

On a much later occasion when La Fontaine was in Paris, Racine and
Boileau urged him to pay more attention to his wife, declaring that his
continued absence from home was unbecoming. Thereupon he set off
to Château-Thierry, where he lodged with a friend whom he met and
who entertained him, and returning the next day to Paris he said 'my
wife was at Mass so I did not see her.' This episode illustrated the mixture of simplicity and indifference with which the poet treated domestic
matters. In October 1653 their only child, Charles, was born and was
baptised in the church of Saint-Crépin at Château-Thierry. Maucroix
was his godfather and Genévrine wife of Jean Josse was his godmother.
When he was eight years old Charles was placed under the care of
M. Harley who lived at Troyes, after which his father appears to have
completely forgotten him, and years later passing him without recog-
nising him, remarked 'I think I have seen that young man before.'
Events left little impression on La Fontaine's mind, his imagination
wandered off into other worlds.

During this demi-bourgeois life at Château-Thierry La Fontaine
was laying the foundations of his future poetry. He was studying
Rabelais for whom he had a strong admiration, regretting that such
vivid language was no longer current. He also felt an intense interest
in the 'ancients'. All this was to be assimilated, to become part of his
equipment, and part of himself. Finding delight and endless meditation
in such studies, it was not surprising that he turned to the congenial
occupation of writing, or rather translating, a comedy. This was the
Eunuque, first published in 1654, printed by Augustin Courbe in Paris.
In his *avertissement au lecteur*, which serves as preface to this version of
Terence, La Fontaine shows a fine critical judgement and a wide
knowledge of Latin writers. He modestly describes his own work as
une médiocre copie d'un excellent original, and explains in what the
excellence of the original consists. Apart from a sincere effort to conform to the taste of his age for classical eloquence, and close fidelity to
the Latin text, the play presents no new force either of translation or
imitation. In fact the translation is sometimes rather weak: for instance
Terence's admirable description of the girl Pamphila, *color verus,*

corpus solidum et succi plenum, which may be literally rendered into French as *teint naturel, corps ferme et plein de sève,* or less vividly into English as 'a natural complexion, a compact body full of vigour,' is translated by La Fontaine by *elle est jeune, en bon point.* At that time *en bon point* meant 'in good health'. Yet his industry in writing dialogue, so evident in his *Eunuque,* was of great value in his apprenticeship to poetry.

At this time La Fontaine liked to go to Paris whenever he could, and when there he lodged with Jacques Jannart on the quai des Augustins, where he came and went as he felt inclined. It was about the time of the publication of his *Eunuque* that he met the elderly poet Guillaume Colletet, in whose house in the Faubourg Saint-Marceau he was often invited to supper. Colletet had lost his first wife in 1641, he had lived for ten years with his servant, whose niece Claude Le Hain, known as Claudine, he married in 1652. Claudine was twenty-six years younger than her husband and was much courted by young men. She was on good terms with Furetière who had her portrait painted by Scève. She was very lively and La Fontaine found her most attractive. In the intervals of discussing fifteenth century verse with the husband, who specialised in that period, La Fontaine made love to the wife. Claudine declared that she too wrote poetry, and she sent verses to her admirers, and published them under her own name, though in reality they were the work of her husband. La Fontaine, desiring her favours, fell an easy victim to this fraud, and he wrote a sonnet, a madrigal and an epigram to her, sending her a laurel wreath to accompany the epigram:

> (Une Muse parle)
> Recevez de nos mains cette illustre couronne,
> Dont l'éclat immortel a des charmes si doux;
> Nous n'avons encor vu personne
> Qui la méritât mieux que vous.
> Vos vers sont d'un tel prix que rien ne les surpasse;
> Ce mont en retentit de l'un à l'autre bout;
> Vous saurez régner au Parnasse:
> Qui règne sur les cœurs sait bien régner partout.[25]

When Guillaume Colletet died his wife's muse died with him, which she had foreseen, for shortly before his death she had insisted that *le pauvre chrétien* should provide her with verses suitable for a widowed poet, in which she cried: *J'ensevelis mon cœur et ma plume avec vous.* It is said that she had so little learning that she could barely write her own name. La Fontaine having enjoyed a passing love affair with her, wrote a letter, to a perhaps imaginary friend, saying: 'Inconstancy puts everything to rights, so do not be astonished at my recantation, I really never cared whether she was a poet or not. When I am in love I bring all my arms to my aid.' And now being no longer in that happy state, he wrote:

> Les oracles ont cessé;
> Colletet est trépassé.
>
> Dès qu'il eût la bouche close,
> Sa femme ne dit plus rien;
> Elle enterra vers et prose
> Avec le pauvre chrétien.
>
> En cela je plains son zèle
> Et ne sais au pardessus
> Si les Grâces sont chez elle;
> Mais les Muses n'y sont plus.
>
> Sans gloser sur le mystère
> Des madrigaux qu'elle a faits,
> Ne lui parlons désormais
> Qu'en la langue de sa mère.
>
> Les oracles ont cessé:
> Colletet est trépassé.[26]

Claudine's mother worked as servant to her daughter, and was completely uneducated, which gave a malicious sense to the current expression '*la langue de sa mère*'. But La Fontaine, always considerate to women, did not publish this till 1671, six years after Claudine's death.

Meanwhile life at Château-Thierry had become for him a monotonous provincial existence; debts and business worries had to be dealt with, and letters had to be written on behalf of his father whose finances were decidedly complicated. Although he was a dutiful son, his attitude to such matters resembled that of many of his most gifted friends, who in their youth were impatient of everything that did not directly touch on their art, and we can only conclude that as artists they were right to give themselves entirely to the development of their genius, and to cultivate an aloof attitude towards the petty cares of daily life. Solitude, a withdrawal from the hum of encircling social relationships, has always been a source and nourishment of poetic consciousness, providing a necessary element in imaginative creation, offering a constellation of possibilities in the skies of Universal poetry from which, according to his capacity and independence, the poet may choose his own world, ranging from active intellectual meditation and communication with other worlds from Sirius to a raindrop, or resting on clouds of fantasy and dream. It was La Fontaine's inclination for this poetic solitude that placed him apart from other men, enabling him to create his world of fables, in which kings are transformed into lions and courtiers become an assembly of animals, more true to life than any ordinary aspect of what is generally considered as real.

Nevertheless life with its cares and events thrusts itself threateningly upon the most retiring of its victims whether they will or not, and almost all the existing documents referring to La Fontaine during the first ten years of his married life are *papiers d'affaires*, and we find him, in 1656–58, corresponding on behalf of his father and himself, with his wife's uncle Monsieur Jannart, on business matters concerning loans and debts. In 1652 Jean had been received *en qualité de maître particulier triennal des eaux et forêts*, having bought this post with money inherited from his mother. In this employment he gained a rich experience; for now he was obliged to bestir himself from the first days of spring, going round the woodlands to inspect the trees in all their different stages of growth; noting whether the annual cuttings had taken place, seeing that the peasants did not take more than their due of wood and supervising the application of the game laws. He had every opportunity of observing the sufferings of the peasants and the habits of animals, and he made good use of all this.

The fortunes of the family deteriorated during Charles de La Fontaine's last years. This was not altogether the fault of father or son, for changes were taking place due to circumstances over which they had no control. The town of Château-Thierry had been acquired by Frédéric-Maurice duc de Bouillon in exchange for the principalities of Sedan and Raucourt, which the King wished to fortify for the protection of his frontiers. By this exchange the Duke took over the duchy of Château-Thierry and the peerage of Albret. By reason of this transfer all the royal functionaries of these duchies lost their posts; the duc de Bouillon had therefore to buy them out, and the holders had the right to keep their office and draw the emoluments due to them until total payment had been made. But La Fontaine was never fully reimbursed, though he did not give up office until some twenty years later. After the death of Frédéric de Bouillon in 1652 and that of his wife in 1657, their son Godefroy became seigneur of Château-Thierry, he married Marie-Anne Mancini, one of Mazarin's nieces, a future protectress of La Fontaine.

In the year 1657 Charles de La Fontaine died, leaving debts that had to be met by Jean. In order to do so without being ruined Jean and his wife annulled by mutual consent their marriage contract of *biens en commun*. Besides his father's debts, Jean had to pay a sum, amounting to some 8,000 *livres*, to his brother who had previously renounced his share in the estate in exchange for a life rent. Claude, who had made his noviciate at the Oratory, had now become a priest, and he sent a bailiff several times to claim the whole of this debt from his elder brother. Jean had inherited his father's two posts of *capitaine des chasses* and of *maître particulier ancien des eaux et forêts*, which brought in a small revenue irregularly paid.

It was not surprising that La Fontaine lost all interest in these employments that interfered with his writing – the only work he enjoyed doing. The thought of fame now spurred him on to consecrate his life to poetry. He had already written a considerable amount, and had mastered the principles of style that best expressed what he wanted to say. It would be a mistake to conclude that during the first thirty years of his life he had not produced noteworthy poetry, for he had already written his carefully constructed *Adonis*, a task that had taught him a great deal about the writing of alexandrines; and also his admirable '*Lettre à M.D.C.A.D.M.*', in which for the first time we hear his authentic voice. Both these remarkable poems, however, were not yet published, though read in manuscript by the poet's friends. It was evident that he required a patron, some generous aristocrat who would give him financial aid. It was therefore fortunate that his wife's uncle Jacques Jannart, with whom he was on friendly terms, was *substitut* to no less a person than the surintendant Fouquet, to whom the poet was now introduced.

TRANSLATIONS

[1]A mother cannot do enough / To show her children all her love.

[2]For the last ten years, we don't know why / The Marne has played such nasty tricks, / That it's sad to see her in a rage. / To keep her in her proper place, / There's nothing for it but hard cash.

[3]I have sometimes told the tale of these quiet hours / Within these dwellings

far from things profane / That I spent in praising the arbiter of my fate. / I pitied then the worldly fortunate. / Alas! I have now lost this blessed peace / My heart is troubled.

⁴To be nurtured on silence and meditation.

⁵Not that M. d'Urfé hasn't written a choice book, / I read his novel when I was a little boy, / And I read it still though my beard is grey / . . . And loud and clear maintain that here and there / Urfé, in his way, teaches us moral precepts.

⁶Desmares wished to teach me theology, they thought he was not capable of doing so, nor that I was capable of learning it. So Desmares amused himself in reading his Saint Augustine and I in reading my Astrée.

⁷Horace has all the tones / I like well authors who model themselves on him. / Those are the people we should imitate today.

⁸The miller and his son. In the past Malherbe recounted this to Racan, / Those two rivals of Horace, heirs to his lyre / Disciples of Apollo, or to put it better, our masters . . .

⁹Master Vincent who would even have praised / Proserpine and Pluto in a playful style / . . . I profited by Voiture / and reading Marot / Greatly helped me, I must confess.

¹⁰Two demons share our life between them as they wish. / And they have driven Reason from her heritage. / I see no heart that does not bow to them, / If you enquire from me their state and name, / One I call Love, and one Ambition / Whose empire stretches further than the other, / And even enters into Love's domain.

¹¹A young man of letters who writes verses.

¹²At last, the night I was waiting for, spread its veils, / And concealed me even from the eyes of the stars: / Neither gambler, thief nor dog, disturbed me. / My luck seemed assured this time; / I approached the house; someone came and said: / Come back tomorrow, the key is mislaid. / The next day it happened that the husband had returned.

¹³For as to these pleasures, no one till now / Has made known to me any that are not also pains. / I loved, I was happy: / Love was favourable to me / At an age when I could not accept her gifts; / Cloris came one night: I thought she was frightened. / Innocent! Ah! why hasten my luck? / Cloris was too hurried, on the contrary Amarillis / Waited too long before giving her favours.

¹⁴Epistle go and sing insults, / Gross insults, to this perjurer / Who strangely, like a hunted quarry, / Took himself off to Château-Thierry. / May a fine quartan fever / Smite you, Sire de La Fontaine, / Who so quickly left this place, / Without deigning to say goodbye / Truly the troop are making a book / That will teach you to look out.

¹⁵But Mistress Courtesy, I pray you / Don't let yourself be vexed unduly / La Fontaine is a good boy / Who never does things to annoy, / He did not

leave us out of spite / Fine laziness is all his plight / And maybe when he fled, / He was hardly out of bed.

¹⁶Wine and pretty country girls, dainty enough for any king.

¹⁷A cassocked shepherd.

¹⁸I have a mania for Virgil, and I shall always insist that his *Georgics* are the finest work that ever came from the hand of the Muses.

¹⁹Happy, without care to increase his estate / He wanders heedlessly, where his desire leads him / Far from frequented places. / He strolls through the fields, through the green pastures, / And nourishes with such sweet thoughts his dreams, / That the bright sun-lit day all too short for him seems.
And softly cushioned under dark foliage, / Sometimes beneath a tree he reposes, / His mind free from cares; / He delights in the beauty of the earth, / He admires the azured plains of the heavens / And he enjoys alone his secret bliss.
He laughs at those prudent who through too much wisdom / Examine future prospects to find distress / And aching cares; / Uncertain prospects never disquiet him, / And his contented mind, always well-balanced, / Cannot be troubled, even by present ills.

²⁰May the earth open up under my feet to engulf me / If I seek in loving aught else than to love her / That is all my desire; because if I love, / It is uniquely for her, and not at all for myself. / You jealous, so convinced of my good fortune, / See if your suspicions are not ill-founded, / Or if you can accuse me of the least licentiousness, / And if ever love was so full of innocence.

²¹Look you, the body is so close to the mind, that one hardly knows how to separate them.

²²A great religious lady, not at all shy.

²³Very reverend Mother in God, / Who reverend scarcely are, / And even less are mother / You are adored in a certain place.

²⁴I am a man of Champagne / Who has nothing against the king of Spain / From Cupid only I take my orders . . .

²⁵(A Muse speaks) Receive from our hands this illustrious crown / Whose immortal radiance has such pleasant charm; / We have not met any person / Who deserves it better than you, / Your verses are so fine that nothing can surpass them / This mountain rings their praise from end to end; / You will know how to reign on Parnassus / Who reigns over men's hearts may reign everywhere.

²⁶The oracles have ceased / Colletet has deceased. / As soon as his mouth closed / His wife said nothing more; / She buried verse and prose / With the poor Christian's lore. / In this I lament her zeal / And above all I know not / If the Graces are in her house; / But Muses there are not. / Without explaining the mystery / Of the madrigals that she wrote / We will speak to her henceforth, / In the language of her mother. / The oracles have ceased / Colletet has deceased.

III

CHEZ FOUQUET

La Fontaine had reached the age of thirty-six when, in the year 1657, his work was first brought to the notice of Nicolas Fouquet, surintendant of the royal finances, one of the richest and most powerful men in the kingdom. Connoisseur of arts and letters, Fouquet befriended and employed artists and the new generation of poets; the former were to surround him with the magnificence of their creations, and the latter were to amuse him with their plays and exalt his glory in their verse.

Fouquet had two residences, one at Saint-Mandé near Vincennes where he liked to retire to work, and the other at Vaux-le-Vicomte between Melun and Fontainebleau where in the midst of sumptuous surroundings and art treasures, he gave magnificent entertainments; employing the artists Louis Le Vau, Charles Le Brun and André Le Nôtre, to construct and decorate the château and design the gardens, where the fountains, cascades and grottos artificially lit through water, anticipated those of Versailles, emulating the sixty feet of arching water in the garden of Richelieu's villa at Rueil. There is no doubt that the fêtes which took place at Vaux inspired the later splendour of Versailles which might never have been built in all its grandeur but for the group of architects and artists who had been employed by Fouquet.

Vaux-le-Vicomte was a court in miniature with all its luxury and *douceur de vivre*. Painters, musicians, poets and dramatists, gravitated round the beau monde composing this garden of art in flower, of thought pruned to elegance, of language restrained to just proportions – as the fountains shaped to fall in their marble basins. Here culture reigned such as that of the Hotel Rambouillet a generation earlier, but freer and more audacious, unchecked by pedantry or ceremonious etiquette. Wit and beauty were the *sine qua non*, and the essential for each individual was *charmer tout par sa présence*.

It was Pellison, Fouquet's *premier commis*, private secretary and minister of letters, science and art, *avocat de mont Parnasse*, who had first spoken of La Fontaine to his chief, and had given copies of the '*Lettre à l'abbesse de Mouzon*' to him and to Mme de Sévigné, who had both been much impressed by it. In June of the following year La Fontaine presented Fouquet with a manuscript copy of *Adonis* – a fine example of calligraphy by Nicholas Jarvey. The result of this offering was that Fouquet asked La Fontaine to compose a work in praise of Vaux, and thus the nine fragments known as the *Songe de Vaux* took shape in the author's mind and were worked on for the next three years. In this rather conventional and artificial poem written in a mixture of verse and prose, Architecture, Painting, Gardening and Poetry, contest the honour of being responsible for the chief beauties of Vaux. But La Fontaine was most at home when he described how, when wandering alone in the park, he talked by the fountain to a salmon and a sturgeon who related their adventures and their reason for coming from the sea.

At this time La Fontaine undertook to provide Fouquet with a *pension poétique* to be paid *tout en belle monnoie de madrigaux, d'ouvrages ayant cours* . . . in return Fouquet was to protect the poet's glory – naturally enough in providing him with a quarterly allowance, the actual amount was not mentioned, but usually such grants were generous. Fouquet was amused by the poet's happy idea of promising *him* a pension made up of poems. This *pension poétique* was to be paid four times a year. La Fontaine excelled in this kind of poetic journalism, and the group of miscellaneous pieces consisted of a varied selection of *épitres*, principally to his patron; *ballades, odes* and *dizains*, dealing with various subjects, addressed to the surintendant, his wife and his friends, or royal personages. The easy familiar manner of Marot was more or less adopted when speaking directly to Fouquet with whom La Fontaine seems to have been on very friendly terms, if we may judge by an '*Épitre*' written towards the end of 1659, in which the poet complains that having gone to Saint-Mandé to present his compliments he had not been received, and

> Il fallut prendre patience,
> Attendre une heure, et puis partir.
> J'eus le cœur gros, sans vous mentir
> Un demi-jour, pas d'avantage:[1]

for he must not exaggerate, it would be a pity if Fouquet whose heart is *tendre et bon* should take it too seriously, so

> Je me console, et vous excuse –

because Fouquet is so run after that

> C'est qu'à la fin vous n'aurez pas
> Loisir de prendre vos repas.
> Le Roi, l'État, votre patrie,
> Partagent toute votre vie:
> Rien n'est pour vous, tout est pour eux.
> Bon Dieu! que l'on est malheureux
> Quand on est si grand personnage!
> Seigneur, vous êtes bon et sage,
> Et je serais trop familier
> Si je faisais le conseiller,
> A jouir pourtant de vous-même
> Vous auriez un plaisir extrême.[2]

And so the whole troop must be dismissed, and the only people to be admitted should be lovers of the arts:

> Mais que pour les amants des Muses
> Votre suisse n'ait point d'excuses,
> Et moins pour moi que pour pas un:
> Je ne serai pas importun:
> Je prendrai votre heure et la mienne.[3]

For the poet would wait peacefully in the *superbe apartement* – the gallery of Fouquet's library – to admire the two sarcophagi of the neo-Memphite epoch that had been bought by Fouquet on their arrival at Marseilles in 1632, and La Fontaine takes the opportunity to describe these *merveilles de Vaux*, according to his own ideas on Egyptology, suggesting that they may have held the mummies of Kefren and Cheops. Now he spent most of his time either in Paris or at Vaux. As Fouquet's protégé he enjoyed a life of comparative leisure in a society that sought amusement and disdained dull care. It was a new experience. this prelude to the fulfilment of his genius, and he felt a pleasant release from the atmosphere of his native town. In the agreeable surroundings of Vaux he met his friends Pellison and Maucroix, and made the acquaintance of Charles Perrault, meeting for the first time Saint-Évremond who remained his lifelong friend, even when separated by exile.

Speaking of this period La Fontaine said: *pour moi le monde était plein de délices*: and he remembered how one day while he stood in the doorway beside Maucroix, at one of the gay receptions at Vaux, while the guests strolled from hall to garden chatting and laughing, he had noticed Pellison talking to a tall dark-complexioned woman whose thought-beaten face was remarkable for its high much lined forehead, crowned by natural black hair; her expression was disdainful and she spoke in a deep commanding voice.

'Who is she?' asked La Fontaine. 'Madeleine de Scudéry,' replied Maucrois. 'They say she is Pellison's *amie*, she is no beauty, but then neither is he. Tallemant says she is intensely proud, and when she speaks of the fall of her ancestral home in Sicily, one would think that she was talking of the overthrow of the Roman Empire. But she is less of a bore than her brother Georges, though they are both long-winded; her novels are remarkable.' 'I know them,' said La Fontaine. Later in the *Songe de Vaux* he paid a discreet homage to the description of Vaux in her novel *Clélie*, of which the last three of the ten volumes are devoted to the glory of Fouquet (Cleonime) and of Vaux (Valterre). And he also said in a ballade:

> Chacun prise Cyrus et la carte du Tendre
> Et le frère et la sœur ont les cœurs partagés.[4]

In this new and friendly environment La Fontaine found that ideal atmosphere of grace and charm that he had first discovered in reading his beloved *Astrée*, and in the works of Latin and Italian poets. Now for the first time he met the human counterparts of the goddesses and shepherds whose beauty had always shed a magic light on his solitude, and who held a place apart from the whoring, wrong-headed women drawn so successfully in his *Contes*. For a time his disorderly *affaires du cœur* were forgotten and we may discern a new poise in his character; he now became the friend and companion of distinguished men and women. In his dedications and his poems we find the names of Mme de Sévigné, Mme Fouquet, the duchesse de Bouillon and her sisters, the princesse de Bavière (sister of the duc de Bouillon), and later Mme de La Sablière and many other ladies often designated under pseudonyms. Yet he kept his independence and his own solitude, and his modest discretion was part of his attraction for his friends, whom he flattered although he did not presume to make love to them. In his sincere simplicity he was withdrawn to a point where he could observe and record, unobtrusive, yet attentive to all he saw. His wide knowledge of the ancients and his passion for poetry were enough to make him a pleasant companion for the society that looked for new sources of amusement, and above all wished to be diverted from care. Added to this the poet's store of romantic tales, his understanding of the perennial interest in love and the delicate problems of the heart, added greatly to his prestige in the social world for which he was to write his *Contes*. He had now a well defined *métier*, a much respected profession, in which he held the attention of a critical and cultivated audience of both men and women, who would criticise by accepted standards and who expected objective entertainment obeying general rules.

Most of the pieces in *La Pension poétique* fell into the class of occasional verse, easy and topical without much poetic significance, yet sustained by classical allusions and comparisons. It was not until the disgrace of his patron that real urgency struck a more profound chord in the *Elégie pour N.F.* and *L'Ode au Roi* on the same theme.

Unfortunately for his protégé, Nicolas Fouquet was not only a connoisseur of the arts, he was also an unscrupulous financier, a bold speculator, a vastly ambitious man who gave every external sign of self-importance. He came of a family of *parlementaires*, his father had been one of Cardinal Richelieu's confidential agents. He himself was received as a parliamentary advocate, and had risen rapidly to power and fortune through a mixture of lucky chance, his own decided talents and vaulting ambition. Something of his personality is revealed in his portraits: his thin pointed face has a ferret-like intelligence combined with cunning, though his bold thoughtful eyes suggest a proud challenge. A strong desire to be surrounded by beautiful objects, and also a sort of *folie des grandeurs* and urge for power, led him to appropriate large sums from the state, to such an extent that he had become the richest man in the kingdom and in some ways more powerful than the King. It is true that the general disorder in the administration of the finances, when Fouquet first took them in hand in 1657, gave some excuse for his transactions and speculations, and a point made by his advocate Ormesson, at the time of the trial, was that the King had never lacked funds. But in his want of caution Fouquet over estimated his own value to his sovereign.

Along with his financial dealings, Fouquet's privately constructed fortifications on Belle-Isle off the coast of Brittany were enough to rouse suspicion as a preparation for another Fronde; added to this the lavish display in the frequent festivities at Vaux were more than enough to waken the jealousy of the youthful Louis XIV whose policy was to gather social prestige round his own person.

Things came to a crisis at the time of Mazarin's death in March 1661. The dying Cardinal considered Fouquet as a danger to the state and put Louis on his guard, at the same time recommending Colbert as a safe and trustworthy counsellor. Louis made secret enquiries into the intrigues of his surintendant, with the help of Colbert who was profoundly shocked by the extravagance and display of Fouquet's way of life, so different from his own methodical and well-ordered ideas of economy. It was also whispered that there were other reasons, secrets of state known only to the protégé of Richelieu, that complicated the whole affair.

However the King, hiding his suspicions, showed every sign of graciousness, repeatedly calling Fouquet to council meetings and listening to his advice without criticising it. And when, in August of the same year, a sumptuous fête at Vaux was offered in homage to the monarch, it seemed to mark their reconcilation; in reality the King was about to strike. Fouquet, though informed by his own secret agents, reassured himself with the idea that Louis cared only for amusements and had easily enough pardoned the illegal transactions which had been brought to his notice. But things went far deeper than any mere question of personal gains. The question was fundamentally political, comprising an attack upon the system of finance as represented by the elder financiers whom Louis wished at all costs to overthrow.

Yet so far no one knew that the fête at Vaux was to be the last. It is true that Fouquet felt anxious, and his state of uncertainty as to the future explains why Molière had been asked, only a fortnight in advance, to produce a new comedy to be played before the King in the *théâtre de verdure* – an open air theatre constructed at Vaux by the Italian engineer Giacome Torelli. Molière had hastily composed his comedy *Les Fâcheux*. Pellison wrote the prologue, Beauchamps arranged a ballet and Le Brun painted the scenic decorations, all in the same short space of time. So that the whole performance had something of the charm of an impromptu.

Molière had already played *L'Etourdi* at Vaux in July, in presence of the queen of England (widow of Charles I), and of Monsieur – the King's brother, and Madame – Henriette d'Angleterre. La Fontaine and Maucroix had applauded *Les Précieuses Ridicules* at the Petit Bourbon theatre in 1650. And now La Fontaine, present at Vaux on this occasion, wrote an account of the evening to Maucroix, who was in Rome on a mission for Fouquet.

★

The royal party had left Fontainebleau at three in the afternoon and arrived at Vaux about six o'clock. The weather was very fine: the King drove in a large calash in company with Monsieur, the Duchess of Valentinois and the Counts of Armagnac and Guiche; Madame travelled in a horse-litter. The Queen was not present, as she was expecting a child, but the Queen-mother with her suite followed in her coach; for some time she had depended on Fouquet for large sums, but influenced by her son, she had broken off friendly relations, though she consented to attend the fête at Vaux. The princes, with the Grand Condé at their head, followed the royal cortège.

The King, smiling as usual, was welcomed by Fouquet and his charming wife Marie-Madeleine de Castille. If it is true that she and her husband had been warned that same day that they might be arrested, they showed no sign of anxiety and did their utmost to charm and please their royal guests.

The company arrived on the wide terrace before the château, an imposing and dignified building with its double court, moat and leaping fountains, its façade of gray stone decorated with pillars and statues, below a pediment bearing the carved emblem of the squirrel with the device *Quo non ascendet*, at which the King gave a rapid glance. Then, on the royal request, they went into the palace to see the interior decorations designed by Charles Le Brun.

Crossing the vast square hall supported by doric pillars and lined with antique statues, they entered the large oval salon below the central dome of the building. Here, above the imposing decorations, the paintings on the cupola, though not completely finished, could be seen to represent a sort of aerial temple, where the sun in the form of a squirrel received the gods and goddesses of Olympus, the seasons, the months, weeks, days and hours, who had all come to pay homage and offer the gifts of earth and sky.

Louis XIV looked at these sketches, hiding his feelings beneath vague compliments. Was not the sun his own symbol of beauty and power? Yet as he passed from room to room decorated with gold and allegorical pictures all dedicated to the glory of Fouquet, he showed

no surprise. There was nothing in his attitude to reveal his disapproba-
tion. He, who as a child had feigned to be asleep while the rioting mob
of Paris passed through his bedroom in the Louvre, had learnt at an
early age the virtues of discretion and self-control. And now the amiable
remarks made by the monarch were taken as signs of approval by his
hosts.

After the visit to the château the company went through the gardens
to admire the ornamental fountains and the display of flowers. Never
had Vaux looked more beautiful, everything seemed to wish to delight
the King, and the ladies vied with each other to please him:

> Toutes entre elles de beauté
> Contestèrent aussi chacune à sa manière:
> La Reine avec ses fils contesta de bonté
> Et Madame, d'éclat avec la lumière.[5]

I remarked, said La Fontaine, that the Nymphs of Vaux always had
their eyes turned towards the King. All through his account of the
fête, the poet made a point of flattering and praising the royal guests, as
was usual on such occasions.

Fouquet and his wife accompanied the King and the Queen-mother
through the magnificent gardens; not in the least apologetic for so
much grandeur, but pointing out, here and there, statues by such
artists as Michel Anguier, or other masters. The vast formal garden
with its wealth of flowers and yew trees, the canal, the water-falls, and
the fountains shining and vivacious in the rays of the setting sun,
terminated at the massive silhouette of Hercules reposing after his
labours, set before a raised half-moon of close planted shrubs.

The royal party then returned to the château where a sumptuous
feast was served in the room known as the *chambre du roi*; a six course
dinner, prepared by the famous Vatel, was served on plates of chased
gold, while twenty-four violinists led by Lulli played delightful muted
music. In the neighbouring rooms, the Court, seated round immense
tables covered with flowers, partook of the feast.

After supper Nicholas Fouquet and Mme Fouquet led their Majesties
into the grounds, where the theatre was set up at the end of an avenue
of pine trees:

> De feuillages touffus la scène était parée,
> Et de cent flambeaux éclairée:
> Le Ciel en fut jaloux. Enfin figure-toi

> Que, lorsqu'on eut tiré les toiles,
> Tout combattit à Vaux pour le plaisir du roi:
> La musique, les eaux, les lustres, les étoiles.[6]

The prologue was spoken by Madeleine Béjart, who represented a nymph coming out of a shell; and then the comedy began; the theme was that of a man stopped by all sorts of bores when on his way to meet his lady-love:

> C'est un ouvrage de Molière:
> Cet écrivain par sa manière
> Charme à présent toute la Cour.[7]

A ballet was incorporated in the play and both were much applauded. After this entertainment every one returned to the gardens to see the fire-works, which were truly impressive:

> Figure toi le tintamarre,
> Le fracas et les sifflements.[8]

The rolling of drums succeeded the noise of detonations; the King having given orders for his return to Fontainebleau that night, his bodyguard of mousquetaires was on duty. As the spectators proceeded in silence towards the house, there suddenly burst almost over their heads a thunder of rockets and coloured serpents of fire that filled the sky, darkening it with terrific coloured clouds.

'Should one say darkened or lit,' asked La Fontaine, 'one thought that all the stars, great and small had fallen from the heavens . . .' So terrible was the noise that two horses yoked to one of the Queen's carriages took fright, reared sideways, fell into the moat and were drowned. Only La Fontaine seems to have paid attention to this accident at the time, though later it was considered an ill-omen. At the end of his letter the poet commented on it thus:

> Ces chevaux, qui jadis un carrosse tirèrent,
> Et tirent maintenant la barque de Caron,
> Dans les fosses de Vaux tombèrent
> Et puis de là dans l'Achéron,[9]

After a final collation of all sorts of pastries, fruits, sweets, comfits, rare and rich liqueurs, enjoyed to the soft strains of violins, the company drove away in the gray dawn. It seemed to the courtiers that they had spent an evening in fairyland. But they noticed that the King was tired and silent and had a serious expression. He had now decided to take action.

La Fontaine, thinking still of the drowned horses, murmured to himself as he went sleepily to bed: 'I did not think that things would end tragically and so piteously.' And this might almost be considered as a forecast of coming events.

*

Fouquet was arrested at Nantes on Monday 5th September. On the following Saturday La Fontaine wrote to Maucroix who was still in Rome: 'I cannot say anything about what you wrote concerning my own affairs, my dear friend, for they do not touch me as much as the misfortune that has fallen on the surintendant. He has been arrested, and the King is violently against him, to the point of declaring that there is sufficient evidence to hang him. Ah! If the King does that, he will be even more cruel than his enemies, in so much as he has not, as they have, interest in being unjust. Mme de B. has received a note telling her that there is cause for anxiety about M. Pellison. If this is so, it makes matters much worse. Farewell, my dear friend. I would tell you much more if I were less anxious, but the next time I will make up for today.'

The Madame B. mentioned in this letter was Suzanne de Bruc, marquise de Plessis-Bellière. She was related to Fouquet and was his faithful friend. Saint-Simon said of her that she was witty and amiable with the intelligence of a man. She suffered rigorous imprisonment, terrifying threats and final exile on behalf of the surintendant. However, she lived to be very nearly a centenarian, dying in 1705.

Pellison, for his part, was arrested at Nantes on the same day as his master. He was taken to Angers on the 22nd November, then to Saumur on the 1st of December, four days later he was moved to Amboise, and thence to the Bastille. The surintendant was also moved from prison to prison and finally in June 1664 to the Bastille. It seems as if the King feared some organised plan of escape for his victim. The official trial did not begin till 14th November 1664, that is three years after Fouquet's arrest.

La Fontaine was deeply shocked by the misfortune that had overtaken his patron in which

> Thoughts of ambition, or delicious banquet
> With beauty, youth and love, together perish.

All his indignation was expressed in his '*Elégie pour M.F.*', in which Fouquet is referred to as Oronte. Evidently written quite soon after the arrest, it was printed anonymously in italics, on a single sheet of paper, about a year later, and although it was handed round among Fouquet's friends, it was not actually published till 1666.

> Remplissez l'air de cris en vos grottes profondes;
> Pleurez, Nymphes de Vaux, faites croître vos ondes . . .
> Les Destins sont contents: Oronte est malheureux,
> Vous l'avez vu n'aguère au bord de vos fontaines,
> Qui, sans craindre du Sort les faveurs incertaines,
> Plein d'éclat, plein de gloire, adoré des mortels,
> Recevait des honneurs qu'on ne doit qu'aux autels.
> Hélas! qu'il est déchu de ce bonheur suprême!
> Que vous le trouveriez différent de lui-même!
> Pour lui les plus beaux jours sont de secondes nuits:
> Les soucis dévorants, les regrets, les ennuis,
> Hôtes infortunés de sa triste demeure,
> En des gouffres de maux le plongent à toute heure.
> Voilà le précipice où l'ont enfin jeté
> Les attraits enchanteurs de la prospérité!
> Dans les palais des rois cette plainte est commune,
> On n'y connait que trop les jeux de la Fortune,
> Ses trompeuses faveurs, ses appas inconstants;
> Mais on ne les connaît que quand il n'est plus temps . . .
> Ah! si ce faux éclat n'eût point fait ses plaisirs,
> Si le séjour de Vaux eut borné ses désirs,
> Qu'il pouvait doucement laisser couler son âge!
> Vous n'avez pas chez vous ce brillant équipage,
> Cette foule de gens qui s'en vont chaque jour
> Saluer à long flots le soleil de la Cour:
> Mais la faveur du Ciel vous donne en recompense
> Du repos, du loisir, de l'ombre, et du silence,
> Un tranquille sommeil, d'innocents entretiens;
> Et jamais à la Cour on ne trouve ces biens.[10]

The nymphs are then called upon to soften the King's heart:

> Du titre de clément rendez-le ambitieux:
> C'est par là que les rois sont semblables aux dieux.[11]

And the example of Henri IV, *le magnanime Henri*, is recalled. The poem ends with a final appeal to the King, for

> La plus belle victoire est de vaincre son cœur.[12]

In this well-knit musical *Elégie*, strong in its classic substance, sure in its delicately woven texture, La Fontaine reached the zenith of a certain poetic manner which became generally adopted. He shows shrewd insight and common sense, together with a warm-hearted devotion and pity for Fouquet's misfortunes. Here there is nothing of the spacious declamations into which this form of expression was to deteriorate in pseudo-classical verse of a later period.

The *Ode au Roi*, on the same theme, was written in the year 1662. The poet dares to criticise and admonish the monarch in dignified and compelling verses. The main argument is that the King should use his power to crush his enemies and show mercy to his own subjects for:

> Les étrangers te doivent craindre;
> Tes sujets te veulent aimer.
>
> L'Amour est fils de la Clémence;
> La Clémence est fille des dieux:
> Sans elle toute leur puissance
> Ne serait qu'un titre odieux.[13]

La Fontaine had managed to have the Ode passed in to Fouquet, who returned it with certain criticisms, finding it too poetical to please the King, to which the poet replied:

> Quant à ce que vous trouvez de trop poétique pour pouvoir
> plaire à notre monarque, je le puis changer en cas que l'on
> lui présente mon ode; ce que je n'ai jamais prétendu. . .
> J'ai composé cette ode à la considération du Parnasse.
> Vous savez assez quel intérêt le Parnasse prend à ce qui
> vous touche. Or se sont les traits de poèsie qui font valoir
> les ouvrages de cette nature. Malherbe en est plein, même aux
> endroits où il parle au roi. . .[14]

These words deserve to be remembered as illustrating La Fontaine's independence.

★

Fouquet's examination began on November 14th 1664, in the Chamber of Justice of the Arsenal; the judgement was not pronounced until December. The public followed the case with the greatest attention, and an atmosphere of feverish interest surrounded the whole trial. Although the proceedings in Court were not made public, every one knew the accusations brought against the former surintendant, his means of defence, his allies and his enemies. The leading juge was the ancient chancellor Seguier, whose fine house still stands in the Paris street of that name. He himself had passed through some delicate situations, having been on the side of the princes against the King, at the time of the Fronde. Ormesson, Fouquet's advocate, spoke of his client's admirable integrity, and laid the blame for extravagance and financial irresponsibility on the late Cardinal Mazarin, who had demanded large sums for war expenses, and in particular for munitions for the army and navy. In his final speech for the defence Ormesson deplored the 'odious irregularities of the procedure in this so-called trial.'

Mme de Sévigné considered this speech a masterpiece of legal argument. She was an old friend of Fouquet – whose success with women was notorious. He had been in love with her, but she had firmly refused to become his mistress, preferring to remain his friend. A correspondence had passed between them concerning the affairs of a certain Mme de La Trousse, a distant cousin of Mme de Sévigné. *Les lettres les plus innocentes du monde*, were found, after the arrest, in the surintendant's famous casket that contained all the love letters from his mistresses. Indeed it was only after a valiant defence of her honour, by her cousin Bussy-Rabutin, that Mme de Sévigné's reputation was saved.

Greatly preoccupied as to the fate of her old friend, Mme de Sévigné referred constantly to the trial in her letters to her daughter. She noted the dignified calm and strength of character shown by Fouquet; and remarked that Colbert was feeling anxious in the face of the prisoner's admirable replies during the instruction. She also related how, one morning when passing on foot from his prison to the Arsenal where he was being tried, Fouquet stopped to watch some workmen who were making a fountain, and going towards them, gave them some advice. 'In the past I was clever enough at that sort of thing,' he said to the Captain who accompanied him.

Before the final verdict, Fouquet's friends had prayers said for him in every church in Paris. At last, after what seemed an interminable trial, they had the joy of knowing that he would not be condemned to death. Of the twenty-two judges, thirteen voted for his banishment, and nine for the death penalty. Had he been condemned to die, it was amply shown by contemporary evidence that the King would have done nothing to save him. As it was, Louis exercised his sovereign right of grace in the inverse sense – changing the sentence of perpetual banishment, pronounced by the Chamber of Justice, to imprisonment for life; a penalty which in fact did not figure in the code of legal criminal sentences of the time.

Public feeling was widely expressed in a spate of epigrams and popular songs, carefully copied out and abundantly distributed, all showing how strongly the Parisians were in favour of the prisoner.

> A la venu de Noël
> Chacun se doit bien réjouir
> Car Fouquet n'est point criminel
> On n'a pu le faire mourir.[15]

La Fontaine's unpublished fable '*Le Renard et l'Écureuil*', with its promise of Colbert's downfall, was passed round among the friends who had so often enjoyed themselves at Vaux.

A last glimpse of the château is given us by Mme de Sévigné when, twelve years later, on her way to Paris, she stopped at Vaux after a gruelling journey during which she had pictured to herself her arrival at Vaux, with all the fountains filling the air with their cool delight. But alas! the fountains were not flowing. The impoverished family had recently been allowed to return, and the comte de Fouquet, the surintendant's eldest son, received his guest most graciously, and explained that the fountains were out of order – temporarily. But during an excellent supper, Mme de Sévigné found herself comforting him with 'the great value of his own merits.'

TRANSLATIONS

[1]One had to be patient, / Wait for an hour and then go away, / I did so with a heavy heart; to tell the truth / Sad for half a day, not more. / I console myself and forgive you.

[2]It comes to this, that in the end / You will not have leisure to take your meals. / The King, the State and your country, / Divide between them your whole life: / Nothing is left for you, everything is for them. / Good God! It is unfortunate / To be so great a personage! / Sire, you are good and wise, / And I would be taking liberties / If I gave you my advice, / All the same, to enjoy your own life / Would give you pleasure extreme.

[3]But lovers of the Muse / Your Swiss should not refuse / And me less than any other. / I will not be importunate, / I will come when it suits you and me.

⁴Everyone praises Cyrus and the Map of the Sentiments / And the brother and sister share all hearts . . .

⁵All with each other vied in beauty, / Everyone in her own way; / The Queen vied with her sons in graciousness / And Madame in brilliance with the light.

⁶The scene was decked out with thick foliage / And by a hundred torches lit: / The sky was jealous. Just imagine / How, when the curtains were pulled back / Everything competed at Vaux to please the King: / The music, the fountains, the chandeliers, the stars.

⁷ It is a work by Molière / This writer by his manner / Charms at present all the Court.

⁸Imagine all the hullabaloo / The crashing and the whirring!

⁹ Those horses who formerly drew a coach / And now draw the bark of Charon, / Fell into the moat at Vaux / And from thence into Acheron.

¹⁰Fill the air with cries in your grots profound / Weep, Nymphs of Vaux, increase your streams / . . . The Fates are satisfied: Oronte is unhappy, / You saw him not long since, at the brink of your fountains, / Who, without fear of Fortune's uncertain favours, / Brilliant, and glorious, the adored of all mortals, / Received honours that should be offered to the gods. / Alas! How he has fallen from that supreme fortune! / How changed you would find him, how unlike himself! / For him the brightest days are second nights. / Devouring cares, regrets, anxieties, ill-fated guests of his sad abode / The whole time plunge him in gulfs of despair. / This is the precipice where at last he is thrown / By the enchanting lure of prosperity! / In the palaces of kings' this complaint is common, / There the tricks of Fortune are too well known, / Her deceiving favours, her fickle attractions, / But one only knows them when it is too late . . . Ah! If this false glamour had not been his delight, / If the domain of Vaux had limited his desires, / How peacefully he could have let the years flow by! / You have not in your abode this brilliant train, / This crowd of people who go by each day / In long procession to honour the Sun of the Court. / But the favour of Heaven grants you in recompense / Repose and leisure, silence and shade, / Tranquil slumbers, innocent converse / And never at the Court does one find these blessings.

¹¹ Make him ambitious to be called merciful / It is in this that kings resemble the gods.

¹²The greatest victory is to conquer one's inclinations.

¹³Foreigners should fear you / Your subjects wish to love you. Love is the daughter of Mercy, / Mercy is the daughter of the gods / Without her all their power / Would be only an odious name.

¹⁴In regard to what you find too poetical to please our monarch, I can change this in the event of any one presenting him with my Ode; which I never intended. I composed this Ode for the approbation of Parnassus. You are well

aware what interest the Parnassians take in whatever touches you. Well, it is the poetic passages that give value to a work of this sort. Malherbe is full of them, even in places where he speaks to the king.

[15]At the coming of Christmas / Everyone should greatly rejoice / For Fouquet is no criminal / He could not be put to death.

IV

AN INTERLUDE

When in Paris La Fontaine and his wife lodged with her uncle Jannart on the Quai des Orfèvres in the Enclos du Palais. Jannart was a man of solid parts, and as *Substitut au Parlement de Paris* for Fouquet held an important position. He had accompanied the surintendant to Nantes at the end of August 1661, and was near him at the time of his arrest. Jannart arranged the documents intended for the defence of his master and remained as adviser to Mme Fouquet, warning her against the possible abuses and misuse of documents by the King's council. Mme Fouquet was exiled to Limoges at the time of her husband's arrest: it was not until 1672 that she was allowed to send to Fouquet a memoir dealing with the family affairs which were in a state of considerable confusion. In the meantime Jannart did what he could to help her, till as a result of his efforts he was exiled to Limoges in August 1663.

La Fontaine decided to accompany Jannart on this journey. It seems unlikely that he himself was under orders to do so. In his first letter to his wife he says: 'the fantasy of travelling had filled my mind for a long time. I was ashamed to have lived so long and seen so little.' Had he been banished we may imagine the epistles, the moving letters in verse that would have been addressed – to what great names! But as those were never written, we may conclude from the carefree letters to his wife, that it was the spirit of adventure that made him take the road. In any case he was back in Paris in the autumn for he took out a privilege there for his *Nouvelles en Vers* early in January.

In six letters addressed to his wife at Château-Thierry, probably intended to be handed round in their intimate circle of friends and even among a wide circle of Fouquet's friends, La Fontaine describes the places he visited and gave his impressions of the people he met. Besides giving an account of his reactions to the journey, the letters tell us something of the poet's married life, for they show that he and Marie were at this time on fairly good terms, and that she evidently enjoyed his pleasantries. The free and easy tone of comradeship, if sometimes condescending, is nevertheless remarkable between a married couple of that time. The little Charles, whom La Fontaine was said to neglect, is sent a kind message and the promise of a present – *un beau petit chaperon* – on his father's return. The general tone is friendly and often ironical; at the beginning of the first letter, he teases Marie for her taste in novels.

> 'You have never wished to read any other voyages than those of the knights of the Round Table; but our journey well deserves that you should read my account of it. However there may be things which do not suit your taste, so it is up to me to flavour them, if I can, in such a way that they will please you, and you should praise my intentions in this even when I am not successful. It may even happen that if you like this account you will afterwards enjoy more serious things. You neither play, nor work, nor do you take any care in house-keeping; and beyond the time that your good friends devote to you through charity, nothing amuses you but novels, of which the supply is soon exhausted. You have read the old ones so many times that you know them by heart; and there are very few new ones, and among the few not all are good, so you are often left high and dry with nothing to read.
>
> I beg you to consider, how useful it would be to you, if in amusing you I had given you the habit of reading the history of people and places; you would then have the means of diverting yourself for the whole of your life; provided that you had no intention of remembering and still less of quoting anything. It is not a good quality in a woman to be learned, and to affect to appear so is a very bad one.'

This playful and ironic letter serves as an introduction to La Fontaine's account of his journey. It also explains the simplicity and brevity of his descriptions, and the homely and humorous reflections throughout the letters. Here, as in his other prose works, he often lightens his text with verse, and the style is always well balanced.

On August 23rd 1663 Jannart left Paris, accompanied by La Fontaine and escorted by an officer of the crown, the *lieutenant criminel*, as was usual in such cases. They were given a great send off by friends and neighbours, there was much embracing, laughter and some tears, and condolences of *une quantité de personnes de condition et de ses amis*. The officer behaved with tact and generosity, opening his purse and inviting them to take from it any money they wanted. La Fontaine started in high spirits. 'It is indeed a pleasure to travel,' he noted, 'one always meets with something remarkable.' Their first stop was at Clamart under the hill of Meudon about three leagues (seven and a half miles) from Paris. 'You would not believe what excellent butter we eat here,' reported the poet, 'I wished twenty times that I had the same cows, and the same grass and water, and everything to do with it except the dairy-maid who is a bit old.'

At Clamart they stayed with Mme C. who was evidently a friend of the family, for La Fontaine asks his wife whether she had ever seen the garden, which he describes with enthusiasm, greatly admiring the lawns and ancient trees; speaking of the terrace with its grass and covered steps he ends his description in verse:

> Deux châtaigniers, dont l'ombrage
> Est majestueux et frais,
> Le couvrent de leur feuillage,
> Ainsi que d'un riche dais.
>
> Je ne vois rien qui l'égale,
> Ni qui me charme à mon gré
> Comme un gazon qui s'étale
> Le long de chaque degré.
>
> J'aime cent fois mieux cette herbe
> Que les précieux tapis
> Sur qui l'Orient superbe
> Voit ses empereurs assis. . .
>
> De quoi sert tant de dépense?
> Les grands ont beau s'en vanter:
> Vive la magnificence
> Qui ne coute qu'à planter![1]

'Nevertheless, in spite of these moralities, I advised Mme C. to have a house built in some proportion to the beauty of her garden, and if necessary to ruin herself for it.'

On the 25th they went on to Bourg-la-Reine where they were to take the coach that passed every Sunday for Poitiers. Here the Lieutenant left them in the charge of M. de Châteauneuf, the officer under orders to accompany M. Jannart to Limoges. Mme Jannart, accompanied by Mme C., who had come so far, now bade them tearful and tender farewells. At last the coach arrived and they were hurried into it, having waited for three hours.

Leaving Sceaux on their right, they passed by the ruined fifteenth century fortified castle of Montléry which at one time the English had repaired; it was wrongly said to have been built by them. As the coachman had no intention of lingering, La Fontaine had to be content with Jannart's description of the interior and of the English paintings in the two remaining rooms on the first floor.

In the coach there were three women, a merchant who did not say a word, and a notary who sang out of tune all the time. He was taking four volumes of song back to his own town. Among the women there was one from Poitiers who said she was a Countess; she seemed fairly young and had a good figure and a certain wit. She would not disclose her name, but said she had been suing for a separation from her husband – a circumstance that La Fontaine would have considered as a good sign if she had been beautiful. 'For me,' he wrote, 'beauty is an essential quality. I defy you to make me find a grain of salt in any woman who is not divinely fair.' Happily the Countess had wit and entertained him with gossip about the people of her country.

They stopped to dine at Châtres (which in 1720 changed its name to Arpajon), and after dinner continued their journey through a wild and hilly country, passing many fine châteaux on the road to Torfou. The valley of Torfou, ill-famed as a haunt of robbers, made La Fontaine tremble – for like Panurge *'il craignait naturellement les coups.'*

> C'est un passage dangereux,
> Un lieu pour les voleurs, d'embûche et de retraite;
> A gauche un bois, une montagne à droite
> Entre les deux
> Un chemin creux.
> La montagne est toute pleine
> De rochers faits comme ceux
> De notre petit domaine.'[2]

The small domaine of which he speaks was La Fontaine-Regnard near Château-Thierry, from which the family were said to have taken their name.

As the hill was steep, all the men were obliged to get out of the coach, much to the poet's discomfort, and he wished it had been war-time, for war had a great advantage of giving employment to robbers. He even reflected that since the forest was said to be crawling with cut-throats, it deserved to be burned – which was contrary to his usual respect for

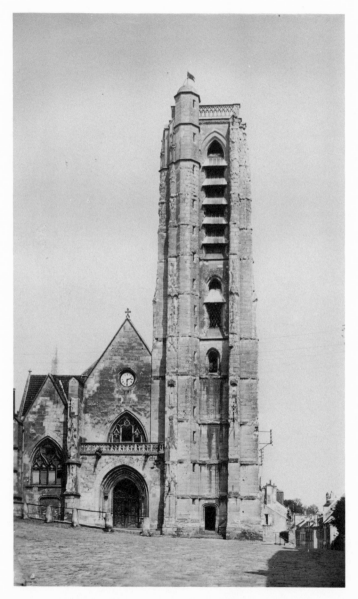

Church of Saint Crépin, Château-Thierry (p. 22)

Vincent Voiture
de l'Academie francoise ne a
Amiens et mort a Paris dans un
age fort avance

Gravé par E. Desrochers rue de Foin prés la rue St Iacques a Paris.

En prose ainsi qu'en Poësie
D'un Stile delicat et fin ;
Dans tes escrits Voiture alie
Le tendre et le galant, le Simple et le badin

Portrait of Vincent Voiture (p. 28)

Honorat de Buül Marq
de RACAN poëte, et de l'Académie
Françoise né en Touraine il mourut
en 1670 fort âgé

Tout chantre ne peut par cür Ac ton d'un Orphée
Entonner en grands Vers la discorde étouffée,
Peindre Bellône en feu Tonnant de toutes parts,
Et le Belge effraye fuyant sur ses remparts,
Sur un ton si hardi sans estre temeraire
Racan pouroit chanter au deffaut d'un Homere.

Portrait of Honorat de Racan (p. 28)

Portrait of Marie Héricart (Mme. de La Fontaine) (p. 36)

trees. But he was not too scared to note details, used to such fine effect in his fable '*Le Coche et la Mouche*':

> Dans un chemin montant, sablonneux, malaisé,
> Et de tous les côtés au soleil exposé,
> Six forts chevaux tiraient un coche.
> Femmes, moine, vieillards, tout était descendu:
> L'attelage suait, soufflait, était rendu. . .[3]

As evening fell they passed through the suburbs of Étampes, and remarked with pity the devastations of the civil war: '*quelques monuments de nos guerres*' La Fontaine called them. 'Lines of houses without roofs or windows, pierced with holes on every side, there is nothing more ugly, more hideous. It made me think of the ruins of great Troy. Truly fortune mocks at the works of man.' That evening the poet read aloud his poem on this subject, to entertain the company. Here is the last verse:

> Beaucoup de sang français fut alors répandu:
> On perd des deux côtés dans la guerre civile;
> Notre prince eût toujours perdu,
> Quand même il eût gagné la ville.[4]

The next day they crossed the plain of Beauce, a boring country, and they were only kept awake by a lively discussion on religion, between M. de Châteauneuf and the lady from Poitiers, she being a Calvinist. Finally Jannart and La Fontaine fell asleep, while the notary kept on singing. After dinner, to prevent the discussion from continuing, La Fontaine asked the unknown Countess if there were handsome people at Poitiers; and she mentioned among others a very beautiful girl whose face had brought her a handsome fortune. This story amused the company until they reached Orléans. Here La Fontaine and M. de Châteauneuf went to admire a magnificent sunset from the bridge. Looking round about him, the poet noticed the statue of Jeanne d'Arc and Charles VII kneeling before a *Pietà*. This monument, dating from 1458, had been mutilated and restored. La Fontaine felt no enthusiasm for it, finding that *la Pucelle* had neither the bearing, nor the figure, of an Amazon; and he added, 'if M. Chapelain had not written about her, I would not have mentioned her.' Which shows that he respected the pontiff of letters who later praised his *Contes* – though perhaps rather as the dispenser of pensions than as poet.

Those who see the Loire for the first time are impressed by the beauty
of its wide clear surface and the measured grandeur of its surroundings.

'It is three times as wide at Orléans as the Seine is at Paris. The horizon is
fine on all sides and limited as it should be. So much so that this river being
comparatively low, its clear water, its smooth course, make it seem like a
canal. From each side of the bridge one continually sees barges with sails,
going up and down stream; one can count them and notice the distance
between them. This is one of the attractions, for it would be a pity if such
pure water was entirely covered with boats. Their sails are very full which
gives them the majesty of sailing ships, and I imagined that I was looking
at a small sized port of Constantinople.

Looked at from the Sologne – the region of marshy land in the curve
of the river – Orléans has a fine aspect. . . . The mall and the other trees
planted all along the ramparts, make the town appear to be half enclosed
in green walls . . . I had not enough time to see the ramparts thoroughly,
but I let myself praise them and also the church of Sainte-Croix.'

At last the whole company, who had gone off in all directions,
returned satisfied. One spoke of this, another of that. It being now
supper time they all sat down at their tables, rather badly served, then
they went straight to bed.

La Fontaine was as pleased with the country between Orléans and
Amboise as he had been bored with that of the Beauce. They were
now at the beginning of the Sologne, a much less fertile province than
that of the Vendômois which lies on the other side of the river. 'It is
because of this,' said La Fontaine, 'that rustics may be hired for very
little, for they are not so crazy as those of Champagne or of Picardy.
I think the maids cost more.' The next place they stopped at was Cléry.
La Fontaine went at once to visit the church.

'It is collegiate,' he reported, 'and well enough endowed for a small market
town, not that the Canons would agree to this. Louis XI is buried here, on
his tomb one sees him kneeling, four children at the corners; they could be
four angels, or four cupids, if their wings had not been taken from them.
Here this hypocritical king poses as a saint, and he has been completely
caught, even more than he was when the Duke of Burgundy led him
captive to Liège.

        Je lui trouve la mine d'un matois;
        Aussi l'était ce prince, dont la vie
        Doit rarement servir d'exemple aux rois,
        Et pourrait être en quelques points suivie.[5]

At his knees are his book of Hours, his rosary, and other small objects: his hand-of-justice, his sceptre, his hat and his Notre-Dame; I do not know why the sculptor did not also put in the Provost-marshal Tristan l'Hermite. The whole monument is of white marble, and seems to me to be well enough done.'

Coming out of the church, La Fontaine mistook another hostelry for one they had stopped at, and he all but ordered dinner there; then going to walk in the garden, he became so absorbed in reading Livy, that for more than an hour he never thought about his appetite till a man-servant of the inn called his attention to this forgetfulness. He then hurried to the place where they had got off, and arrived just in time. It was only four leagues from Cléry to Saint-Dié which was the ordinary stopping place, and as the road was agreeable and bordered by hedges, La Fontaine did part of the way on foot. He had no adventures and only met some beggars and some pilgrims from Saint-James of Compostella. As Saint-Dié was not a borough, and as the hostelries were badly stocked, 'our Countess' not being satisfied with her room – M. de Châteauneuf always wanting the best accommodation for M. Jannart – they thought that they were going to fall into the same controversy as that between Potrot and the lady from Nouaillé, during the Fair of Niort, when the servants of Potrot and those of the lady put the belongings of their respective master and mistress on the same bed in the hostelry, which led to a dispute. Potrot said: 'I am going to sleep here.' 'I do not say that you should not,' retorted the lady, 'but I am going to sleep here too.' As a point of honour neither of them would give in, so they both slept in the same bed.

'But this time,' says La Fontaine, 'things happened differently. The next day the Countess complained of fleas. I don't know if it was this that woke the coachman; I mean *his* fleas – not those of the Countess – but the fact remains that he made us all leave so early in the morning that it was just eight o'clock when we found ourselves opposite Blois with nothing but the Loire between us and the town.

'Blois, like Orléans, is built on a slope, but it is smaller and more compact, the roofs of the houses are arranged in such a way that they resemble the steps of an amphitheatre. This seemed to me very fine and I think it would be difficult to find a more agreeable and cheerful plan. The castle is at one end of the town and the church of Saint-Solenne at the other . . . I did not hear anything about the ancient custom of the town, but the manners of the present occupants are very pleasant;

whether this has always been so and if the climate and beauty of the
country contribute to it, or whether the presence of Monsieur, or the
number of pretty women, gave it this politeness, I cannot say. I asked
the names of some of the ladies. Beside these, several hunchbacks were
pointed out to me. At Orléans they were even more common. I
believe Heaven, friend of these people, gave them wit through this
means, for they say that a hunchback is always witty; and yet there are
old traditions which give another reason for it, that also explains the
formation of La Beauce.

> La Beauce avait jadis des monts en abondance,
> Comme le reste de la France:
> De quoi la ville d'Orléans
> Pleine de gens heureux, délicats, fainéants,
> Qui voulaient marcher à leur aise,
> Se plaignit, et fit la mauvaise:
> Et messieurs les Orléanois
> Dirent au Sort, tous d'une voix,
> Une fois, deux fois et trois fois,
> Qu'il eût à leur ôter la peine
> De monter, de descendre, et remonter encore. . .[6]

To this complaint the cunning Fate replied, that if they did not like
to make their feet work they could have the hills on their backs'

The château, La Fontaine tells us, was built at different times. One
part dates from François I and the other from Louis XII; the living-
rooms in front were begun by Gaston d'Orléans who died at Blois in
1660. 'These three sections of the château follow no regular design.
Thank God they do not seem to have any particular relation to each
other.' The part built by François I pleased La Fontaine more than the
rest, and this is not surprising, for its small windows and finely proportioned balconies, with the delicate decoration of salamander and
crown set above them, are made to charm. Unfortunately he had no
time to visit the interior, for he would have appreciated the well
proportioned rooms, with their narrow windows through which
marvellously happy landscapes seem to shine like illuminated pages,
leaving a lasting impression of strength and beauty. But what he regretted most was that he did not see the room in which Gaston d'Orléans –
'*feu Monsieur*' had died. In singing the praises of this prince, he was not
altogether disinterested, as he hoped to receive his brevet as gentlemen

in the household of the prince's widow Margaret of Lorraine, which in fact he did a year later.

There was no time to visit the herb garden made by the prince, said to be the finest in the world. Evelyn had also remarked on it when he was in France some twenty years earlier, and had said in his Diary (1644) that he had seen 'a large garden, esteemed for its simples and exotic plants, in which the present Duke of Orléans takes great delight.' La Fontaine who adored gardens, would very much have liked to see it. But the coachman showed no interest, and after gobbling a huge dinner, he cracked his whip and off they went, down through the town and along the wide embankment that cost so much to make and keep in repair. As for the country, the poet found it entirely to his liking, and as they drove through the low wooded hills lit by a gentle afternoon sun he wrote a poem about it in which this verse occurs:

> J'y rencontrai de si charmants appas
> Que j'en ai l'âme encore tout émue.
> Coteaux riants y sont des deux côtés:
> Coteaux non pas si voisins de la nue
> Qu'en Limousin, mais coteaux enchantés,
> Belles maisons, beaux parcs, et bien plantés,
> Prés verdoyants dont ce pays abonde,
> Vignes et bois, tant de diversités
> Qu'on croit d'abord être en un autre monde.[7]

They arrived at Amboise in very bad weather, and La Fontaine hurried off to visit the château which is built on a high rock overlooking the great forest, with the town nestling at its foot, and the Loire flowing below. Of the view he said, 'it is wide and majestic and of an immense extent; there is nothing to limit it and no objects to spoil it. One imagines that the town of Tours is visible although about fifteen or twenty leagues away. One sees the most happy and varied landscape, and at one's feet the river waters a wide field.'

In the château the unfortunate Fouquet had been imprisoned in a room of which all the windows were blocked. There was only one small hole high up in the wall. La Fontaine asked to see his cell, '*triste plaisir, je vous confesse, mais enfin je le demandai.*' But the soldier who took them there had not got the key; so not being able to go inside, the poet lingered there all afternoon looking at the door and picturing the miseries of his friend and benefactor – a characteristic gesture, touching in its simple sincerity. He asked many questions as to how the prisoner had been treated, and he recounts all this in verse:

> Qu'est-il besoin qui je retrace
> Une garde au soin nonpareil,
> Chambre murée, étroite place,
> Quelque peu d'air pour toute grâce,
> Jours sans soleil,
> Nuits sans sommeil,
> Trois portes en six pieds d'espace?
> Vous peindre un tel appartement,
> Ce serait attirer vos larmes;
> Je l'ai fait insensiblement:
> Cette plainte a pour moi des charmes.[8]

At dusk he was obliged to tear himself away without having seen the interior, and he reluctantly returned to the hostelry.

The next day they left the river-side, which La Fontaine regretted, but remarked that there was no lack of waterways for

> Depuis ce lieu jusques au Limousin,
> Nous en avons passé quatre en chemin,
> De fort bon compte au moins qu'il m'en souvienne:
> L'Indre, le Cher, la Creuse, et la Vienne. . .[9]

When they had crossed the Indre, they met three men, who might have been characters from *Guzman d'Alfarache;* one of them wore his hair plaited down his back (which was to become the fashion of the next generation). But the more enthralling were the gypsies, a troop of Zingari, often called Egyptians in the seventeenth century. These horrible creatures, all toothless hags, uncovering their skeleton shoulders, came towards the travellers, dancing and hopping about with looks of scorn and hatred in their sunken eyes. They could not have been more disdainful if they had been young and beautiful. 'I trembled with horror at this spectacle,' says La Fontaine, 'and I have been unable to eat for more than two days.' After the hags came two blonde women, dressed in embroidered skirts, white capes and coloured taffeta caps *à l'anglaise* with silver tassels. Compared to the others they seemed well enough and the travellers saluted them respectfully; they in return scarcely seemed to notice the people they passed, but walked with the gravity of goddesses. Then came more women followed by a Franciscan friar, and finally the baggage in carts or on beasts of burden, after which four empty carts and some men-servants with dogs, made up the procession the whole being escorted by M. de la Fourcade, *garde du corps*. As this cavalcade had stayed at the hostelry where the coachman intended to stop, our travellers took fright at the idea of sleeping in the same beds and drinking out of the same cups as these disreputable creatures had used, the Countess in particular was horrified at the idea. But whether they did so is not recorded, for La Fontaine only says: 'we went the following day to sleep at Montels,' (perhaps the modern Manthelan), and the day after dined at Port-de-Pilles where the company began to separate. The Countess sent a lackey, not to her husband, but to her relatives, to announce her arrival and to order a carriage with an escort.

It was decided that La Fontaine should make a détour to see Richelieu which was only five leagues off the road. M. de Châteauneuf who knew the road offered to accompany him, while M. Jannart was to go straight on to Châtellerault where he had friends, and where the other two would meet him early the next morning. Port-de-Pilles was a place where one found all sorts of commodities and even incommodities for there was a horse fair at which a quantity of very poor animals were offered for sale. '*Méchants chevaux*,' La Fontaine called them, meaning wretched rather than vicious:

> Encore mal ferrés, et mal embouchés
> Et très mal enharnachés.[10]

Of these they chose the best they could find and had them shod and made ready. A guide was hired who rode pillion, and they set off for Richelieu.

The little town of Richelieu had been constructed on the site of the family property of Plessis-Richelieu where the great Cardinal was born. La Fontaine considered the spot badly chosen because of the poverty of the ground and the distance from the river. He commented on the emptiness of the houses, the population having dwindled so much that the town seemed deserted. Twenty years earlier Evelyn had reported: 'the town is on low marshy ground, having a small river cut by hand, very even and straight, capable of bringing up a small vessel . . . but since the Cardinal's death the town is thinly populated, standing so much out of the way and not well situated for health or pleasure.' At that time the town consisted of only one street, the houses built uniformly on each side. Besides a well built church, paved and adorned, the town boasted of an academy where all the sciences 'are taught in the vulgar French by professors paid by the Cardinal.'

Beyond the town lay the château and its magnificent grounds, approached by a long avenue leading to the domed entrance surmounted by a *Renommée*, a bronze statue of Fame. La Fontaine was deeply interested in all he saw. Before describing the château he reminded his wife that he was no authority on architecture and that those who looked for a learned discourse in his descriptions would be disappointed; and he recommended her to read the *Promenades* of M. Desmarets, particularly the fourth which describes birds nesting on the statues:

> Mainte hirondelle passe avec son aile aiguë,
> Consulte de ces dieux la réponse ambiguë
> Va cent fois et revient, gazouillant à l'entour
> De Jupiter, de Mars, de Vénus et d'Amour.
> Mais n'en vois-je pas une, insolente et profane,
> Qui gâte de son nid le carquois de Diane?
> Une autre a pour abri la harpe d'Apollon;
> Cette autre, de Pomone habite un creux melon;
> J'admire celle-ci qui, simple, s'aventure
> De confier sa race à ce larron Mercure.[11]

These statues had delighted La Fontaine as he crossed the wide court in front of the château. Most of them were antiques, such as the Caesar in oriental alabaster; the Faustine whom he took for Venus, and the Venus 'divinely beautiful' – which Poussin had said was finer than the Venus de Medicis. Michael-Angelo's famous statue of the Two Captives also greatly impressed him. He would have liked to linger in the interior admiring the great staircase of marble, but he was obliged to hurry along and follow M. de Châteauneuf and the concierge who acted as guide. However, he did spend some time in a room tapestried with portraits of the Richelieu family, of the kings of France and the great men of French history. They then passed through many splendidly decorated rooms: in the Queen's chamber there was so much gold that he got quite tired of it, preferring those which were decorated with tapestries.

After that they visited the chapels of which there were three, but they had only time to see the two that were upstairs. In one of these he found 'the original of that *dondon* – the plump girl that our cousin has placed above the chimney-piece in his hall. It is a Magdalen by Titian.' She was so alluring that after describing her he added: 'she has just become a penitent, and these recent penitents are dangerous, and all men of sound judgement fly from them. It seems that I have not spoken very devoutly of the Magdalen, but it is not my habit to argue about spiritual things, I have always been unwilling to do so.' The only other thing that he describes in the chapels is the mosaic representing Saint Jerome – 'so finished that it could not have been better done with a paint brush, and it looks like a painting, even when seen close up.'

The next treasure to attract his attention was the famous inlaid table (now in the Louvre), of which he says:

> Elle est de pièces de rapport,
> Et chaque pièce est un trésor;
> Car ce sont toutes pierres fines,
> Agates, jaspe, et cornalines.[12]

and in the middle '*la reine des agates*.' Passing from treasure to treasure, he admires the busts of the Roman Emperors, and after looking at a magnificent bust of Alexander the Great, he finally comes to a halt before the portrait of the Cardinal 'dressed in black, mounted on a very fine horse – a '*barbe blanc*,'' and encouraging his troops by his presence.' All along the gallery were pictures representing the conquests made during the ministry of Richelieu, and after glancing at the principal ones, La Fontaine and M. de Châteauneuf descended into the garden.

Nothing separated the gardens from the extensive park, and looking out from where he stood the poet saw before him a wide lawn, and beyond this green deep shaded walks, where, he says, it would have been pleasant to have had an amorous adventure. It was now evening, and as M. de Châteauneuf was tired, La Fontaine wandered off by himself, through those groves which Evelyn had said 'were a real paradise.'

'I strolled down a wide path, and had only gone a few steps,' says La Fontaine, 'when I felt myself obliged by a secret power to begin some verses to the memory of the great Cardinal . . . I should have liked to have put the finishing touches to these verses in the same place. Indeed if M. de Châteauneuf had not come to tell me that it was getting late, I would still be there. Imagine that I am in an alley where I meditate on what ensues:

> Mânes du grand Armand, si ceux qui ne sont plus
> Peuvent goûter encor des honneurs superflus,
> Recevez ce tribut de la moindre des Muses. . .
> On leur ouit chanter vos faits, votre sagesse,

Vos projets élevés, vos triomphes divers;
Le son en dure encore aux bouts de l'Univers.
Je n'y puis ajouter qu'une simple prière:
Que la nuit d'aucun temps ne borne la carrière
De ce renom si beau, si grand, si glorieux!
Que Flore et les Zéphyrs ne bougent de ces lieux;
Qu'ainsi que votre nom leur beauté soit durable...[13]

Together the two men strolled through the bowling greens, which were placed so as to have shade at different hours of the day. Now it was quite dark, and it took them some time to reach the main entrance of the château; La Fontaine well content and M. de Châteauneuf, who was wearing heavy boots, very tired.

Before he went to bed La Fontaine wrote to his wife, giving an account of all he had seen, ending his letter thus: 'look how grateful you should be; it is only a quarter of an hour before midnight, and we will have to get up before dawn, in spite of the fact that the setting sun promised to rise early. Nevertheless I employ these precious hours in order to write to you, I who am the child of sleep and idleness. Let them talk of husbands who sacrifice themselves for their wives! I maintain that I surpass them all, and that you will never be able to repay me, unless you wish me as many good nights as I shall have bad ones before this journey is finished.'

Though tired by their long day at Richelieu they had to get up before dawn, so as to rejoin M. Jannart at Châtellerault. 'It would be a fine thing to travel, if it were not necessary to start so early,' sighed La Fontaine as they groped their way into the still dark street. To make matters worse, the seneschal had ordered the gates of the town to be locked, because of a murder in the locality, and now M. de Châteauneuf had to prove that he was the king's messenger, before they could get out. However they arrived sooner than they had expected at Châtellerault, where they found the good uncle waiting for them at his friend's house. He had been promised horses to finish his journey, and provided that La Fontaine did not mind, had decided to cut out Poitiers, as it made the voyage longer. So on the friend's invitation they rested there for another day: the obliging M. de Châteauneuf being as anxious to please them as to carry out his orders.

At Châtellerault, beside the river Vienne, they were very well entertained: all that could be imagined of friendliness, of good cheer and politeness was lavished on them. They feasted on delicious carp, and ripe melons. Not only were they among friends but also found family connections, for their host had married a sister-in-law of one of the Pidoux, a kinsman of La Fontaine's mother. This M. Pidoux to whom the poet was introduced, bore out all the traditions of the family: he was born in 1581, had been married three times, and was to have a daughter born to him in 1664, having reached the respectable age of eighty-three years. La Fontaine said: 'all the Pidoux have long noses, and live to a very great age, death, which is such a common accident to other men, is considered as something most unusual among those of this line. I would be extremely curious to know if this is true! In any case my relative at Châtellerault can ride his horse for eleven hours without any fatigue, although he is over eighty. What is peculiar to him, and lacking in his relatives at Château-Thierry, is that he likes hunting and playing bowls; knows the scriptures and writes controversial books . . . This testifies to a happy old age in which pleasures, love and grace keep company till the end.'

In the family of this old man, La Fontaine found no great interest except for a girl whom he thought attractive; she was called Marie-Louise and he was pleased to accept her as his cousin, though his short stay at Châtellerault prevented him from discovering whether or not she was 'capable of secret passion.'

After an excellent and prolonged breakfast, they took the road to Chavigny, a miserable place, and from there the bad roads began and also the smell of garlic – two characteristics that distinguished the Limousin from other provinces. Their next night was spent at Bellac, of which La Fontaine said: 'the approach to this place was so bad that out of ten persons who pass there without getting out of their carriage, or off their horse, every three or four break their necks, for

> Ce sont morceaux de rochers
> Entés les uns sur les autres,
> Et qui font dire aux cochers
> De terribles patenôtres
>
> Des plus sages à la fin
>   Ce chemin
> Épuise la patience.
> Qui n'y fait que murmurer
>   Sans jurer,
> Gagne cent ans d'indulgence.

M. de Châteauneuf l'aurait cent fois maudit,
  Si d'abord je n'eusse dit:
'Ne plaignons point notre peine;
Ce sentier rude et peu battu
  Doit être celui qui mène
  Au séjour de la vertu,'[14]

M. Jannart would have liked to change their route, insisting that though there were honest people at Bellac, an unfortunate event had given the place a bad name: and he told the story of how an official of this town had bribed a miserable beggar to replace a man condemned to be hanged, by promising him twenty pistoles with the assurance that a reprieve was coming. The poor idiot accepted, only to discover his mistake when it was too late. M. Jannart had been one of the commission who judged the Provost responsible for this trickery. Perhaps, though La Fontaine does not say so, Jannart feared some sort of vengeance on account of his part in administering justice to the Provost.

The interior of the town was as disagreeable as the approach to it had been; the streets were sordid and the houses badly arranged: 'you who are so clean will dispense me from telling you details,' he adds, in a domestic compliment to his wife. The kitchens – on the upper floor – were such that those who saw them had no great curiosity about the sauces prepared there. In fact bad dishes were produced from good material, and the wine was only fit to dye clothes, and was generally known as *la tromperie de Bellac* – a name given to it by Louis XIII. The only attractive person was the serving maid, and La Fontaine would have liked to flirt with her. However, he slept soundly and alone on his hard bed.

M. Jannart was up betimes and anxious to be off before dawn. But as the horses had lost their shoes on the bad roads they had to be re-shod before they could start. And as Limoges was not far from Bellac, the travellers had plenty of time once they started, to lose themselves in a country where French was replaced by a patois difficult to understand; yet considering that they knew neither the language nor the country they got along very well.

As soon as they arrived at Limoges, their fidus Achates – M. de Châteauneuf – made arrangements to ride back to Paris as messenger, leaving next day. La Fontaine was sorry to part with this amiable companion who had kept them amused with court gossip. But there was no time for regrets, as they had to install themselves in their new retreat. The authorities received them with great affability, notably the bishop who kept the best table in the country and lived in considerable style. But don't imagine, said La Fontaine, don't imagine that the rest of the diocese are therefore unhappy and expelled from heaven as one supposes in our provinces. For the people of Limoges are as tactful and polite as the people of France: the men of this country are witty and the women fair; but their customs, their way of life, occupations, and above all their compliments, do not please me.' In fact he finds that:

> Ce n'est pas un plaisant séjour:
> J'y trouve aux mystères d'amour
> Peu de savants, force profanes;
> Peu de Philis, beaucoup de Jeannes;
> Peu de muscat de Saint-Mesmin,
> Force boisson peu salutaire;
> Beaucoup d'ail et peu de jasmin:
> Jugez si c'est là mon affaire.[15]

And with this verse the last letter ends. Happily he did not remain there long, and he was back in Paris before the end of the year.

TRANSLATIONS

[1]The shade of two chestnut trees, / Majestic and fresh / Cover it with their leaves, / As with a rich canopy. / I know nothing that equals this, / Or that is more to my taste / Than a lawn that is laid / On the length of every step. / I love ten times better this grass / Than the most precious carpets / On which the proud Orient / Sees its emperors seated. / Of what use so much expense / The greatest in vain may boast: / Long live the magnificence / That costs only the planting.

[2]It is a dangerous passage / A place of ambush and retreat for robbers; / To the left a wood, a mountain to the right, / Between the two / A sunken road. / The mountain is all covered / with rocks like those / Of our small domain.

[3]Up a steep road, sandy and rough, / Exposed on all sides to the sun / Six stalwart horses dragged a coach. / Women, a monk, old men had all got out, / The sweating, panting team were quite dead-beat.

[4]Much French blood was then shed; / Both sides lose in civil war; / Our prince would have been defeated, / Even if he had taken the town.

[5]I think he looks a sly old fox; / And indeed such was this prince: his life / Should rarely serve as an example to kings, / But could be followed on some points.

[6]La Beauce had many mountains long ago / As had the rest of France: / Of this the town or Orléans, / Full of successful, refined and lazy people / Who wished to walk at their ease, / Complained, and sulked and took offence. / And

the gentlemen of Orléans / said to Fate, with one voice / Once, twice and again, / That Fate should free them from the trouble / Of climbing, descending and climbing again.

[7]I found there such charming attractions, / That my soul is still deeply moved by them. / On both sides there are smiling hills: / Hills not such close neighbours to the sky / As those of Limousin, but hills enchanted, / Fine houses, lovely parks, and all well planted, / Green meadows everywhere in this rich country, / Vines and woodlands, so much diversity, / That at first one seems to be in another world.

[8]What need is there to describe / A strict and watchful guard, / Walled-in room, narrow place, / A little air for all grace, / Days without sun / Nights without sleep, / Three doors in six foot of space? / To describe to you such a lodging / Would reduce you to tears; / I have done it unintentionally: / And this plaint has charms for me.

[9]Between this place and the Limousin / We have passed at least four rivers on our way, / The Indre, the Cher, the Creuse, and the Vienne.

[10]Also badly shod and hard-mouthed, / And very badly harnessed.

[11]Many a swallow passes on pointed wing, / Consults the ambiguous answer of these gods / Goes and comes a hundred times, twittering round / Jupiter, Mars, Venus and Cupid: / But do I not see one, insolent and profane, / Who spoils with her nest Diana's quiver? / Another has for shelter the harp of Apollo; / That other, inhabits Pomona's melon; / I admire this one, simpleton who ventures / to confide her offspring to that thief Mercury.

[12]It is a rich mosaic / And each piece is a treasure / For they are all precious stones, / Agates, jasper and cornelian.

[13]Shades of great Armand, if those who are no more / May still enjoy honours superfluous; / Receive this tribute from the least of Muses ... We hear them praising your deeds, your wisdom, / Your noble projects, and your diverse triumphs: / The sound still rings to the ends of the Universe. / I can only add to it a simple prayer; / That no night of time will limit the career / Of this renown, so grand and glorious; / That Flora and zephyrs never leave this place, / And that like your name their beauty may endure ...

[14]These are lumps of rock / Piled on top of each other, / That make coachmen repeat / Terrible paternosters. / In the end this road exhausts the most patient / Those who only murmur / Without swearing / Gain a hundred years indulgence. / Monsieur de Châteauneuf would have cursed it a hundred times / If at first I had not said: / Don't complain of our discomfort; / This rude and rough path / Must be the one that leads / To the dwelling of the virtuous.

[15]This is not a pleasant resort: / I find here in the mysteries of love / Few wise, many profane; / Few Philis, many a Jane; / Little muscat from Saint-Mesmin, / Much drink of an inferior sort, / A lot of garlic and little jasmin, / Judge whether it is to my taste.

V

FOUR FRIENDS

1. Life in Paris

La Fontaine had known Molière as early as 1659. It was probably about a year later that he met Racine who had come to Paris in 1658, where he finished his studies at the collège Harcourt, and stayed on in the rue St Dominique with his cousin Nicolas Vitart to learn the business of administration. Vitart, intendant to the pious duc de Luynes, was a good friend and had many literary connections. He introduced his young cousin to the celebrated authors Perrault and Chapelain. Racine was also a cousin of La Fontaine's wife Marie Héricart, and the two poets probably met for the first time at the tavern kept by another of Racine's relatives, the Captain Antoine Poignan with whom La Fontaine had remained on friendly terms since their mock duel at Château-Thierry.

Racine had his first literary success with his Ode *La Nymphe de la Seine* composed for the Queen's entry to Paris in August 1660. This poem had been praised and corrected by Chapelain, and Racine amusingly suggested that the corrections in their turn should be corrected. From their first meeting La Fontaine and Racine became friends. The elder poet's amiable manners and easy way of life made him a very pleasant companion. Above all his knowledge and love of poetry delighted and inspired his young friend, who thoroughly agreed with him that the art of writing verse was of the greatest consequence. The constant discussions on books and authors, and the freedom of speech and liberty of morals in the taverns they frequented, seemed to the former seminarist of Port Royal a very pleasant change.

It may have been Furetière who introduced Racine and La Fontaine to the young critic Boileau Despréaux. He was three years older than Racine and they became very friendly. Boileau had started his career as critic in Paris, and he invited his two new friends to dine with him at his flat in the rue du Colombier to meet Molière. This was the beginning of a sort of quadruple alliance between four of the most remarkable poets of the age. Very soon they took the habit of meeting regularly, and for a considerable time they dined together two or three times a week, generally at Boileau's flat, to discuss their ideas and laugh at their contemporaries. Whether or not they went so far as to consider that their theories constituted the principles of a new movement, that would replace the burlesque and artificial style that still held favour with the public, they certainly agreed that their intention was to introduce into their works *le beau, le naturel et le vrai* while maintaining their respect for the ancients. Each in his own way followed this precept: it was a principle that gave wide scope to individual interpretations within contemporary conditions.

Racine's son Louis has recorded that when the four poets dined together *chez* Boileau, there was an open copy of Chapelain's *Pucelle* on the table, and if any one of them broke the rules of the company by using an affected or a hackneyed word, or did not take in good part the criticisms made by the others on his work, he was condemned as a penalty to read a number of lines from the poem. Such was the perpetual mockery with which these young poets treated this worthy but boring authority whom they wished to overthrow. In this they were helped by Chapelain himself whose verses were in general more admired than read.

Molière was the accepted leader and to a great extent the lawgiver of the group. He was older than the others, and was already celebrated as the author of *Les Précieuses Ridicules* – played in Paris from December to April 1659 – and his reputation and that of his troupe was well established. He stood high in the King's favour, and this added to his prestige in the eyes of the younger poets who honoured him particularly as the founder of a new movement towards natural comedy. La Fontaine had been much impressed by the trend of naturalism in *Les Fâcheux* when he saw this comedy played at Vaux. Writing to Maucroix at that time he said:

> C'est un ouvrage de Molière,
> Cet écrivain par sa manière
> Charme à présent toute la Cour.
> De la façon que son nom court,
> Il doit être par delà Rome:
> J'en suis ravi, car c'est mon homme.
> Te souvient-il bien qu'autrefois

Nous avons conclu d'une voix
Qu'il allait ramener en France
Le bon goût et l'air de Térence?
Plaute n'est plus qu'un plat bouffon;
Et jamais il ne fit si bon
Se trouver à la comédie;
Car ne pense pas qu'on y rie
De maint trait jadis admiré,
Et bon *in illo tempore*;
Nous avons changé de méthode:
Jodelet n'est plus à la mode,
Et maintenant il ne faut pas
Quitter la nature d'un pas.[1]

Jean Baptiste Poquelin, known as Molière, was Parisian by birth, he came from a good bourgeois family of successful merchants. His father held the inherited position of tapestry merchant and upholsterer to the King. Molière was the eldest son, he was received as day-boy at the college of Clermont, a renowned school run by Jesuits, where the sons of the nobility and those of the middle class were taught a little Greek and much Latin, with two years of rhetoric followed by two years of philosophy. In class the young noblemen sat apart separated from the commoners by a small gilded balustrade. The Prince de Conti – father of La Fontaine's future patrons – had attended the school at the same time as Molière, but he was several years younger than the dramatist. A school-fellow, in a truer sense, was the gifted Chapelle, whom we find in company of poets and wits at the time of Molière's first successes. When he had finished his school days the young Molière graduated as *Avocat de la cour de Paris* in 1640. But his real vocation became apparent as little by little he freed himself from his family to seek the company of comedians, discovering with enthusiasm the adventurous life of the theatre. He soon became acquainted with well known players such as Turlupin and Bruscambille, going regularly to see their popular farces. In 1642 his father sent him to Narbonne as *tapissier valet* to Louis XIII then in the last year of his reign. It was after this journey that Molière declared his intention of devoting himself to the stage and shortly afterwards linked his fortunes with the Béjart family and began his career as a comedian, joining with the Béjarts in the enterprise of the *Illustre théâtre* in the rue de l'Ancienne Comédie, of which he became the manager, principal playwright and leading actor.

The various adventures of those early years of touring through the country and the final success in Paris, would be too long to relate here; nor is it possible to dwell on his comedies, which hold their own when compared with the work of the greatest Greek comedians. One of his outstanding qualities was his complete intellectual honesty and this sincerity is reflected in all his works. It made for him many bitter enemies. His deep respect for logic and reason is shown also in the preface to his plays. For him the most dramatic situation was that in which passions were opposed to reason, and he considered that the art of comedy consisted in demonstrating and ridiculising the humiliations that arose from these painful adventures of the spirit. In this he was the most original dramatist of his time, expressing his own truth through his own methods. His characters appear on the stage with all the assurance of real life while their exaggerations and hypocrisy are held up to ridicule. There is nothing mysterious or sophisticated in these graphic portraits. Such plays as *Tartuffe* show clearly the force and rectitude of their author who, in spite of calumny and unrequited love, could conclude *il vaut mieux rire que pleurer.*'[2]

Yet beneath his strong common sense Molière hid an extremely sensitive response to life and literature. This is revealed in the *Misanthrope* where, in the ironic plight of the proud and solitary Alceste, the poet's own isolation is played on the scene; so that though the public are invited to laugh at Alceste, in the words of the author *il dit les choses fort justes*. The sonnet scene is a fine summary of the attitude to art on which his work is based; but when first played, the audience at once applauded the verses that were intended to be laughed at. Thus when Alceste condemns the school of Marot and Voiture: *ce style figuré, dont on fait vanité*. Molière speaks for himself, and concludes:

> . . . J'ai le défaut
> D'être un peu plus sincère en cela qu'il ne faut.[3]

It says much for Louis XIV that, even though he showed his usual caution in such matters, he protected his favourite comedian to some extent against the calumnies of the ecclesiastics, and in this he was encouraged by the opinion of Boileau, who replied to the King's question as to who was the greatest writer of the century: *Sire, c'est Molière*. This opinion surprised Louis, and may well have astonished the courtiers whose language was highly refined, whereas Molière's characters spoke in a perfectly natural and expressive manner. Boileau considered Molière as his master and founded many of the laws in his *Art poétique* on the ideas expressed in the comedies and their prefaces or in Molière's conversation. It was in fact evident that the comedies had turned the taste of the Court towards a new life-like rendering of society, enlarging the comic scene to include ruthless satire side by side with laughter and light jest.

*

In the autumn of 1661, shortly after the arrest of Fouquet, both La Fontaine and Racine fell ill, probably from an epidemic that had broken out in Paris. This was one of the immediate causes of Racine's departure for Uzès in Provence to stay with his uncle, chanoine régulier de Sainte-Geneviève, from whom the family had hopes of an ecclesiastic appointment for the young man, this however came to nothing. In two letters to La Fontaine, Racine gave his first impressions of the Midi: in the first, dated 11th November 1661, he recalled the happy time when they met every day:

> Avant qu'une fièvre importune
> Nous fit courir même fortune
> Et nous mit chacun en danger
> De ne plus jamais voyager.[4]

He had, he said, been writing very little verse, and told how he had first tasted olives, picking them off the tree and eating them 'with the greatest appetite,' so that for hours his mouth was in a sorry state, and he learned later there had to be 'many ceremonies and soakings to make them palatable.' He spoke also of the beauty of the Meridionals, and the warnings he had received from his pious hosts to be blind to all such attractions, and he concluded: '*voyez-vous, il faut être régulier avec les réguliers, comme j'ai été loup avec vous et avec les autres loups vos compères.*'[5] He remained at Uzès for eighteen months. In July of the following year he wrote again, in answer to a letter from La Fontaine, unfortunately now lost, which had greatly pleased him: 'I don't know anything that could better console me for my absence from Paris. I imagine myself right in Parnassus for you have described so well all that is worth recording of what happens there.' The letter ends with an appreciation of La Fontaine's judgement: 'I don't dare to think anything is good or bad till you have judged it.'

Orphaned at the age of four, Racine had been brought up by his paternal grandfather, after whose death he had been sent to the college of Beauvais, and at the age of seventeen went to continue his studies at Port-Royal, where his grandmother's sister had been a nun, and one of his aunts, Agnès Racine, became Abbess. Port-Royal was not a regular college, but a retreat where certain learned and devout men holding Jansenist doctrines had decided to retire from the world to live and work in common. They took a small number of pupils, giving them an excellent classical education, with special attention to the teaching of Greek. The pupils read the tragedies of Sophocles and Euripides whose works were explained and commented on by the well known grammarian Lancelot and other classical scholars. Ardour for their particularised faith, for the imposed solitude on which they prided themselves, and their courage in face of persecution, gave their cause dignity and strength. None of them were great writers. Lancelot's well known *Grammaire raisonnée* was edited by Arnauld, the leading spirit of the community, who as a polemist had a clear and modest style.

Racine spent three years at Port-Royal, at his most impressionable age. A difference of opinion between him and his learned but biased masters, arose from his insistence on reading profane authors; the Greek novel the *Loves of Theagenes and Chariclea* was taken from him and burned. This however, did not prevent him from obtaining another copy, which later he handed to Lancelot, saying that he had no further use for it, as he had learned it by heart. His enthusiasm for secular Greek authors had roused his need to assert himself, which La Fontaine noted in the character of Acanthe in *Les Amours de Psyché*. This incident also throws light on the point of view of the masters of Port-Royal, who allowed and encouraged the study of Greek drama provided it was subordinated to the rules of the church.

The double study of profane and sacred antiquity – Greek tragedy and Jewish Biblical history – was of incontestable value in animating and nourishing Racine's imagination, and providing him with themes of high drama. The classical inspiration reached its apogee in the great tragedy of *Phèdre*, and the Christian doctrine triumphed in the pure beauty of *Athalie* where the Muse of Port-Royal raises her voice in Biblical grandeur. The riches of those sources of drama provided Racine with the foundations of poetic resonance and nobility of language, which have never been surpassed. Notes made by him at Port-Royal for a concordance between classical and biblical terms, show how profoundly he was interested in such matters. His tastes were above all classical, and he had that particularly Greek quality of musical expression that fuses mind and matter, thought and feeling, into great poetry. Conforming perfectly to the taste of his time while enlarging the scope of the theatre, he turned radically against the trivial sophistication of his lesser contemporaries, replacing it by his genius and culture. In this he was enthusiastically supported by Boileau who, as a Greek scholar, ardently approved of the qualities of measure and reason found in Greek and Latin authors.

Nicolas Boileau Despréaux *le créateur du bon goût*, was the man about town of the group. The least gifted of the four poets, when young he was lively and sociable; his critical faculties extended from literature, good taste and morals, to the domain of wine and cookery. He was always ready to advise all comers on the choice of where to dine and what to drink, and though he did not make good living the object of his life, he liked to entertain his friends and he frequented wits of note, such as the duc de Vivonne – that *bon viveur* who excelled in mimicking and parodying actors and authors. Boileau was educated at the college of Beauvais where he studied law and theology. But he had strong leanings towards literature and when his father died leaving him *beaucoup d'honneur et peu d'héritage*, he devoted himself to writing satirical verse. Having a strong aversion to the generation of poets who had immediately preceded him, he attached himself with enthusiasm to Molière and Racine. From the beginning of his association with them he upheld Molière against the opinion of Chapelain who admired the fashionable Italian comedies. Boileau wrote his *Satire II* in 1662 after *L'École des Femmes* had been attacked, and his *Épitre VII* appeared in 1677 after the cabal against Racine's *Phèdre*. In his admiration for those two great men he showed much foresight, for they were to dominate, by their individuality and art, the age whose expression they created. The critic may be forgiven for running after them with his axioms taken from the classics, borrowing from Horace what he wanted to say. Indeed he translated much wisdom from Latin into French, but when he depended on his own talent he was greatly inferior to his masters, and he was later to be surpassed by the author of *The Rape of the Lock*, who was still in his cradle. For when left to himself Boileau's moral was commonplace and his realism heavy, his mind was that of a pedant and too often his verse lacked charm. Yet how useful he was, this rhyming critic, providing just what was needed to dispel the influence of the fripperies and fret-work, the decorative patterns of the Hôtel de Rambouillet, the extravagances of Madeleine de Scudéry, and the over refinement of Quinault and Cotin. And in his whole-hearted admiration for the classical art of his friends, he strengthened the ties of literary companionship and defined the doctrines of their work.

Yet Boileau showed little understanding of La Fontaine's genius, and always considered the *Fables* as a minor form of poetry, and in this he showed his limitations as a critic. In speaking of the tale of *Joconde*, an early work of La Fontaine, he did however say: 'all that La Fontaine writes is simple and natural, and what I particularly admire is a certain inimitable naivety of language which is so much esteemed in the works of Horace and Terence.' But he attacked the same story on moral grounds.

Boileau is said to have composed part of his third Satire during the autumn of 1665, when on a visit to La Fontaine at Château-Thierry, in company with Racine. On this occasion, the Lieutenant-General of the town invited Boileau to dine with him, but did not include the other two in the invitation. The satirist revenged himself for this slight on his friends by graphically describing the stupidity of provincial manners, and the heaped dishes of untempting food; making fun of the absurd opinions of the guests and their host which ended in a brawl while the author slipped away unnoticed. The boredom and discomfort of the whole entertainment are well described and must have caused much merriment to Racine and La Fontaine.

In this poetic alliance La Fontaine was the poet and dreamer who appeared to live in a sort of Epicurean leisure, yet there was nothing apathetic or devitalised in his meditations, which were principally concerned with poetry and poetic technique if not with his ephemeral love affairs. After listening with apparent indifference to his companions discussing the problems of their work, he would suddenly break into the conversation, his eyes shining with an inner light, his gestures dominated by an irrepressible rhythm. Completely absorbed in what he was saying, he paid no attention to remarks or contradictions from his friends but continued with enthusiasm to express his own ideas till, as suddenly as it had arisen, his ardour would fall, his face would change, as a sunlit landscape over which the shadow of a cloud passes, and he would retire again to his own solitude. Sunk in this state of reverie he was oblivious to what the others were saying. On one occasion – after dining with the flute player Descoleaux, Molière,

Racine and Boileau – La Fontaine, deep in his own thoughts, paid not the slightest attention to the jeers of the two youngest members of the party, Racine and Boileau; till Molière, thinking they were going too far, drew Descoleaux into the window recess and with warm-hearted conviction assured him: 'our fine wits work themselves up in vain, they will not get the better of the good fellow.'

Molière and La Fontaine were in many ways alike, they were nearer to nature than the other two poets whose learning and high spirits enlivened the dinner parties, at which they were sometimes joined by Furetière and Chapelle or other congenial wits. Such meetings, when not at Boileau's flat, generally took place at one of the cabarets frequented by men of letters.

It was Chapelle who introduced the four friends to the *Croix de Lorraine*, one of the most renowned meeting places of poets and wits. There remains no trace of its exact whereabouts, Chapelle refers to it as being '*à l'autre bout de Paris*,' and he celebrated its steep and narrow stair:

> C'était à la Croix de Lorraine,
> Lieu propre à se rompre le cou
> Tant la montée en est vilaine,
> Surtout quand, entre chien et loup,
> On en sort chantant mirondaine.[6]

Chapelle was the son of a rich bourgeois called Huiltier who was a friend of the philosopher Gassendi; he sent his son to the Jesuit college of Clermont in the rue Saint-Jacques, where Molière was also a pupil. The high-spirited and precocious younger boy greatly admired Molière's gift of mimicking popular actors. In Parisian circles Chapelle soon acquired the reputation of being a brilliant wit, and he also passed for a poet, having the gift of composing verses. On one occasion when asked by Racine for his opinion of *Bérénice*, he reduced the author to despair by replying:

> Marion pleure, Marion crie
> Marion veut qu'on la marie.[7]

Chapelle's most important work was *Le Petit Voyage* which he wrote in partnership with his friend Bachaumont. It is the description of an imaginary journey in the Midi, its tone is satirical, and it describes, in a mixture of verse and prose, whom they met and what they ate. Boileau said it was the only good thing he wrote, but today it seems very flat and decidedly dull. It was his conversation and high spirits that made him a welcome guest at dinner parties. When with the poets he amused himself by teasing Boileau and refusing to take him seriously, contradicting him and sometimes even persuading him to get drunk. But it was Molière for whom Chapelle had a real affection, and he gave sympathetic advice when consulted about the difficulties of theatre management, such as the distribution of the rôles of the three important actresses in Molière's troupe, for those ladies had to be treated with extreme tact; and we find Chapelle writing to Molière from the country:

> Il faut être à Paris pour en résoudre ensemble, et, tâchant de faire réussir l'application de vos rôles à leur caractère, remédier à ce démêlé qui vous donne tant de peine. En vérité, grand homme, vous avez besoin de toute votre tête en conduisant les leurs. Je vous compare à Jupiter pendant la guerre de Troie.[8]

Chapelle always remained a faithful friend to his *grand homme*, and when Molière, later in life, lived in a comfortable villa at Auteuil, Chapelle was a constant guest there.

During the early years of their friendship, the four poets met and dined or supped in various cabarets which Chapelle recommended to them, and it is thanks to him that the names of these places became associated with Molière, La Fontaine, Racine in his youth, and Boileau; and the legend of their indisputable comradeship is closely connected with the joyous intercourse of this bon viveur who had the precious faculty of amusing his friends.

The *Mouton blanc* near the church of Saint-Gervais in the Marché Saint-Jean where only a street of that name exists today, was one of the places where the poets liked to dine. It was here that Racine made his first draft of *Les Plaideurs*, in the company of Furetière and Boileau who both knew the modes and manners of the law-courts. They also frequented the *Pomme de pin* in the rue de la Licorne near Notre-Dame. This became an active centre of libertinage where gentlemen of the Court such as the marquis de Liancourt, Cyrano, and their friends met, sometimes dangerously, to discuss religion. The former proprietor had

made a fortune and sold the cabaret to Crenet, of whose wine Boileau
said:

> ... un rouge bord
> D'un Auvernat fumeux qui, mêlé de Lignage
> Se vendit chez Crenet pour vin de l'Hermitage.[9]

As Auvernat and Lignage are both inferior wines from the vineyards of
Orléans, this was an affront to the critical palate of a connoisseur.

Most of the cabarets had their special clients: there was the *Cabaret
du Bel Air* in the Faubourg Saint-Germain where the King's musicians
met. It was run by the sieur Dupuis whose daughter had married Michel
Lambert; Lulli the violinist who was compared to Orpheus went there,
and also Jacques le Pailleur and Damien Mitton – the latter was a
neighbour of La Fontaine. Not only musicians but also mathematicians
were habitual customers of this tavern; when the former were occupied
at the Palace, Etienne Pascal and his son Blaise would come to discuss
physics and astronomy with their friends, before Blaise had moved to
Port-Royal.

In the best of the cabarets the wine was excellent, the customers drank
Beaune, Gondrieux, Bourgogne, Champagne – not at this time a
vin mousseux, and Spanish wines. A Venetian ambassador writing from
Paris at this date to his government said:

> The French spend their money on nothing so willingly as on food and
> what they call 'good cheer.' That is why butchers, caterers and proprietors
> of eating-houses, retailers, pastry-cooks, restaurants and taverns are found
> in such quantity ... There is not a street no matter how insignificant that
> has not its share ... The eating-houses and pastry-cooks, in less than half
> an hour, will arrange for you a dinner, or a supper for ten, twenty or a
> hundred guests ... The foreigners flock there; not only the provincials
> who come for their pleasure or to visit the Court, but also Germans,
> Flemish, Northerners, Scots and English, Italians, Spaniards, Portuguese
> and others ...

But it was not only to eat well, but also to talk well, that Parisians
dined in town. The tradition of good cooking led to cheerful social
relations; people met to talk, and the taste for animated conversation
and for a certain luxury and elegance went with carefully chosen wine
and 'good cheer.' *Bien dîner*, in Parisian circles was also *bien causer*
according to a phrase of the time. This was particularly apparent in the
meetings of poets and wits; it was there that *bons mots*, vaudeville and

drinking songs originated, and in general a convivial atmosphere of jovial friendliness prevailed:

> On est savant quand on boit bien
> Qui ne sait boire ne sait rien.[10]

At this period the upper middle class on the whole hated domesticity: they liked to emulate – even at a distance – something of what they imagined resembled the gaiety of the Court, and willingly left their dark houses and narrow streets to enjoy themselves in the social atmosphere of the restaurants. The result of this trend of life was that most love was outside marriage, and most good eating was outside the home. Cheerfulness and recreation were rightly considered as essential to good health. To eat well and sleep well were the first conditions of happiness, and love-making was the finest game in the world. On the other hand, a woman's good name was her glory, as honour was essential to a gentleman. No one was ashamed of being drunk, what counted was how one behaved when in this precarious state.

2. A Picnic at Versailles

The most entertaining record of the friendship of the four poets is found in La Fontaine's *Amours de Psyché et de Cupidon*, dedicated to the duchesse de Bouillon and published in 1669, having been announced in the Epilogue of the *Fables* of 1668. The *Psyché* is a fairy tale in verse and prose, founded for the most part on the story as told by Apulius, and combined with a literary dialogue between four friends who are traditionally identified as Molière, Racine, Boileau and La Fontaine. This interpretation has been questioned, and other names have been suggested, such as Pellisson in place of Boileau for Ariste, Maucroix instead of Molière for Gélaste and La Fontaine as Acante in place of Racine, leaving the narrator Polyphile, who so much resembles La Fontaine, without any certain model. Maucroix had been the Gélaste of the *Songe de Vaux*, but this does not prove much, for we have ample evidence that throughout his works La Fontaine constantly gave the same *nom de Parnasse* to different friends both men and women. Also although certain dates have been introduced to confound tradition, as was the critical habit of the eighteen nineties, a careful reading of the *internal* evidence seems to show that the *Psyché* was probably written in the autumn following the fête at Versailles of May 1664, mentioned in the text as having recently taken place – and described elsewhere by Maucroix – though of course fêtes were fairly frequent at Versailles. This date would place it before the rupture between Molière and Racine in 1665, that is, at the time when the four poets were constantly in each other's company.

The excursion to Versailles may not actually have taken place, yet the arguments used in the conversations are founded on the opinions of Molière, Racine and Boileau, and recorded by their seemingly absent-minded companion. So too, the unquestionable resemblance between La Fontaine's portraits and those well-known authors is supported not only by the expression of their authentic theories, but also in the careful recording of their individual characteristics and tastes and their essential differences. We may therefore assume that Polyphile – the author of *Psyché* – is La Fontaine; Gélaste is Molière, who good-naturedly makes fun of the more sentimental parts of the story in truly Molièresque fashion, and is in general 'serious without being a bore'; Boileau, the lively Ariste, has much in common with Acante, who is Racine, and who upholds tragedy and loves gardens, flowers and shady places; In this he resembles Polyphile 'who loves everything'; 'the passions that filled their hearts with a certain tenderness were extended to their writings. They both had strong leanings towards lyricism, with this difference, that Acante's verses had something more moving, more impressive, and Polyphile's were more flowery.' This is an admirable observation on the part of La Fontaine, for what is moving in Racine is his deeply human interest expressed in musical and therefore lyrical verse; while La Fontaine's verses are also musical and 'flowery' in the contemporary sense of being fluent and light.

It is perhaps necessary to add, in a desire for accuracy, that the characters are to some extent imaginary: thus Acante may well be a sort of composite embodying Racine's arguments and La Fontaine's love of ease in pleasant shade of gardens. Yet this does not alter the fact that the arguments that form the background of the *Psyché* give us a general idea of the intercourse that the poets enjoyed.

We are told that it was 'the love of literature and the knowledge of Parnassus that had brought them together and the first rule they made was to banish all academic teaching from their conversation. When they had discussed their amusements, if they touched on some question of science or literature they did so without lingering on any subject: neither envy nor spiteful gossip found place in their intercourse.'

Moreover, 'they adored the works of the ancients, but did not refuse the moderns their due, and spoke modestly of their own work, giving each other sincere advice when any one of them caught the malady of the age and wrote a book.'

This is, of course, an idealised picture, such as we find in other works of the time describing picnics or excursions in which real, or imaginary characters take part. For La Fontaine was not alone in framing his story in the fiction of a party of friends, who comment on the tale read aloud or told by one of the group. Both Lemoyne in his *Peintures morales* whose characters were purely fictional, and Mademoiselle de Scudéry in her *Promenade à Versailles* (1669) whose characters were portraits, used the same method with great success.

It was at the suggestion of Acante that the four friends went together to spend the day at Versailles to hear Polyphile read his romance and admire the latest improvements in the palace and gardens. In the intervals of reading the manuscript they visited first the *Ménagerie* 'a place filled with many kinds of beasts and birds,' where they particularly admired the Ibis, *les demoiselles de Numidie*: Polyphile observing the extreme whiteness of the pelicans' plumage, 'lighter than a swan's, even from close up it appears flesh-coloured and becomes slightly rose towards the roots.' They next visited the *Orangerie* and were full of admiration for the mass of flowering shrubs. Acante, noticing that there were no other people near, recited a poem in praise of orange trees with their flowers, fruit and leaves, growing in such profusion:

> Sommes-nous, dit-il, en Provence?
> Quel amas d'arbres toujours verts
> Triomphe ici de l'inclémence
> Des aquilons et des hivers?
>
> Jasmins dont un air doux s'exhale,
> Fleurs que les vents n'ont pu ternir,
> Aminte en blancheur vous égale,
> Et vous m'en faites souvenir,
>
> Orangers, arbres que j'adore,
> Que vos parfums me semblent doux!
> Est-il dans l'empire de Flore
> Rien d'agréable comme vous?[11]

The three last verses sing of the beauty of these trees, and Aminte is not again mentioned. May this not be taken as further evidence that Racine is identified with Acante, for we know that he had spent eighteen months in Languedoc?

After they had dined, they visited the château and stopped to admire the King's bedroom and dressing-room, where the bed and chairs and also the walls, were all covered in Chinese tapestries representing the religious figures of China, 'but as there was no Brachmane (sic) present to explain, they understood nothing of the legends.' Returning to the gardens, they were amused by the ingenuity of the fountains and artifices with whistling birds, carved nymphs and tritons, described in verse by Polyphile, who adds that they scorned the shower-bath reserved for 'Germans and bourgeois sight-seers.' Then finally they sat down on the short grass round Polyphile who drew out his manuscript and began to read aloud.

When they had listened to the tale of Psyché for some time, a discussion arose as to whether gaiety or pity, laughter or tears, were the most desirable effects to be produced in a work of art. Having come to the point of his story where Psyché drops oil from the lamp and wakes the sleeping Cupid, Polyphile declared that he could go no further:

> Ce n'est pas mon talent d'achever une histoire
> Qui se termine ainsi.[12]

for you would weep to hear of the sufferings of a beautiful woman.' The impetuous character of the young Racine is well expressed in Acante's reply. 'Well then, we shall weep, don't let that stop you. The heroes of antiquity wept a lot. The charms of compassion are not less than those of laughter. I even maintain that they are greater, and I think that Ariste would agree with me. Be as tender and moving as you like, we will both listen to you all the more willingly.' 'And I,' said Gélaste, 'what becomes of me? God has had the grace to give me ears as well as you. When Polyphile consults me, and doesn't become too pathetic, things will go even better, considering the way he has chosen to write.' This opinion was received with approval by Polyphile, but Ariste who so far had said nothing, now joined in, 'I wish you would melt my heart with the adventures of your heroine, I would weep for her with the greatest pleasure. Pity is one of the most pleasing motives in a discourse, I prefer it above all others. But don't be tied down by that; it is a good thing to adapt oneself to one's subject, but it is still better to act according to one's genius. That's why you should follow Gélaste's advice.' Thus spoke the critic of the party. 'I am obliged to follow it, how could I do otherwise,' replied Polyphile. 'I have already mixed gaiety with the most serious parts of my story in spite of myself, and I can't be sure that I won't mix it with the saddest parts. It is a fault that I don't know how to correct, no matter how much trouble I take.' This is a good self-criticism of La Fontaine, for in his *Fables* the most tragic events are often treated with an amiable lightness or a sort of organic irony. 'Fault for fault,' replied Gélaste, 'I much prefer to be made to laugh when I ought to weep, than to be made to weep when I should laugh. That is why I say again, continue as you have begun . . .' Thus Molière gives the comedian's point of view, with which La Fontaine agrees, while Racine and Boileau defend tragedy.

At this point Acante suggested that they should walk about and see more of the gardens as the sun was now less hot. So they strolled along for some time without speaking, till Gélaste broke the silence. 'Just now,' he said, 'I let you put the pleasure of laughing lower than that of weeping; shall I cure you of that error? You know that laughter is the friend of man and of me in particular. Did you think that I was capable of abandoning its defence, without contradicting you?' 'Alas! no,' retorted Acante, 'for, if it were merely for the pleasure of contradicting, you would find it enough excuse for a long and stubborn dispute.' These words, which Gélaste had not expected, disconcerted him a little; after a short derisive laugh he continued: 'You think you will escape that way, but avoid the combat as much as you like, as long as you admit that your statement is absurd, and that it is better to laugh than to weep.'

'Taking it in a general way as you do,' admitted Ariste, 'that is true, but you falsify our text. We only said that pity is one of the emotions that we consider the most noble and the most excellent in an oration. I go even further and declare that it is the most agreeable; observe the boldness of this paradox!'

'O immortal gods!' exclaimed Gélaste, 'are there really people in the world mad enough to hold such an extravagant opinion? I don't say that I am not better entertained by Sophocles and Euripides than by a great many writers of comedy; but given that the two things are of equal excellence, would you miss the fun of seeing two old men cheated by a rascal like Phormion, to go and weep with the family of king Priam?'

'Yes! I would leave Phormion,' replied Ariste.

So they argued, each one illustrating his point of view with examples from classical authors, till Gélaste concluded the discussion by saying that laughter was peculiar to man, but that some animals could weep. 'I defy you,' he said, 'to let fall tears as big as those of a stag at bay, or the horse of that poor prince whose funeral is described in the eleventh book of the Eneid. I shall leave you to weep in company with the horse of Pallas, and I shall laugh with all men.'

This conclusion made the three others laugh. But as the discussion threatened to continue, Polyphile, feeling that they were wandering far from his text, began to praise the gardens in verse, saying:

> On ne connaissait point autrefois ces beautés
> Tous parcs étaient vergers du temps de nos ancêtres. . .[13]

Then under the withered branches that formed the roof of the vast gallery, especially constructed for the recent fête, they sat down and Polyphile continued to read aloud the adventures of his heroine interwoven with reflections, to which the others listened with interest. The reading ended with a hymn to Volupté the daughter of Psyché. This summed up the author's preferences and delighted them all by the warmth and truth of its imaginative power and the perfection of its form.

> O douce Volupté, sans qui, dès notre enfance,
> Le vivre et le mourir nous deviendraient égaux;
> Aimant universel de tous les animaux,
> Que tu sais attirer avecque violence!
> Par toi tout se meut ici-bas.
> C'est pour toi, c'est pour tes appas,
> Que nous courons après la peine. . . .
>
> Ce qu'on appelle gloire en termes magnifiques,
> Ce qui servait de prix dans les jeux olympiques,
> N'est que toi proprement, divine Volupté.
> Et le plaisir des sens n'est-il de rien compté?
> Pour quoi sont faits les dons de Flore,
> Le Soleil couchant et l'Aurore,
> Pomone et ses mets délicats,
> Bacchus, l'âme des bons repas,
> Les forêts, les eaux, les prairies,
> Mères des douces rêveries?. . .
>
> Volupté, Volupté, qui fus jadis maîtresse
> Du plus bel esprit de la Grèce,
> Ne me dédaigne pas, viens-t'en loger chez moi;
> Tu n'y seras pas sans emploi.

> J'aime le jeu, l'amour, les livres, la musique,
> La ville et la campagne, enfin tout; il n'est rien
>   Qui ne me soit souverain bien,
> Jusqu'au sombre plaisir d'un cœur mélancolique.
> Viens donc; et de ce bien, ô douce Volupté,
> Veux-tu savoir au vrai la mesure certaine?
> Il m'en faut tout au moins un siècle bien compté;
>   Car trente ans, ce n'est pas la peine.[14]

When Polyphile had finished reading, after a few brief reflections on the work, Ariste remarked: 'do you not see that the parts that gave us the most pleasure were those that excited our compassion?' 'What you say is very true,' replied Acante, 'but I beg you to look at this linen-gray, this colour of dawn, this orange and above all this purple, which surround the king of the stars.' And indeed it was a long time since they had seen such a magnificent setting of the sun:

> Dans un nuage bigarré
> Il se coucha cette soirée
> L'air était peint de cent couleurs;
> Jamais parterre plein des fleurs
> N'eut tant de sortes de nuances. . .[15]

Now the moon being at the full, the poets and their coachman took her for their guide.

The discussions that take place throughout the *Psyché* on the relative value of laughter and tears, comedy and tragedy, explain to some extent the inevitable disagreement between Molière and Racine, but the immediate cause of their quarrel was more sordid and materialistic. Molière behaved with generosity, first in lending Racine money, and secondly in putting on the stage at the *Palais Royal* his tragedy *Les Frères Ennemis*; and till the representation of his *Alexandre* at the same theatre, Racine had been grateful and amenable. But his ideas as to how his verse should be spoken, and the disdain of Molière's troupe for the phrasing of tragedy at rehearsals, were bound to lead to trouble. Racine's pride was wounded, he was dissatisfied and angry. So although his *Alexandre* was acted in a manner that pleased the Court, without saying anything to Molière, he managed to have the play put on at once at *l'Hôtel de Bourgogne*. This representation at a rival theatre was the only intimation that the comedians of the *Palais Royal* received to tell them that the play was withdrawn, and for two nights the piece was

played at both theatres. At this time there were no laws or legal contracts between authors, players and their producers and theatre mana-
gers. So this insulting behaviour merely resulted in a break in the
friendship of Molière and his protégé; and a coldness remained between
them, though Racine always kept his admiration for Molière's work,
and when some one criticised the *Misanthrope* in his presence, he
replied: 'it is impossible that Molière could have written a bad play, go
and see it again and consider it more carefully.'

This breach in the poetical alliance accounts for the fact that Racine
may not have been present on the impressive occasion when Boileau
invited La Fontaine, Molière and Chapelle to supper at the small house
which he rented at Neuilly-sur-Seine. The excellent wine provided by
their host made them all intensely serious, and led them to moralise
upon the futility of life, and to agree with the maxim of the Ancients
'that the greatest good fortune would be not to have been born and the
next best thing was to die as soon as possible.' These conclusions made
them decide to go at once to the river and drown themselves, and
through the darkness they set out to the banks of the Seine, only a short
distance from the house. However, when they got there, the dark water
looked uninviting, and Molière, who doubtless saw the comic side of
the adventure, remarked that such a fine action as they contemplated
should be carried out in the full light of day, and not hidden in the
shadows of night. La Fontaine was the first to agree with him, the
others hesitated for a moment and then concluded, 'after all he is right.'
And Chapelle added: 'No Sirs, we won't drown ourselves in anything
but wine until tomorrow morning.' So the tragedy turned to comedy
as Molière had intended it should, but if Racine had been there things
might have been different! It was Racine's son Louis, who in telling of
this adventure, which he considered the height of folly, added: *heu-
reusement mon père n'en était pas.'* Yet tradition has decided that he *was*
present on this occasion. But in the words of Molière's Sceptics, 'We
assert nothing – no, not even that we assert nothing.'

TRANSLATIONS

[1]It is a work by Molière, / This writer by his manner / Charms at present all
the Court. / So famous has his name become, / It must by now have reached to
Rome: / I am delighted, for he's my man. / Do you recall how in the past / We
all concluded with one voice / That he was bringing back to France / The good

taste and the style of Terence? / Now Plautus is a flat buffoon; / And never has it been such fun / To go and see a comedy; / For don't suppose when at the play / We laugh at things already seen / And praised *in illo tempore*; / For we have modified our method: / Jodel is no more *à la mode*, / At every step the whole way through / To nature we must now be true.

²It is better to laugh than to weep.

³I have the failing of being a little more sincere in this than is necessary.

⁴Before a fever importunate / Threatened us both with the same fate / And danger that all men deplore / Never to travel any more.

⁵For you see, one must be correct when with the correct, as I have been a gay dog with you and the gay dogs your cronies.

⁶It was at the Croix de Lorraine, / A proper place to break one's neck, / So dangerous is the stair, / Particularly when at dusk / One comes out singing mirondaine.

⁷Marion wept, Marion cried, / Marion wished to be married.

⁸ We must be in Paris to work things out together, and try to fit your rôles to your actresses' characters, so as to put an end to the contentions that give you so much trouble. Truly, great man, you need all your wits in guiding theirs. I compare you to Jupiter during the Trojan war.

⁹A coarse red wine from Auvergne, which mixed with Lignage / Is sold at Crenet's for a bottle of Hermitage.

¹⁰One is learned when one drinks well: / Who drinks not has nothing to tell.

¹¹Are we, said he, in Provence / What mass of trees always green / triumphs over the inclemency / Of cutting blasts and winters wild. / Jasmins that exhale sweet air, / Flowers that the wind cannot wither, / Aminte is as fair as you, / And you remind me of her. / Orange trees that I adore / How sweet is your perfume, / Is there in Flora's realm / Anything as agreeable as you? / Your fruits with their solid rind / Are a veritable treasure / And the garden of the Hesperides / Had no other apples of gold.

¹²I have not the aptitude to finish a story / That ends thus.

¹³Long ago these beauties were unknown / All the parks were orchards in the time of our ancestors.

¹⁴O sweet Voluptas without whom from our childhood, / Living or dying would have been the same thing, / Universal loadstone of all living creatures, / Whom you know how to attract with violence! / By you all things on earth are moved, / It is for you, it is for your charms, / That we all run after trouble. / What in magnificent terms we call glory; / That which served as prize in the Olympic games / Is you, and you alone, divine Voluptas. / And the pleasure of the senses does it count for naught? / For what are the gifts of Flora, / The setting sun and Aurora, / Pomona and her delicate fruits, / Bacchus, soul of all good feasts, / The forests, water-ways and meadows / Mothers of sweet reveries. / Voluptas, Voluptas, who long ago were mistress / Of the finest

spirit of all Greece, / Do not scorn me, come and dwell with me, / You will not be without employment: / I like gaming, love, books and music, / Town and country, there is nothing / That for me has not supreme worth, / Even to the sombre pleasure of a melancholy heart. / Come then: and of this boon, O sweet Voluptas, / Would you like to know truly the sure measure? / I would need at least a full century / For thirty years is not worth while.

[15]In a dappled cloud / The sun that evening set, / The air was painted with a hundred colours / Never flower-bed full of bloom / Had so many varied hues . . .

VI

THE BOUILLONS AND THEIR CIRCLE

La Fontaine's relations with the Bouillons had always been friendly, and he readily adopted the Duke and Duchess as his protectors when the occasion arose. The Duke, Godefroy de Bouillon, after his marriage with Marie-Anne Mancini in 1662, came frequently to Château-Thierry; he was *Grand chambellan de France*, a steady, submissive, rather colourless sort of man, but a good friend. It was about this time (1663) that La Fontaine, who since the arrest of Fouquet had been supervised by Colbert's officers, was condemned to pay an exceedingly heavy fine, amounting to 2,000 livres, on the charge of usurping the title of *écuyer* in signing two contracts. In the past his father had sometimes used this title, but since 1661 any false assumption of nobility was fined, particularly as holders of titles were exempt from payment of certain taxes.

La Fontaine realising that he would be ruined, wrote an *Épitre à Monsieur le duc de Bouillon* begging for his intervention. In this poem – a masterpiece of its kind – after praising the illustrious family of his protector, who was the nephew of Turenne, the poet pleads his cause:

> Digne héritier d'un peuple de vainqueurs,
> Ecoutez-moi; qu'un moment de contrainte
> Tienne votre âme attentive à ma plainte:
> Sur mon malheur daignez vous arrêter;
> En ce temps-ci, c'est beaucoup d'écouter.[1]

Then after alluding in veiled terms to the arrest of Fouquet, and his other anxieties concerning Jannart and his friend Pellison, he speaks of his own troubles and of himself:

> Mais le moins fier, mais le moins vain des hommes,
> Qui n'a jamais prétendu s'appuyer,
> Du vain honneur de ce mot d'écuyer,
> Qui rit de ceux qui veulent le paraître,

> Qui ne l'est point, qui n'a point voulu l'être
> C'est ce qui rend mon esprit étonné.
> Avec cela je me vois condamné,
> Mais par défaut. J'étais lors en Champagne,
> Dormant, rêvant, allant par la campagne,[2]

and he says that he had always paid his dues, and that he had not even read the contracts which described him wrongly:

> Signés de moi, mais sans les avoir lus:
> Et lisez-vous tout ce qu'on vous apporte?
> J'aurais signé ma mort de même sorte...[3]

For who in the world reads all the boring business papers brought to him; and he continues:

> Sous le chagrin mon âme est accablée;
> L'excès du mal m'ôte tout jugement.
> Que me sert-il de vivre innocemment,
> D'être sans faste et cultiver les Muses?[4]

And now he fears that he and his brother, his little son and the child's nurse, will all have to go to the hospital – the poor-house – if they have the luck to find a place there. The little Charles was at this time about eight years old, here a poetic licence makes him appear younger. Claude de La Fontaine had not yet been fully paid the money owed to him from his share in the family estate, and was probably living at his brother's expense in the old home. This pathetic epistle ends with an appeal to the young Duchess:

> Comme elle sait persuader et plaire,
> Inspire un charme à tout ce qu'elle dit,
> Touche toujours le cœur quand et l'esprit,
> Je suis certain qu'une double entremise
> De cette amende obtiendrait la remise.[5]

Evidently the Duke took steps to soften Colbert's heart and the charge was cancelled. In the dedication of *Psyché* to the Duchess, La Fontaine said: For a long time Monseigneur le duc de Bouillon has done me the greatest favours, all the greater because I do not deserve them, and all I can do to thank him is to bear witness to his glory...

It was in the early summer of 1664, that La Fontaine, then living in his house rue des Cordeliers at Château-Thierry, climbed slowly up to the château to pay his respects to the Duchess. As he climbed the slope, all sorts of poetic compliments passed through his head, to be at once forgotten when, having entered by a postern gate, he arrived on the terrace to find himself in the presence of a very young lady surrounded by a whole pack of barking lap-dogs. She was sitting on a wide stone bench, leaning back on a red velvet cushion, precariously balancing on one white foot a red embroidered shoe, just showing beneath her ample skirts. She was slim and well proportioned, her nose was short and slightly tip-tilted, her unpowdered complexion peach-coloured, and her long hair fell in a mass of brown curls that glinted in the sunlight on her white shoulders. La Fontaine never forgot this first impression and years later he wrote:

> Peut-on s'ennuyer en des lieux
> Honorés par les pas, éclairés par les yeux
> D'une aimable et vive princesse,
> A pied blanc et mignon, à brune et longue tresse,
> Nez troussé, c'est un charme encor selon mon sens;
> C'en est même un des plus puissants.
> Pour moi, le temps d'aimer est passé, je l'avoue,
> Et je mérite qu'on me loue
> De ce libre et sincère aveu,
> Dont pourtant le public se souciera très peu:
> Que j'aime ou n'aime pas, c'est pour lui même chose;
> Mais, s'il arrive que mon cœur
> Retourne à l'avenir dans sa première erreur,
> Nez aquilins et longs n'en seront pas la cause.[6]

The Duchess, in whose presence he so unexpectedly found himself, swearing at her dogs rose to meet the poet, greeting him with smiles. He had already been presented to her and she had read some of his *Contes* in manuscript. La Fontaine was soon quite at his ease, while his amiable hostess made him sit down beside her, and spoke of his work which she had enjoyed, showing that she was no prude, and begging for more of his 'fascinating and wicked tales.' She talked a great deal, and he was sorry when presently a lady-in-waiting joined them, and the young Duchess rose offering him her small white hand to kiss. The poet now gracefully withdrew, with many respectful bows, promising to be always at her command, while she insisted laughingly that he must come again and read some of his new *Contes to* her.

In a delicious dream La Fontaine departed taking the same short-cut by which he had come. At this the Duchess laughed and the lady-in-waiting remarked: '*il est distrait*.' This was the beginning of a long and friendly patronage. Very often La Fontaine would pay a morning call and find the Duchess surrounded by a perfect menagerie of monkeys, dogs and bright-winged parakeets, all of which she controlled as best she could, while listening to the poet reading his own verses or those of earlier authors. Years later he reminded her of those happy days:

> Nul auteur de renom n'est ignoré de vous;
> L'accès leur est permis à tous.
> Pendant qu'on lit leurs vers, vos chiens ont beau se battre!
> Vous mettez les holàs en écoutant l'auteur;
> Vous égalez ce dictateur
> Qui dictait tout d'un temps à quatre. . .[7]

Continuing in prose: 'it was, it seems to me, Julius Caesar, who dictated at the same time four dispatches on four different matters. You do not owe him anything in that direction. I remember one morning, reading verses to you, I found you at the same time attentive to my reading and to three different quarrels among your animals. It is true that they were on the point of strangling one another. Jupiter the conciliator could not have done better. One may judge by that, Madame, how far your imagination can go when there is nothing to distract it. You give judgement on a thousand different works, and judge them well.'

This was not entirely base flattery, for Mazarin's youngest niece had a ready gift of picking up subjects discussed at supper parties, and giving an opinion with a seeming authority that lost nothing from her graceful gestures and bright eyes. In a letter to La Fontaine (1687), Saint-Évremond, then in England, said in speaking of her: 'In ordinary arguments, she disputes with spirit, often to my shame she is right, but her rightness is so animated that it appears to be passionate, and people of mediocre judgement, even those with more delicate observation, would find it difficult not to think that she was angry – were she less amiable than she is.' This was written during her exile in England when she had passed through many told and untold adventures.

Marie-Anne Mancini, who had married the duc de Bouillon, was the youngest of the five notorious Mancini sisters, nieces of Mazarin, the daughters of the Cardinal's younger sister Hieronyme who married a Roman baron, Lorenzo Mancini. The Mancini sisters, installed by their uncle in the Palais-Royal, when they first arrived in France were popularly known as the Mazarinettes: thin drooping little girls with long straight hair, dark eyes and sallow faces, they drifted across the Parisian scene, mournful as Pirandello's characters in search of an author. The appearance of these mysterious unpromising actresses in the comedy of French society did not pass unnoticed by the composers of *Mazarinades*:

> Elles ont les yeux d'un hibou,
> L'écorce blanche d'un chou,
> Les sourcils d'une âme damnée
> Et le teint d'une cheminée.[8]

But they were soon to change all that; their development was rapid and each of them learnt to make the best of her appearance and charm. They admirably represented the Italian race, and their natural nobility combined with adventurous instincts made them popular. Like their cousins the daughters of Mazarin's elder sister Laure-Marguerite Martinozzi, they had beauty, daring and ability; and enlivened French society, bringing new movement to the humdrum decorum of the Court by their impulsive spirits and agility. One never knew where one was with them, they disturbed other people's serenity, but were so amusing and lively that when they were not there one sighed for their company.

Perhaps the first women to be entirely cosmopolitan, owing no allegiance to any one country, they were European, neither strictly Italian nor French in their fickle and opportunist outlook. This trait, inherited by their respective sons, was to be the cause of continuous anxiety to the careful Louis and his ministers.

The eldest sister Laure was married to Louis duc de Vendôme, the son of a legitimised bastard of Henri IV; she was the mother of the two Vendômes, the Duke and the Grand Prieur, two of the most rebellious and irresponsible malcontents of Louis' reign. The second of the five sisters, Olympe Mancini, was loved with gallantry by the young King and was appointed surintendante of the Queen's household. At the beginning of his reign Louis was constantly in her company to the great displeasure of his queen. But Olympe spoilt her own chances by her insatiable pride and passion for intrigue, and she was finally exiled from the court. By her marriage with the count of Soissons she had two sons, the younger of whom became the celebrated prince Eugène. This youth inherited the bitterness of his disillusioned mother; he took part in all the escapades of his cousins the Contis and became the most brilliant general of the Imperial armies.

The third sister, Marie, had been loved tenderly by the young King whose passion for her was never satisfied: she was not beautiful but she had great vitality. When Louis became engaged to the Infanta Marie-Thérèse, Marie Mancini was sent from his mother's household to the sad little town of Brouage. When taking leave of Louis, who was greatly moved, she said: 'I go away, you weep; and you are king:' words which were repeated in Racine's *Bérénice*, played before the court ten years later. Eventually Marie married Lorenzo Colonna, constable of the kingdom of Naples. In 1661 the fourth sister Hortense, Duchess of Mazarin, to escape the jealous tyranny of her husband Charles de La Porte, who took his ducal title from Mazarin, retired to England to join her confidant and friend, Saint-Évremond. She and her companion Madame de Courcelles were described by a contemporary as '*deux demons sous forme d'anges.*'

The duchess de Bouillon occupied a house on the Quai Malaquais where La Fontaine was always welcome; and here he met Ninon de Lenclos, the marquis de La Fare, the courtier abbé de Chaulieu – at this time attached to the Bouillon household – and other libertines. La Fontaine also frequented the Hotel de Vendôme. Chaulieu, in a letter to his sister, describes an evening there: 'the company was plunged in the furies of bassette. There were seventeen or eighteen players among whom shone Mme de Bouillon, and her husband. The duc de Vendôme, following his usual custom, lost at least the value of half the Hôtel de Vendôme.' In this circle the lively Marie-Anne de Bouillon was so conspicuous for her gallantry that after a particularly daring intrigue with the husband of a lady of the Court, the dissolute Duchess was confined to the care of the convent of Montreuil in 1674. Three years later she and her brother the duc de Nevers took the lead in the cabal against Racine's *Phèdre* – presented at l'Hôtel de Bourgogne – in favour of Pradon, an obscure dramatist, chosen by Mme Deshoulières to compose a play on the same subject as that of Racine; the uneasy conscience of Mme de Bouillon having discovered in Racine's tragedy a slight on her behaviour with her nephew the Grand Prieur. These intrigues were known to the King, who disapproved of the Duchess and disliked her bold manners, but said, when the Dauphin was growing up, that she would be a suitable person to instruct him in the art of love-making.

La Fontaine never lost touch for long with the Bouillon family. In 1669 the duc de Bouillon's youngest sister Mauricette Fébronie de La

Tour had married the Duke of Bavaria. The marriage had taken place at Château-Thierry, and apparently at the bride's request, La Fontaine wrote an account in verse of '*les affaires de France,*' in which the progress of events concerning the international situation was admirably presented: the exploits of the family were recounted and praised. The poem was published in the *Fables Nouvelles et autres poésies* of 1671. In the same year as Mauricette's marriage, her uncle the duc d'Albret, younger brother of the duc de Bouillon, received his cardinal's hat at the age of twenty-five. This was an occasion not to be missed, for La Fontaine had known him since boyhood and now joyously addressed him as '*Vous voilà deux fois Prince*' which must have pleased this ambitious prelate who was made Grand Aumonier de France within the year. La Fontaine dedicated to him the *Poème de la Captivité de Saint Malc.*

The third part of the *Contes et Nouvelles en vers* was published in January 1671 and the *Fables nouvelles et autres poésies* followed in March of the same year. And in June we find La Fontaine at Château-Thierry writing to the duchesse de Bouillon to remind her that the year before she had given orders to her *prévôt* M. de La Haye (who as a young man had taken part in the ballet *Les Rieurs du Beau-Richard*), that La Fontaine was to be allowed to stay at the château for as long as he liked, and that he was not to be bothered about anything. Now he also reminds her that he had already given her the name of Olympe as her *nom de Parnasse* (in spite of the fact that she had a sister of that name), and he pays her many pretty compliments:

> Qu'Olympe a de beautés, de grâces et de charmes!
> Elle sait enchanter les esprits et les yeux:
> Mortels, aimez-la tous; mais ce n'est qu'à des Dieux
> Qu'est réservé l'honneur de lui rendre les armes. . .[9]

Again some years later, after the sale of the house in the rue des Cordeliers, La Fontaine, now staying in the château, writes to the Duchess, who, he says, had not been there for some time.

> 'here I am, Madame, in a dwelling that in the past had the honour of your presence, for it seems that your Highness has not been here for a long time. I very humbly beg you to allow me to cultivate flowers in the high flower-bed above the terrace; my chief reason for asking this favour is to decorate a place where you may come some day. M. de La Haye tells me

that you wish me to have a room in the château whenever I am staying at
Château-Thierry. I will accept this favour; but I very much doubt whether
I shall be able to stay more than two months, on account of my business
affairs. Paris will see me again sooner than I thought. Nevertheless I cannot
imagine that there is such a fine view anywhere else in the world as there is
here. Only your presence could compensate me for it. I will give you proof
of this in the future more often than I have done for some time. . . Does
your Highness remember that you amused us for four hours at the abbé
de Chaulieu's? We were four fine wits – not counting Mademoiselle de
Lenclos – so charmed to listen to you that we had not a word to say. . .

Continuing his letter he hopes that Chaulieu will invite them all again
and that there will be some general discussion, and ends in a less sub-
servient tone, declaring that he himself is not bad at debating but
almost as good in that line as her nephew the duc de Vendôme.

La Fontaine was at Château-Thierry on business during the summer
and autumn of 1684, and if this undated letter was written then, the
Duchess's prolonged absence from Château-Thierry would coincide
with the famous Poisons case in which she was involved. This was the
greatest scandal of the age, lurid in its horrible details, and piteously
childish in the crude faith in magic shown by those who took part in it.
A sort of mass hysteria possessed a group of credulous and jealous
women, ready to risk everything for their own triumphs.

It is difficult to say how far the duchesse de Bouillon was guilty of
any criminal intention towards her husband the bland Duke. Probably
it was merely the desire to be in the fashion, to follow the King's
mistress, together with the excitement of a new adventure, that
brought her into direct contact with fortune-tellers, venders of love-
charms, and suchlike sorcery that haunted the borders of evil. Certainly
when denounced and called up for examination before her judges, she
replied to their questions with cool disdain; and Mme de Sévigné gives
us a graphic account of the proceedings:

> Yesterday Mmes de Bouillon and Tingry were both questioned at the
> Arsenal. They were accompanied by their noble families. Really they
> received this affront on the slightest grounds – or so it seems up to the
> present. After she had been questioned the duchesse de Bouillon left the
> court and was received by all her friends and relations with adoration,
> for she was so pretty, naive, natural and fearless and looked so well and
> care-free.

Unfortunately she was not content to keep quiet about her trial, but boasted so much of her own cleverness in the replies she had made to the judges, that she brought on herself a month later a *lettre de cachet* – a royal warrant ordering her to go to Nerac in Guyenne near the Pyrennees. 'She left with much regret,' records Mme de Sévigné, and adds, 'there is food for thought in this departure: if she is innocent, she loses infinitely in not having the pleasure of a triumph; if she is guilty, she is lucky to avoid the shameful confrontations and convictions that would have ensued. All her family escorted her for half a day's journey from here ... Look at the four sisters,' continues Mme de Sévigné, 'what wandering star dominates them; in Spain, in England, in Flanders, and in the depth of Guyenne!'

Olympe, comtesse de Soissons, at the same time as her sister, was compromised in the vile accusation of having plotted to poison the King, who, to avoid having her arrested, sent a *lettre de cachet* by the duc de Bouillon, who told her that she must leave France at once or go to the Bastille. She did not hesitate, and leaving the card table where she was entertaining her friends, without saying a word to them, packed up and left that night for Brussels. Hearing of her departure, her lover the marquis de Villero, in whose interest she was said to have acted, shut himself in his rooms and saw no one for several days.

In 1687 the duchesse de Bouillon was again sent away from Paris for some escapade, and went to England to join her sister Hortense.

TRANSLATIONS

[1]Worthy heir of a race of conquerors, / Listen to me, and let a moment of restraint / Hold your mind attentive to my plaint: / Deign to pay attention to my misfortune / In these days even to listen is an effort.

[2]But the least proud, but the least vain of men, / Who has never claimed to depend upon / The vain honour of the word esquire / Who laughs at those who could appear as such / Who has not, who never wanted to have this title? / It is this that astonishes me. / In spite of this I see myself condemned,/ But by default. I was then in Champagne, / Sleeping, dreaming, going about the country ...

[3]Signed by me, but without having read them: / And do you read everything brought to you? / I would have signed my own death warrant in the same way.

[4]My soul is overwhelmed by grief / The burden of this ill destroys my judgement. / What good is it to live in innocence, / To be temperate, calm, and cultivate the Muse?

⁵As she knows how to persuade and please, / And gives charm to all she says, / And always touches both heart and mind, / I am sure that a double intervention / Would obtain release from this penalty.

⁶Could one be bored in this place / Honoured by the footsteps, lit by the eyes / Of an amiable and lively princess, / Dainty white feet, long and brown locks, / Turned-up nose, to my mind that's also a charm, / It is even one of the most powerful. / For me the time of loving is past, I admit / And I deserve to be praised / For this free and sincere admission, To which the public will pay little heed; / Whether or not I love, is for them the same thing; / But should it happen that my heart / Returns in future to its first imprudence / long aquiline noses will not be the cause.

⁷No author of renown is ignored by you / All of them are allowed an audience. / While one reads to you, your dogs fight in vain! / You call them to order while listening to the author; / You equal that dictator / Who dictated four texts at the same time.

⁸They have eyes like owls, / Skin as white as cabbage / Eyebrows of the damned / And complexions black as chimney-pots.

⁹What beauty, grace and charms has Olympe! / She knows how to enchant our minds and our eyes; / Mortals, you all must love her; but it is only the gods who are worthy of her.

VII

AT THE LUXEMBOURG

In July 1664 La Fontaine entered the household, at the Luxembourg
Palace, of Marguerite of Lorraine duchesse douairière d'Orléans, from
whom he received his *brevet de gentilhomme servant*, and became one of
her nine gentlemen in waiting, taking his oath of fidelity at Paris. This
appointment was badly paid but the duties were light and he was often
free to go and come as he liked. At first he lodged with Jannart and
later, when his wife retired to Château-Thierry, he had a room in the
rue d'Enfer just beyond the park. He still held his offices at Château-
Thierry, but went there less and less and seldom saw his wife. He
remained in the service of the Duchess until her death eight years later.

The Luxembourg palace had been built for Marie de Médicis in
1615–1620, under the direction of Salomon de Brosse. The English
diarist Evelyn, who visited the palace in 1644 said:

> 'I went to see more exactly the fine rooms ... The gallery is full of the
> paintings of Rubens, being the history of the Foundress's life, finely
> designed; at the end is the Duke's library well furnished with excellent
> books, all bound in moroquin and gilded, the *valans* of the shelves being
> of green velvet fringed with gold. In the cabinet joining it are only smaller
> volumes with six cabinets of medals, and an excellent collection of shells
> and agates whereof some are prodigiously rich ... There are other spacious
> noble and princely furnished rooms, which look towards the gardens and
> are nothing inferior to the rest.'

At the time of La Fontaine the park extended about a square mile
enclosed by walls as when Evelyn had visited it. The immediate
gardens were laid out in trimmed box, and the flower beds were gay
with flowers, though less resplendent than in the days of the late Duke.
All round the parterre with its statues and fountains, a border of
freestone decorated with pedestals for figures and vases, divided the
garden from the slightly higher level of the woods, opening to reveal

the Medici fountain on the left, as it does today. Paths led in all directions through rows of magnificent lime trees. A thick hornbeam hedge
sheltered the palace and gardens. Here people from the town came to
walk in the shade, lie on the grass, or play bowls. Yet the grounds were
so large that they never seemed to be crowded. On the north side
beyond the palace entrance lay the town residence of the Conti family,
with its extensive gardens on the slope of the hill.

In the time of the late Gaston d'Orléans the palace had been filled
with merriment and feasting, but under the rule of his widow it had
become extremely austere and dull. It was now a divided household in
more senses than one, for the *vieille Madame* – as Mme de Sévigné
called the dowager Duchess – lived in the east wing; and the Grande
Mademoiselle, daughter of Gaston by his first wife and thus first
cousin to the King, inhabited the west side with her suite of attendants
and servants. The two ladies were not on speaking terms, and during
the Duchess's last years their relations did not improve.

Of Madame's three daughters, the eldest, Marguerite-Louise
d'Orléans, was married to the Grand-Duke of Tuscany whom she left
in 1676; the second, Elizabeth d'Orléans duchesse d'Alençon, who was
a hunch-back, married the duc de Guise in 1667; and the youngest,
Françoise-Madeleine who had married Charles-Emmanuel duc de
Savoie, had died in January of the year in which La Fontaine took
service at the palace. The *vieille Madame* was a sombre figure, gloomy
and devout; in mourning for her favourite daughter, she received few
guests, and was under the influence of the more forbidding type of
spiritual advisers of whom the most notable was François de Batailler,
bishop of Bethlehem, who was her almoner till 1668 when he was
succeeded by Mallier who became later bishop of Tarbes. La Fontaine
was much in awe of his disillusioned and parsimonious patroness, but
he kept his independence, as indeed he always had done. Now he
expressed no opinion on the encircling melancholy of the palace,
perhaps agreeing with Tallemant that the Duchess was *une pauvre
idiote, et qui pourtant a de l'esprit*; and was therefore to be treated with
special deference and at best avoided as much as possible.

The young Elizabeth d'Alençon and her maids of honour provided
the only relief from the heavy boredom that weighed down the occupants of the east wing of the palace, though the ceremonious visits,
connected with her proposed marriage to a Spanish prince, did little to
enliven the atmosphere. La Fontaine, easy-going and ready to be

Portrait of Nicolas Fouquet, by Nanteuil, 1661 (p. 45)

Veue du Chasteau de Vaux le Vicomte du costé de l'Ecurie
A Paris chez N. Langlois Rue S.t Jaques à la Victoire.   avec Privil.   fait par Perelle.

Château de Vaux-le-Vicomte (p. 51)

Le Coche et la Mouche, engraved by J. B. Oudry (p. 65)

View of Orléans in 1690 (p. 66)

View of Blois, 'profile from west' (p. 67)

amused, or to retire into his own world of dreams inspired by visible beauty, found a meagre diet for reflection in his immediate surroundings. However, he made the best of what he saw and wrote a sonnet to Elizabeth d'Alençon, in which he referred to her problematic marriage that should bring peace to France.

Ne serons-nous jamais affranchis des alarmes?
Six étés n'ont point vu la Paix dans ces climats,
Et déjà le démon qui préside aux combats
Recommence à forger l'instrument de nos larmes.

Opposez-vous, Olympe, à la fureur des armes;
Faites parler l'Amour, et ne permettez pas
Qu'on décide sans lui du sort de tant d'Etats;
Souffrez que votre hymen interpose ses charmes.

C'est le plus digne prix dont on puisse acheter
Ce bien qui ne saurait aux mortels trop coûter;
Je sais qu'il nous faudra vous perdre en récompense.

Un souverain bonheur pour l'empire françois,
Ce serait cette paix avec votre présence;
Mais le Ciel ne fait pas tous ses dons à la fois.[1]

This sonnet was written in 1665, perhaps in September of that year, when owing to the death of Philip IV of Spain, the European situation had again become critical. But it was to a Frenchman, the eighteen year old duc de Guise, that Elizabeth became engaged, and their marriage took place on 15th May 1667. Shortly after this event the palace was enlivened by the arrival of the youthful Mlle de Poussay, whose mother was lady-in-waiting to the newly married duchesse de Guise, now installed in her new home. Mlle de Poussay was extremely pretty, she had been taken from a convent to be presented to the King in the hope that he would be seduced by her charms. But the young Duke's sister, Mademoiselle de Guise, fearing that her brother would fall in love with the new-comer, had obliged both her and her mother to retire to the Luxembourg in the household of the old Duchess. This, together with the fact that La Fontaine had not paid any compliments to her looks, seems to show that the little hunch-backed Duchess was no beauty. There are allusions to this general situation in the sonnet *Pour Mademoiselle de Poussay*. La Fontaine, enamoured of her beauty and roused from a mood of peaceful contemplation, responded at once to the marvel of things immediately seen and felt:

> J'avais brisé les fers d'Aminte et de Sylvie,
> J'étais libre, et vivais content et sans amour:
> L'innocente beauté des jardins et du jour
> Allait faire à jamais le charme de ma vie,
>
> Quand du milieu d'un cloître Amarante est sortie;
> Que de grâces, bons dieux! tout rit dans Luxembourg:
> La jeune Olympe voit maintenant à sa cour
> Celle que tout Paphos en ces lieux a suivie.
>
> Sur ce nouvel objet chacun porte les yeux;
> Mais, en considérant cet ouvrage des Cieux,
> Je ne sais quelle crainte en mon cœur se réveille.
>
> Quoi qu'Amour toutefois veuille ordonner de moi,
> Il est beau de mourir des coups d'une merveille
> Dont un regard ferait la fortune d'un roi.[2]

The atmosphere of tension which pervaded both sides of the palace is amusingly revealed in a poem to the small dog Mignon whom the Grand-Duchess of Tuscany had given to her mother. One of La Fontaine's minor duties from time to time was to keep an eye on this little creature, who would have liked to be on friendly terms with the dogs in the household of the Grande Mademoiselle. The poem is full of discreet allusions to the Orléans family as well as to the sorrows of the little dog. After lines to the glory of the illustrious family and the destiny of Mignon, a dialogue ensues between poet and dog:

> Petit chien, qu'as-tu? dis-le-moi:
> N'es-tu pas plus aise qu'un roi?
> Trois ou quatre jeunes fillettes
> Dans leurs manchons aux peaux douillettes
> Tout l'hiver te tiennent placé;
> Puis de Madame de Crissé
> N'as-tu pas maint dévot sourire?
> D'où vient donc que ton cœur soupire?
> Que te faut-il? un peu d'amour.
> Dans un côté de Luxembourg
> Je t'apprends qu'Amour craint le suisse;
> Même on lui rend mauvais office
> Auprès de la divinité
> Qui fait ouvrir l'autre côté.

- Cela vous est facile à dire,
Vous qui courez partout, beau sire;
Mais moi. . . - Parle bas, petit chien;
Si l'évêque de Bethléem
Nous entendait, Dieu sait la vie.
Tu verras pourtant ton envie
Satisfaite dans quelque temps:
Je te promets à ce printemps
Une petite camusette,
Friponne, drue, et joliette,
Avec qui l'on t'enfermera;
Puis s'en démêle qui pourra![3]

The young girls referred to were the demoiselles de compagnie who attended Elizabeth before her marriage. The marquise de Crissé, an intimate friend of the dowager Duchess, had a passion for law-suits, and she is said to have been the model for Racine's comtesse de Pimbesche. La Fontaine must have written this poem to Mignon some time before 1667, for the *évêque de Bethléem* retired from the Duchess's service at the end of that year. The allusion to the Swiss guard between the two households throws light on the unfriendly relations between the Grande Mademoiselle and her step-mother. The Princess was supposed to disapprove of love, and the drama of her passion for Lauzun did not occur till 1670. Had she not written that her ideal of social life was: 'to be polite without gallantry and at least without love-making, living honestly without having recourse to the vulgar remedy of marriage?'

Now in 1666 she appears as a somewhat lonely figure. A decade older than the King, her triumphs in the role of a Jeanne d'Arc at the time of the Fronde, were now relegated to an unheroic past. Though she often quoted from Molière's *Tartuffe*, which had been played in her salon, she really belonged intellectually to the age of Corneille who was her favourite poet. In her frequent letters to Mme de Motteville her style shows the influence of Honoré d'Urfé both in matter and manner, and she describes at length the happiness of a life of pastoral solitude. When La Fontaine took service at the Luxembourg she was thirty years old, the richest princess in France, and had missed many grand marriages. It was not until 1669 that she began to notice M. de Lauzun who was several years her junior, and favoured by the King. Greatly attracted by this graceful Captain of the Guards, but constantly rebuffed by his extreme regard for ceremonious etiquette, the Princess was obliged to make all the advances. Finally on the pretext of asking his advice as to whom she should marry, she intended to propose to him. But her courage failed her when on the point of naming him as the person she preferred, and sighing softly she breathed on her mirror and wrote his name in large letters on the glass.

The King at first consented to the marriage, and had they taken the advice of Mme de Sévigné and acted immediately on this permission all might have been well. As it was, three days later Louis changed his mind and withdrew his consent when confronted with the strong dis-approval of his intimate circle and of Gaston d'Orléan's heirs. Although both the Princess and her lover were submissive to this order, Lauzun was arrested a year later and cast into prison where he was kept for ten years. At this misfortune Mademoiselle shed many tears, but in a short time she again took up her duties at the Louvre, where she received visitors on behalf of the King. She was not defeated, she was only waiting for time to act in her favour.

Meanwhile the gloom deepened at the Luxembourg. The dowager Duchess was scandalised by her step-daughter's choice of a husband, and showed her spiteful disapproval by cutting down the fine old trees on her side of the palace, thus ruining the gardens. Her health was failing and in the spring of 1671 she was afflicted by what was described as an apoplexy, and remained an invalid. A further misfortune fell on the family when in July the young duc de Guise, the husband of Elizabeth d'Orléans, caught smallpox and died in his residence in Paris, from a too copious blood-letting. 'As soon as one falls ill in Paris one falls dead,' commented Mme de Sévigné in telling the sad news to her daughter. In February of the following year the old Duchess lay dying. But the Grande Mademoiselle was not among those who visited her, and indeed refused to do so, which, as Mme de Sévigné remarked, 'was neither courageous nor Christian.'

★

After the death of the dowager Duchess, La Fontaine

> Sortant de ces riches palais
> Comme l'on sortirait d'un songe,[4]

found himself again thrown on his own resources, as at the time of Fouquet's disgrace; and now, as he had neglected his interests at

Château-Thierry, his finances were at a very low ebb. Just a year earlier he had given his last receipt for payments from the duc de Bouillon, and as he had neither the wish nor the means to buy back his office, his principal source of income came to an end.

However in regard to his literary career he had not wasted his time. During the eight years at the Luxembourg palace he had written a considerable quantity of verse, and before that, since the days of Vaux he had been working on his *Contes – Nouvelles en vers tirées de Boccace et l'Arioste*. These had been widely read in manuscript and were printed in 1664, a second collection had appeared in the following year, together with a slim opuscule containing 'Le Cocu battu,' and the tale of 'Joconde,' with the delightful Ballade – *Je me plais aux livres d'Amour*.[5] Saint Évremond's *Matrone d'Éphèse*, an imitation of Petronius, was included in this publication. The *Contes* were written in verse, '*au style naif, au petit vers leste et campagnard qui aime les mots francs*,'[6] said Charles Perrault. They met with immediate success, and further selections continued to appear. When censured by the government they were passed from hand to hand in manuscript.

The *Contes* were in reality 'pot boilers,' to some extent a concession to the taste of the time and to the libertinage that was accepted by ladies of the Court, such as Mme de Montespan and her sister Mme de Thianges, as well as by the duchesse de Bouillon and her high spirited sisters, who wanted to be amused . . . They were never shocked, for they themselves were proud of having a *réplique* – a witty and ready retort in all circumstances, characteristic of aristocracy as of those who lived by their intelligence. Both aristocrats and wits unquestionably enjoyed the stories retold by La Fontaine in which illicit love is the primary and predominant theme. As far as the subjects were concerned he had invented little, for most of the tales had been told before by such well known authors as Boccacio, Ariosto or Petronius. It was the manner more than the matter that the poet had worked on, and he evolved an irregular and loose sort of verse, in reality adding little of artistic value to the originals. La Fontaine frequently justified himself, declaring that this form was the most suitable for narrative, and that it had given him as much trouble as the writing of regular verse or prose. And indeed there is much merit in certain of his effects. The more immoral and irreverent of the *Contes*, those of 1675, which dealt with priests, monks and nuns, were suppressed by the *lieutenant général de police*, on the grounds that they 'would corrupt good manners and

encourage vice.' La Fontaine said in his own defence that he had merely
followed greater poets than himself, who, as it were, stood guarantee
for that sort of writing, and that a story should not be judged by its
truth or probability, but by the grace and beauty of its form. That, he
said, was the law of Ariosto before him, and of the ancients before
Ariosto. Compared to what is allowed to be published today, the
Contes appear as moral tales.

But those were not the only literary activities of the poet. In 1668
Fables choisies mises en vers appeared. This first collection contained
124 fables, divided into six parts, in one volume, dedicated to the
Dauphin. Its success was immediate. It is said that on this occasion La
Fontaine was presented to the King and his son, and received from the
hands of M. Bontemps, first valet de chambre, a purse containing one
thousand pistoles. But La Fontaine never mentioned any personal
contact with the King, neither in prose nor verse, and it seems more
probable that the presentation took place through the intermediary of
the duc de Saint Aignan in the following year, at the time of the
publication of *Psyché* and the first printing of the *Adonis*.

Although the fables were at once welcomed as fine examples of their
kind and were widely read, they were not immediately given their full
due as a new development in poetics. This is not altogether surprising,
for an important piece of work is more easily recognised and more
widely praised than a masterpiece, which, on account of its apparent
simplicity and perfection, eludes praise, and is only recognised for what
it is by connoisseurs: perhaps this is because it does not necessarily
force open a new door, having, as it were, slipped past the doorway and
established itself within the temple of genius. Thus while seeming to
conform to the classical idea of a fable, La Fontaine had in reality
revolutionised this accepted form in abandoning conventional moralities, and replacing moral reflections by subtle observation of nature. He
had evolved a free, perfectly musical verse-form, that broke accepted
rules with such natural ease and grace, that this passed almost unnoticed. He had in fact created a mature and inimitable development in
the art of the fable bringing it into line with other lyrical creations. Yet
when Boileau published his *Art poétique* six years later, he did not mention fables among the different kinds of poetry discussed, nor did he
include La Fontaine in the list of living poets at the end of the book.

The *Contes* show us one aspect of La Fontaine: the easy-going,
pleasure loving sensualist who is amused by telling a good story well;

but it is in the *Fables* that the real poet appears, that self who both dreams and reasons, whose solitude is concerned and intermingled with imaginative creations.

Just a year after the death of the old Duchess, La Fontaine had the sorrow of losing a friend whose works he had always greatly admired. For some years he had seen less of Molière whose life was fully occupied with the cares of an unhappy marriage, and the wrath raised by certain of his plays, together with the career of author, actor and stage-manager. From first to last Molière belonged body and soul to the theatre; his means of expression existed through the stage and its actors. He voiced his opinions with frankness, showing up the errors of the age in creating the personifications of such faults, and he did this without preaching, or caricaturing his world. When he was at the height of his fame, honoured and rich, but alas, already ill, Boileau tried to persuade him to give up acting and consecrate his life to writing plays. To this the great comedian replied: *Ah! que me dites-vous là? Il y a un honneur pour moi à ne pas quitter.*[7] The presentation of his works was for him the crowning glory, and he said: *'les pièces ne sont faites que pour être jouées.'* Even in the last hours of his life and while greatly suffering he played the role of the *Malade Imaginaire* with exemplary courage, and died in his house at Neuilly that same night.

La Fontaine on hearing of Molière's death wrote an epitaph for him:

'Sur Molière'

> Sous ce tombeau gisent Plaute et Térence,
> Et cependant le seul Molière y git.
> Leurs trois talents ne formaient qu'un esprit
> Dont le bel art réjouissait la France.
> Ils sont partis! et j'ai peu d'espérance
> De les revoir. Malgré tous nos efforts,
> Pour un long temps, selon toute apparence,
> Térence, et Plaute, et Molière sont morts.[8]

After the treatment that the mortal remains of Molière received from the Clergy, is it surprising that his friend La Fontaine should show up some clerical failings and treat them with derision in his *Contes* published a year later?

TRANSLATIONS

[1]Shall we never be free from constant fears? / Six summers have not seen peace in these regions / And already the demon who presides over combats /

Recommences to forge the instruments of our tears. / Be opposed, Olympe, to the fury of arms. / Make love speak, and do not allow / That the fate of so many states be decided without him. / Permit your marriage to interpose its charms. / It is the most noble price with which may be bought / Peace that mortals may never hold too dear. / I know that we will lose you in return for it. / Supreme good fortune for the French empire / Would be to have both peace and your presence / But Heaven does not give all its gifts at once.

²I had freed myself from Aminte and from Sylvie: / I was free, and living content without love: / The innocent beauty of gardens and sun light / Were to be for ever the charm of my life. / When from a cloister Amarante appeared / What charms, good god! All Luxembourg rejoices; / The young Olympe sees now at her court / One whom all Paphos has followed to this house. / All eyes are turned towards this new wonder; / But, in considering this creation of Heaven / I know not what fear awakes in my heart; / Yet whatever love may ask of me, / I would be happy to die struck by this marvel, / whose glance would make the fortune of a king.

³Little dog, tell me what's wrong with you? / Have you not as much comfort as is a king's due? / Three or four little girls / in muffs that softest fur enfurls / All winter make a place for you; / And then from Madame Crissé too / Many pious smiles you had, / Why then is your heart so sad? / What do you want? Love for sure. / On this side of the Luxembourg / I tell you that Love fears the Swiss; / They even carry tales of this / To the Divinity / On the other side who keeps the key. / – Sir, it's easy enough for you to speak / Who everywhere your pleasure seek: / But me ... / Little dog, whisper low in my ear / If the bishop of Bethlehem should hear / What we say, god knows what a life! / Nevertheless, you shall have a wife, / I promise you this very spring / A jolly little snub-nose thing / With whom you'll be shut up all day; / Then let them moralise who may!

⁴Coming from these rich palaces / As one comes out of a dream.

⁵I delight in books on love.

⁶In a naive style, in light unpolished verses, giving preference to outspoken language.

⁷Ah! what is that you say? I am bound in honour not to give up the stage ... The pieces are only made to be played.

⁸In this tomb lie Plautus and Terence, / And nevertheless Molière lies here alone. / Their three talents made up a single genius / Whose great art delighted France. / They are gone and there is little chance / Of seeing them again. In spite of all our efforts, / For a long time, to all appearance, / Terence, Plautus and Molière are dead.

VIII

MADAME DE LA SABLIÈRE

1. Iris

Shortly after La Fontaine had lost his post at the Luxembourg he was taken under the protection of Mme de La Sablière who welcomed him in her house, giving him board and lodging and providing for all his needs. It is probable that they had known each other since the days of Vaux, for Mme de La Sablière had been an intimate friend of Fouquet and kept her friendship for him after his downfall. Among her many gifts she had the capacity of real friendship, and La Fontaine was the type of man for whom intellectual women feel profound sympathy: his very weakness endeared him, and the halo of his genius sublimated his errors, for beyond his failings his gaze was fixed on his art, and if he erred – as he certainly did – it was merely a passing aberration. Mme de La Sablière felt a deep affection for her *fablier*, as she called him, and she agreed with Maucroix that he was the most frank and sincere soul that ever existed. Yet she knew his faults and told him laughingly, *en vérité, mon cher, vous seriez bien bête si vous n'aviez pas tant d'esprit.*[1] La Fontaine richly repaid her generous friendship with his devotion; she inspired much of his best work, and he paid her supreme homage in three 'Discours' to Iris: these were not *vers de circonstances*, they are sincere and moving and are among the finest things he ever wrote.

The first '*Discours*' gives a vivid picture of Mme de La Sablière's modesty and intelligence, and her keen interest in philosophy and science. It was evidently written some time before her liaison with La Fare, and was published for the first time in the second collection of the *Fables* in 1679. It begins thus:

> Iris, je vous louerais, il n'est que trop aisé;
> Mais vous avez cent fois notre encens refusé,
> En cela peu semblable au reste des mortelles,
> Qui veulent tous les jours des louanges nouvelles.
> Pas une ne s'endort à ce bruit si flatteur...

> C'est la louange, Iris. Vous ne la goûtez point;
> D'autres propos chez vous récompensent ce point,
> Propos, agréables commerces,
> Où le hasard fournit cent matières diverses,
> Jusque-là qu'en votre entretien
> La bagatelle a part: le monde n'en croit rien.
> Laissons le monde et sa croyance:
> La bagatelle, la science,
> Les chimères, le rien, tout est bon. Je soutiens
> Qu'il faut de tout aux entretiens:
> C'est un parterre où Flore épand ses biens;
> Sur différentes fleurs l'abeille s'y repose,
> Et fait du miel de toute chose.[2]

He then asks, with a humorous touch of irony, if she has heard of the new philosophy – *subtile, engageante et hardie* – and he proceeds to refute the Cartesian theory that *la bête est une machine*, a subject to which I shall return when discussing the *Fables*.

The second *Discours* was read by La Fontaine on his reception in the Academy on the 24th April 1684. It was probably written at least a year earlier. It is a veritable *apologia pro vita sua*, and magnificently begins:

> Désormais que ma Muse, aussi bien que mes jours,
> Touche de son déclin l'inévitable cours,
> Et que de ma raison le flambeau va s'éteindre,
> Irai-je en consumer les restes à me plaindre,
> Et, prodigue d'un temps par la Parque attendu,
> Le perdre à regretter celui que j'ai perdu?
> Si le Ciel me réserve encor quelque étincelle
> Du feu dont je brillais en ma saison nouvelle,
> Je la dois employer, suffisamment instruit
> Que le plus beau couchant est voisin de la nuit. . .[3]

Here he tells us more about himself than about Iris, who had by then more or less renounced the world and whose example he admires without really being inclined to follow it, at least not for the present.

> Si j'étais sage, Iris (mais c'est un privilège
> Que la Nature accorde à bien peu d'entre nous),
> Si j'avais un esprit aussi réglé que vous,
> Je suivrais vos leçons, au moins en quelque chose:
> Les suivre en tout, c'est trop; il faut qu'on se propose. . .
> Un chemin dont sans crime on se puisse écarter. . .[4]

The third *Discours* is the dedication to Madame de La Sablière which serves as introduction to the fable on friendship of 'Le *Corbeau, la Gazelle, la Tortue et le Rat,*' published in *Ouvrages de prose et de poésie* in 1685 in which the second *Discours* was also printed. This volume was dedicated to Antoine Harlay procureur général du Parlement, on Mme de La Sablière's advice, and in addressing Harlay the poet explains:

> Cette Iris, Harlay, c'est la dame
> A qui j'ai deux temples bâtis,
> L'un dans mon cœur, l'autre en mon livre.[5]

And the dedication to Iris begins:

> Je vous gardais un temple dans mes vers:
> Il n'eût fini qu'avecque l'univers...

and after describing the temple where even the gods would come to adore her, he continues,

> Au fond du temple eût été son image,
> Avec ses traits, son souris, ses appas,
> Son art de plaire et de n'y penser pas,
> Ses agréments à qui tout rend hommage...
> J'eusse en ses yeux fait briller de son âme
> Tous les trésors, quoique imparfaitement:
> Car ce cœur vif et tendre infiniment
> Pour ses amis, et non point autrement:
> Car cet esprit qui né du firmament
> A beauté d'homme avec grâces de femme,
> Ne se peut pas comme on veut exprimer.
> O vous, Iris, qui savez tout charmer,
> Qui savez plaire en un degré suprême,
> Vous que l'on aime à l'égal de soi-même
> (Ceci soit dit sans nul soupçon d'amour;
> Car c'est un mot banni de votre cour;
> Laissons-le donc), agréez que ma muse
> Achève un jour cette ébauche confuse...[6]

Surely this is one of the finest tributes to friendship that has ever been written, and is it not surprising that it has been so little quoted, known and loved, even in La Fontaine's own country where his Fables are given great importance. It is true that the second *Discours* is printed in full in one *Anthologie de la Poésie Française*; but even at the present day, it seems to me that the three *Discours* do not yet receive the attention they deserve.

If we want to know what Mme de La Sablière looked like, we may turn to the admirable prose portrait which appeared in the *Mercure galant* of July 1678, which may have been written by La Fontaine and tells us that:

> her fine silky hair was ash-blonde, her eyes blue, soft and brilliant though not very large; her face was oval, her complexion clear and bright and her skin dazzlingly white, her hands and throat were finely proportioned. Added to this a certain touching air of sweetness and playfulness animated her whole personality. In all that she said or did there was this easy grace and unembarassed character of mind, honest, good-humoured and pleasing manners that would be difficult for others to imitate. . .

This description harmonises delightfully with Mignard's fine painting of her done about the same time.

Marguerite Hessein, 'a lady of great merit and much art,' came from a bourgeois family who held to the reformed religion. In 1654 at the age of eighteen she married Antoine de Rambouillet de La Sablière, known as *le grand madrigalier*, son of a rich financier and councillor to the king. She had three children, one boy and two girls, the youngest of whom was born in 1658. While her husband flirted and wrote madrigals, la belle Marguerite cultivated astronomy and at the age of thirty was considered a veritable Venus Urania. Yet she was neither a pedant nor a *précieuse*; her active and enquiring mind led her to study many different subjects, and she was probably a willing pupil rather than a *savante*. She is said to have written *Pensées chrétiennes* – a hundred maxims which, however, were not published till 1736 when they appeared together with those of La Bruyère, and this is the first we hear of them.

Throwing herself whole-heartedly into the study of science, she spent her mornings in Dalance's laboratory making experiments under the microscope, and sometimes attended a dissection in the evening at the doctor du Verney's. Gilles de Roberval gave her lessons in mathematics and Saint-Évremond corresponded with her. When Boileau, in his fifth Epistle, spoke of an astrolabe without knowing what it was, she mocked freely at his ignorance. To this he replied in spiteful verse, without mentioning her name:

> cette savante,
> Qu'estime Roberval et que Sauveur fréquente

D'où vient qu'elle à l'œil trouble et le teint si terni?
C'est que, sur le Calcul, dit-on, de Cassini,
Un astrolable en main, elle a, dans sa gouttière
A suivre Jupiter passé la nuit entière.[7]

However, Boileau had the good sense not to publish this, and when it did appear after her death, it was much disapproved of by her friends, and the cautious critic saw that he had made a mistake.

Undoubtedly, had she lived today, this *femme savante* of her epoch would have become a doctor or a scientist, for her interest in science and anatomy, her sympathy with human suffering, together with her acute intelligence and self-discipline, show what an admirable physician she would have been.

Separated from her husband in 1668, Marguerite kept open house to savant and poet at her *hôtel particulier* in the rue Neuve-des-Petits-Champs, which was then the new part of the parish of St Roch. Life was gay and care-free in the group of friends who met there; a coterie of scientists, intellectuals and free-thinkers; libertines whose more or less discreet impiety was tolerated by Louis XIV, as being less dangerous to society and the church than the religious disputations of the Solitaries of Port-Royal. The supper parties at rue Neuve-des-Petits-Champs were extremely brilliant: the conversation ranged from metaphysics and the 'new' philosophy to literature and the stage; all subjects were treated with an ironical facility swift as summer lightning:

Propos, agréables commerces
Où le hasard fournit cent matières diverses. . .[8]

As the evening progressed and the wine circulated, the talk became more intimate; affairs of the heart, various degrees of love were discussed, intermingled with gossip, scandalous stories, songs often improvised to fit the occasion by such guests as the abbé de Chaulieu and Chapelle, who both excelled in this accomplishment.

In this sympathetic environment La Fontaine met many of his old friends: there was Charles Perrault of fairy-tale fame whom Mme de La Sablière called her *Maître*, and Paul Barrillon who had been Ambassador in England since 1672, but was often in Paris. Among other distinguished men who frequented the rue Neuve-des-Petits-Champs were Louis de Brancas, François d'Usson seigneur de Bonrepaux, who had been a friend of Fouquet and of the Bouillons, he had made a brilliant career in the French Navy, and was frequently sent to England on missions by the King; Lauzun, before his imprisonment, was often one of the party. It was said that the Grande Mademoiselle disapproved of Lauzun's constant attendance at the house of 'cette petite femme de la ville nommée La Sablière.' It is true that at this time Marguerite had a doubtful reputation among women, who considered that she took too little care of her good name.

In reality Iris was more intellectual than sensual, preferring friendship to flirtation. We find her and Ninon de Lenclos supping in company with Molière and Boileau, amusing themselves in composing the latin of the *Malade Imaginaire.* Among those living in her house were the young geometrician Sauveur who became a distinguished mathematician, and also doctor Bernier, traveller and philosopher.

Bernier was to play an important part in La Fontaine's future. He was born in 1620, and had been a pupil of Gassendi. He travelled much in the East and was for a time doctor to the Emperor Aurangzeb of Hindustan. He had a great deal of common sense, and though anti-Cartesian in so far as he considered that Descartes' conclusions were too affirmative, he did not altogether approve of the easy acceptance of the teaching of Epicurus, which was so fashionable with the materialists. In a letter from Chirus in Persia, in June 1662, he warned his young friend Chapelle against a too positive practice of Epicureanism to which Chapelle was by nature inclined, and in the same letter stated the weak points in Gassendi's doctrine. When Mme de La Sablière came to La Fontaine's aid, Bernier was also enjoying her hospitality, and was making for her an abridgement of Gassendi in twelve volumes.

The first seven years spent with his new patroness were of great significance to the poet, for now he was constantly in the company of people who freely discussed matters in which he took a deep interest. Bernier in particular charmed and instructed him, introducing him for the first time to Eastern myths and fables. But the learned doctor's chief value for La Fontaine lay in his belief in animal intelligence, founded on Gassendi's anti-Cartesian doctrine; and his statements about the soul, and how it differed in man and beasts, were infinitely sympathetic to the fabulist who readily adopted them. Night after night he would listen enthralled to the discussions between Bernier and his hostess's uncle the doctor Menjot who was also a disciple of Gassendi.

This was a time of great intellectual activity for La Fontaine. In the second collection of his Fables there is a wider horizon and a fresh source of inspiration introduced from the works of the Eastern philosopher Bidpay, to whom he makes acknowledgements.

La Fontaine was now as happy as he had ever been. If there was no longer the care-free magic of the days of Vaux when the world had been so full of promise, and faces had seemed lit by a mysterious radiance, there was now a compensating poise, and a keener insight. In this environment he had a fuller intellectual life which suited perfectly his passion for his work, that secret love that came to bear him company in moments of solitude, urging him to perfection of expression the desire for which never left him. He was now well known as a remarkable poet and was liked by every one, his good nature and simplicity had earned for him the nickname of *le Bonhomme; très social, gai, mais sujet à des mouvements et des silences inexplicables*, said a contemporary, *quand une rêverie agréable et profonde occupe son esprit, on a beau lui parler.*[9] At such moments he appeared to spend his time *à ne rien faire.* He was always glad to escape from the present, to wander through a timeless country that had all the freshness and mystery of early dawn:

> Errer dans un jardin, s'égarer dans un bois,
> Se coucher sur les fleurs, respirer leur haleine,
> Écouter en rêvant le bruit d'une fontaine,
> Ou celui d'un ruisseau roulant sur des cailloux.[10]

In this happy mood he was sometimes very close to sleep, and he would fall into a state of mental indolence, a torpor of the senses, a sort of halt in time, so that even his inner life was apt to be inconsequent, passing from one poetic figure to another, from myth to myth, lightly considering every possible form of poetry without dwelling on it, in what would now be called a surrealist manner. Certainly his diversity was most remarkable, and he often referred to this, linking it in his mind with his inconstancy and love of change, and saying of himself:

> Je m'avoue, il est vrai, s'il faut parler ainsi,
> Papillon du Parnasse, et semblable aux abeilles
> A qui le bon Platon compare nos merveilles.
> Je suis chose légère, et vole à tout sujet;
> Je vais de fleur en fleur, et d'objet en objet;
> A beaucoup de plaisirs je mêle un peu de gloire.[11]

On this aspect of himself he is insistent:

> Même beauté, tant soit exquise,
> Rassasie et soûle à la fin.

Il me faut d'un et d'autre pain:
Diversité c'est ma devise.

Je l'ai jà dit d'autre façon,
Car il est bon que l'on déguise,
Suivant la loi de ce dicton:
Diversité c'est ma devise.[12]

A portrait painted in 1672 when the poet was fifty-one, shows us the
dreamer and philosopher who has not changed greatly since the days
of Vaux. His nose looks longer because his mouth is more contracted,
his hair is still light and curling as in the youthful portrait by De Troy,
he has not yet taken to wearing the massive dark wig in which he
appears ten years later – a fashion that tended to make all portraits
resemble Louis XIV. At this time a wig was for men the chief weapon
against old age, neither spectacles nor artificial teeth had as yet come
to the rescue of declining years. La Fontaine now takes less trouble
about his personal appearance than in former days: he is dressed in
black with a neckerchief tied in a simple careless knot with flowing ends,
a style to which he remained faithful. He said of himself 'for me the
time of love-making is past,' but this may be taken as a slight exaggeration, for he had always been promiscuous and he remained so, owing
fidelity to no woman in particular; he was not a constant or faithful
lover:

On m'a pourvu d'un cœur peu content de lui-même,
Inquiet, et fécond en nouvelles amours;
Il aime à s'engager, mais non pas pour toujours.[13]

2. All is Vanity

Five years after the arrival of La Fontaine, Marguerite de La Sablière
became the mistress of the marquis de La Fare. Their passion for each
other was complete and sincere while it lasted. La Fare was a talented
agreeable man of the world; a good soldier, whose military career
seems to have been blighted in consequence of an unfortunate admiration for the marquise de Rochefort with whom the secrétaire d'État,
the all powerful Louvois, was in love. La Fare gave his reasons for
leaving the army: the first being the brutal refusal of Louvois to grant
him a well merited promotion; the second was the bad state of his

Château d'Amboise, from drawing by Monthelier (p. 69)

Château de Richelieu (p. 71)

Portrait of Molière, engraved by Lepicié,
after Coypel (p. 81)

Portrait of Racine, aged 36 (at the time
of Phèdre), watercolour (p. 84)

affairs; the third was laziness, combined with loving a woman worthy of his devotion. When we first meet him he had not yet abandoned himself to excessive gambling and over-eating, a habit of life that later made him enormously fat, for like his friend Chaulieu he was ready to drink and make merry in any company, and frequented the unruly orgies, where the Mancini element predominated, at the Hôtel de Bouillon or the Hôtel de Vendôme. Yet his memoirs are interesting enough to make a strange contrast with what we know of his way of life in his latter years. In his youth he had shown himself capable of action when necessary. Late in life he wrote verses on 'La Paresse,' addressed to Chaulieu, lazy verses on all counts:

> Laisse-toi gouverner par cette enchanteresse
> Qui seule peut du cœur calmer l'émotion,
> Et préfère, crois-moi, les dons de la Paresse
> Aux offres d'une vaine et folle ambition.[14]

When the Marquis fell in love with Marguerite de La Sablière she was thirty-six and he was thirty-three and still good-looking, with no other preoccupation than to pass his life as agreeably as possible. Both lovers believed their attachment to be eternal:

> Je sers une Maîtresse illustre, aimable et sage.
> Amour, tu remplis mes souhaits.
> Pourquoi me laissais-tu, dans la fleur de mon âge
> Ignorer ses vertus, ses grâces, ses attraits?[15]

wrote the Marquis, regretting the time lost rather than lived before they loved each other, and echoing in formal verse the passionate lines of Donne:

> In truth I know not what we did
> Ere we two loved . . .

Now they were always together, and their friends were either amused, or lost in admiration for their fidelity. La Fare appeared as a model lover, and his companions chaffed him: 'one would put you in the place of the turtle-dove as a symbol of love,' mocked Chaulieu; while Mme de Sévigné, with acute perception in judging her contemporaries, expressed her admiration of Mme de La Sablière's perseverance in loving 'son cher Philadelphe.'

The chief adversary of promiscuity is real love and devotion for one particular person; and being in love might be defined as having a preference that excludes all other intimate intercourse. Thus to Mme de La Sablière the trivial relationships of those immediately around her began to appear immoral and absurd as compared with the unique attachment that she felt for her 'Philadelphe.' But alas, after three years, little by little La Fare's sentiments slowly died. Day by day his attentions became less assiduous, he seemed absent-minded and more inclined to consider his own interests than those of his mistress. Now instead of spending all their time together, it was noticed that they were less in each other's company. La Fare was lazy and self-indulgent; lame excuses, embarrassed justifications, stilted conversations and pretexts to go out alone, replaced his amorous attentions; impatient of all restraint, he gradually returned to his old freedom. All the tenderness of his mistress, her distinction and perfect fidelity now only irritated him. It was evident that a passion for gambling was becoming a counter-attraction, and society was quick to comment on this change. Mme de Coulanges reported to Mme de Sévigné that La Fare had never really been in love; it was, she said 'simply laziness, laziness and again laziness, he only went to Mme de La Sablière for company, as the game of bassette showed.' He now sought company in the appartment of La Champmeslé, and he was also interested in Louison Moreau whose sister was one of the Grand Prieur's mistresses.

But it was not women who separated the lovers, but a new game of cards which took Paris by storm, the game of bassette lately introduced into France by the Venetian ambassador. Fontenelle in his *Lettres du Chevalier d'Her*, declared that this new amusement destroyed gallantry, and added, 'one might call it the art of growing old in a short time.' The mathematician Sauveur worked out a table of probabilities to show that certain ways of cutting the cards were more advantageous than others, and the public, believing that this system offered a positive way of winning, redoubled their enthusiasm for the game – the baccarat of the time.

At first Marguerite told herself that in order to maintain a lasting relationship she must be ready to make sacrifices, and she accepted the situation with good humour and patience. But she was too intelligent not to see that her position had become impossible, the idyll had come to an end, and she was obliged to face the cruel fact that La Fare was tired of her. Realising this, she made up her mind and courageously took her final resolution: no matter what it cost her, without a single reproach to her unfaithful lover, without making any scene, asking for no explanations, and with no wish to condemn La Fare, she determined to make a drastic change in the way of living that had become distasteful to her. Betrayed, disillusioned, and suffering from a deep humiliation, she discreetly eclipsed herself, deciding that the worldly life she had so ardently enjoyed was at an end. It was for her the death of earthly love, and this left in her sensitive mind a great desolation: as though wandering through a twilight of closed rooms, disconsolately opening doors, only to find the rooms empty, and to realise that what she was looking for was gone for ever. Funereal images assailed her mind. Yet her courage and will-power showed her a way of escape.

There was only one road to peace, one cure for continual torment; religion, that last resource for dethroned queens and foresaken lovers, was the real refuge and redemption for the world of the seventeenth century. Madame de La Sablière's first step was to join the Catholic church. In this she was encouraged by the friendship of the Père Rapin, Jesuit, a man of great culture, author of Latin poems and of works attacking the Jansenists. He was extremely active in the conversion of Calvinists and his letters on this theme were powerful and persuasive. Marguerite had known him for some time and she now turned to him, putting all her confidence in his guidance and closely following his advice. She had decided to devote herself to the aged poor, and started working at the Hospital for Incurables. Her own misfortune was, she felt, less painful than that of these poor invalids to whom she would henceforth devote her life.

With all the ardour and grace that she had lavished on earthly love, she gave herself up to piety, to the good works and unselfish devotion that are the true signs of real Christianity. Her husband La Sablière had died in 1679, her two daughters were married and her son, who remained faithful to the reformed religion, after being imprisoned had taken refuge in Holland: it was to the poor and suffering that she now turned to offer herself. The Mother Superior and the Sisters at the Hospital were charmed by her spirit. She ruled them all. Her friends, said Mme de Sévigné, went to see her and found her always the best of company, 'for as a reasonable and pretty person she had made up her mind.'

The Hospice des Incurables had been founded by the Cardinal de la Rochefoucauld in 1637, and was described in its charter as being intended 'for men and women deprived of fortune and security and not having the consolation of finding an end to the ills that afflicted them.' Situated on a large tract of ground between the rue du Bac and the rue de Sèvres, in the middle of an extensive market garden, the vast building – now the Hospital Laënnec – had a façade extending for some two hundred and fifty feet. In the grounds there were eleven courtyards, two vegetable gardens, eight wells, a church with a bell-tower and a cemetery.

It was here that Mme de La Sablière came to share with the nuns, *les Soeurs grises*, the care of the aged and afflicted. After she had been there for a year, Mme de Sévigné – with whom she was on friendly terms – reported light-heartedly: 'Mme de La Sablière spends her time at the Incurables, she is quite cured of an ill that for some time one thought incurable, and the recovery from which pleases more than any other. She is in the blessed state of being devout and truly devoted; she makes good use of her free-will; but is it not God that makes her do this?'

It was true that Marguerite now felt that real devotion was a heavenly virtue, which should be directed towards God, and all the rest was only illusion. Yet she was far from the peace of mind that her friends liked to think she enjoyed. There were bitter moments when she told herself that the so-called Epicureans of her former *entourage* were little better than fools, deceiving themselves with too easy conscience, and she blamed herself for her liberal acceptance of all that she was now most ashamed of. Amongst other wrongs, had not her poet and protégé published the most scandalous *Contes* while living under her roof. And was it not partly her fault, for like her friends she had encouraged him, instead of dissuading him from squandering his talent on such unworthy ends. Had she been in a less unhappy state she might have comforted herself by the fact that it was largely due to her influence and to the circumstances of the poet's life under her care, that the second collection of *Fables* had been crowned with well merited success. Added to such reflections there was the spiritual anguish of an increasing isolation, owing to the attitude of friends who did not want her to forsake the world. In this they were supported by her confessors and various spiritual directors, who did not consider that she was a suitable person to retire completely from all social intercourse: did she not appear in their eyes as some one suffering from the shock of circumstances which had cruelly wounded her, rather than as a penitent to whom only the hope of Heaven remained? It was perhaps natural that their disillusioned knowledge of society had made them cautious and mistrustful of passionate desires in what ever form they might appear.

It was not till several years later that she came under the guidance and spiritual direction of the celebrated Armand-Jean le Bouthillier abbé de Rancé, who was then sixty-one and in his twelfth year of retreat. His own life had begun scandalously enough, but the shock of finding the corpse of his dead mistress, Mme de Montbazon, in the most gruesome circumstances, had so completely changed his outlook that he had become a penitent and a recluse. He was a man of indomitable energy and from his monk's cell he disputed with his fellow Benedictines and corresponded with learned men of his time. His knowledge of worldly life admirably fitted him to be the spiritual director of those who like himself wished to retire for ever from society and sin.

In 1680 Mme de La Sablière left her house in the rue Neuve-des-Petits-Champs, which she shared with her brother Pierre Hessein, who was on friendly terms with La Fontaine, Racine and Boileau. She now rented a house in the rue St Honoré, situated beside the gate of the Couvent des Feuillants, in the same parish as the house she had left. La Fontaine went with her to the rue St Honoré, and stayed there for the next eight years till his protectress gave up the lease in 1688. But Marguerite was not content to live all the time so far away from the Hospital where she worked, and wishing to retire more from the world, she decided a year later to rent also a small apartment at the Hospital – on the ground floor, to the right as one approaches the chapel. From time to time, accompanied by one servant, she stayed there for long periods. She furnished this *pied à terre* comfortably; the walls of the narrow rooms were hung with blue silk, some seventy-five volumes, ornaments and china, made quite a cheerful effect in the cramped interior with its small door and windows.

When in 1684 La Fare married Louise de Luz de Ventelet, and the King signed the marriage contract, Mme de La Sablière, in a letter to the Père Rapin, who was then her spiritual director, spoke of 'the cruel circumstances of this affair.' In the following year the King granted her a pension, thanks to the efforts of Rapin; she had already asked for this on the death of her husband in 1679.

Three years later, on giving up the lease of the house in the rue St Honoré, she wrote from the Hospital to the abbé de Rancé – her spiritual guide since Rapin's death in 1687 – telling him: 'I have no other dwelling except this one from where I write, and a small house where I have put the few people left with me.' In a previous letter, written before she left St Honoré she had said: 'I have no other companions here except La Fontaine and my cat and dog.' La Fontaine had now gone to live in the small house near the rue St Honoré, mentioned in the first letter, for he never left the parish of Saint Roch.

But although she would have liked to do so, it was not possible for Marguerite de La Sablière to spend all her life in the little apartment at the Hospital. For one thing, the authorities there could turn her out at any time, and in spite of all the generosity she had shown they were not easy to deal with. This gave her an unhappy feeling of insecurity. So when she had got rid of the house in St Honoré, she borrowed money from her uncle Menjot to buy and furnish a small dwelling in the rue Rousselet, at the corner of the rue Blomet, quite close to the Hospital. Here she retired in 1688, dividing her time between her apartment at the Incurables and this new dwelling. Only four servants went with her, and writing to the abbé de Rancé, she said:

> In regard to my household, I try through gentleness and through quite different conduct from the bad example I have given in the past, to make them return to their duty towards God. For I am little fitted to speak positively to them, and when I am about to blame any one, I remember my past life and say to myself what others might say to me. However there is no positive disorder.

Now more than ever she wished to be alone, refusing to listen to her friends who still tried to persuade her not to give up entirely her social life.

Perhaps the person who missed her most was La Fontaine, even before she left the rue St Honoré. He found it difficult to get used to her long absences. He missed her gay companionship, and his feelings were mingled with admiration and dismay. He admitted to himself that doubtless she had followed the inevitably right path, but he asked himself if she need have done this so early in her life, when they were all living happily together. He did not yet feel ready, or in any hurry, to retire from the world, and letters to his friends at this time show that he regretted the happy past and felt worried as to the future. In writing to his friend Bonrepaux, who was on a mission to London in 1687, he speaks of the absence of Mme de La Sablière and her daughter Mme de la Mesangère, who since her husband's death had lived with her mother in the house in St Honoré.

'The ladies of St Honoré, truly neglect us a little,' he writes, 'I do not dare to say they neglect us a little too much. Monsieur de Barillon will remember the charm of these ladies, which was such that it made a bottle of ordinary wine and an *omelette au lard* pass for nectar and ambrosia. We thought that we were feasting on ambrosia and we maintained that Jupiter would have enjoyed the *omelette au lard*. These days are no more. The Graces of the rue St Honoré neglect us. They are ungrateful, we offer them more incense than they want. On my faith, Sir, I fear that the incense will become mouldy in the Temple. The divinity one comes there to adore (Mme de La Sablière) turns every one away without respect of persons, whether Count, Marquis or Duke: *Tros Rutulusve fuat, nullo discrimine habebo*: be it Trojan or Rutulean I will make no difference. That is her motto.

You are one of those who have most reason to praise her, for we know, Sir, that she wrote to you eight days ago. Also I have nothing to tell you about her health except that it continues to be good except for a cold. . . In the past I would have written a long letter full of her praises; not that she was ever anxious to be praised, she merely tolerated it and was not entirely disdainful. Now all that is changed.

> J'ai vu le temps qu'Iris (et c'était l'âge d'or
> Pour nous autres, gens du bas monde),
> J'ai vu, dis-je, le temps qu'Iris goûtait encor,
> Non cet encens commun dont le Parnasse abonde:
> Il fut toujours, au sentiment d'Iris,
> D'une odeur importune ou plate:
> Mais la louange délicate
> Avait auprès d'elle son prix.
> Elle traite aujourd'hui cet art de bagatelle;
> Il l'endort; et s'il faut parler de bonne foi,
> L'éloge et les vers sont pour elle
> Ce que maints sermons sont pour moi. . .[16]

This was written in August just a year before Iris left the rue St Honoré: La Fontaine soon afterwards installed himself in the small house where she put those who still depended on her generosity. In a letter to his friends in England he speaks of the busts of the philosophers with which he has decorated his room, and he has had them re-cast in terra-cotta. He has also a clavecin, so that he may entertain his friends with

> Quelque musique
> Dans le séjour philosophique.[17]

But Iris was still preoccupied not only with her poet's comfort but a great deal more with his attitude towards moral questions, and at this time she was trying to influence him to reform his ways. So we find him confiding to Bonrepaux: 'The Heaven of which they preach in France requires me to renounce Cloris, Bacchus and Apollo, three divinities whom you recommend to me in your letter. I shall harmonise all this as best I may and for as long as possible, and perhaps you will give me some good expedient for doing so.' This delicate question of conversion from a state of sin to a state of repentance must often have arisen between the poet and his benefactress. For her part she felt responsible for his spiritual welfare, and about this time she almost persuaded him to make contact with the abbé de Rancé's secretary M. Masne. Rancé had offered to give La Fontaine hospitality in the monastery of La Trappe. But the poet was decidedly wary, he did not feel the necessity of religious support and he openly declared *ne point errer est chose au-dessus de mes forces*.[18] In this he was perfectly right, for the *bagatelle* that Iris now despised, the poetry composed with such loving care, was an essential part of his nature, and more, the very breath of his life. So with all possible tact he rightly stood his ground, and we find Mme de La Sablière informing M. Masne, who acted as intermediary between her and the abbé de Rancé:

'I find L.F.s wish to go and see you decidedly cooled. If I were in his place I would profit by your invitation at once. Men take everything that touches their end for a fable: there are minds on which realities flow like water off a duck's back without stopping or penetrating. For myself I cannot understand how any one can count time when thinking of eternity, nor how any one may hope to have enough time to make amends for the past; and one reasons on that, and argues with God. . .

It is easy to recognise La Fontaine's attitude in this description: he very naturally saw God as a superior all-ruling Monarch, and in any approach to this supreme Being one had the right to explain humbly one's own point of view. The poet could not have been expected to share Mme de La Sablière's abhorrence of all that he enjoyed. The whole situation between the poet and penitent is beautifully summed up in the '*Discours à Madame de la Sablière*', which he read to the Academy some time later.

During the last years of her life Marguerite depended more and more on the guidance of the abbé de Rancé, who drew up for her a rule of life, as he had done for other penitents including the Princess Palatine to whom he was spiritual director. The many letters that Mme de La

Sablière wrote to Rancé during the next six years, until her death in 1693, show what an important place his advice and instructions held in her life. She now spent all her time between the wards in the Hospice where she worked long hours and the almost solitary interior of her little house in the rue Rousselet where she felt at peace:

'*Dieu me fait sentir de plus en plus que tout ce qui est au monde est un pur néant, hors d'être à lui,*' she wrote to the abbé de Rancé, while assuring him of her gratitude for all he had done for her. '*Vous savez que vous m'êtes tout en ce monde,*' she told him in a letter dated 15th January 1690, '*et je n'attends aucun secours que de votre charité . . . La solitude seule me porte à Dieu, tout le reste étant rempli de dissipations inutiles, même les occupations les meilleures . . .*'[19]

For some time her health had been gradually failing, and her last poignant letters to the abbé tell him of her terrible illness, cancer, from which she had seen so many of her poor patients die. Yet, in spite of the entreaties of those around her, she refused to have any communications with the outer world concerning her affliction. To one friend alone she spoke of the fatal state of her health, and while begging him not to attempt to visit her, or to make enquiries, she says she will send from time to time to ask for news of his welfare, for he was suffering from gout and was then convalescent in the country and she adds:

'I suppose that you are there to destroy all that puts an obstacle between you and God . . . We have only one duty, and when we abandon ourselves to it we are content and filled with grace. Created things tire us and leave us a desolating emptiness. Believe me that all my life I shall take a sincere interest in all that concerns you, and that the life I lead lends itself to remembering the people one esteems and loves. You see by that that I cannot forget you.'

In another letter to the same friend she implores him 'Monsieur, for the love of God, lay the axe to the root of the tree. It is no use cutting branch by branch. I pray our Saviour to open your heart so that all the brilliance of wit may be dispersed to make way for religion.' and she adds that, though she is neither indifferent to friendship nor to conversation, she does not wish to see him.

It seems probable that these letters were addressed either to La Fontaine or to Fontenelle who had dedicated his *Entretiens sur la Pluralité des Mondes* to her daughter (Marguerite de Rambouillet) Mme de la Mésangère, in 1686, with whom he was on intimate terms. It would therefore not be surprising if Mme de La Sablière had felt a great interest in this brilliant young man, whose ideas on duration were in advance of his time, and to a certain extent anticipate the theory of relativity without, of course, foreseeing the resulting scientific conclusions. He saw time as the manifestation of an infinitely distant Divine energy, and in popularising scientific ideas to explain religious sentiments he might be said to have been the Teilhard du Chardin of his day. This being so, we may wonder why Mme de La Sablière was so anxious to convert him.

On the other hand it does appear as if La Fontaine were the sinner who must repent. The mixture of anxiety for his salvation, and a certain tenderness, in spite of rather formal language, inclines me to think that the letters were written to him. Added to this there is the fact of La Fontaine's suffering from rheumatism – which is referred to as gout – and he may well have gone to the country during his convalescence to stay with his new friends the Hervarts. Above all it is evident that he would remain in touch with the woman whom he trusted and admired and on whom he was still more or less dependent, at least as far as his lodging was concerned.

At this time Mme de La Sablière had to give up her regular attendance at the Hospice on account of her failing health: 'I go less and less to our hospital, and I am here in a more profound solitude which suits me better,' she wrote to Rancé. In her last letter to him, she begged him not to tell any one of her illness either before or after her death, and after thanking him for all he had done for her, she ended her letter saying: 'I feel always the same repose, waiting for the fulfilment of God's will. I desire nothing.' She died in her house in the rue Rousselet, on the 6th January 1693, and was buried by the clergy of Saint-Sulpice in the cemetery that she had seen from her window and of which she had said: 'I see from here every day the place where I shall be buried and I find this view so peaceful that I like it very much. But it seems to me that we should no more desire anything on this occasion than on any other.'

TRANSLATIONS

[1]In truth, my dear, you would be very stupid if you had not so much wit.

[2]Iris, I would praise you, it is only too easy: / But you have refused our compliments a hundred times, / In this most unlike all other mortals / Who daily

wish their praises sung anew. / Not one would fall asleep to this flattering sound / . . . This praise, Iris, is not to your taste. / Other matters for you take its place, / agreeable topics, pleasant intercourse. / Chance furnishes a hundred diverse themes, / In which even frivolous details have a share: / The world does not believe this, / Let us leave the world to its beliefs. / The bagatelle or science, / Fancy or nonsense, all are good. I maintain, / That all things are necessary in conversation: / It is a flower-bed where Flora spreads her riches. / On different flowers the bee reposes, / and makes her honey from everything.

³Henceforth my Muse, as well as my days, / Approaches the inevitable end of her course / And since the torch of my reason is going to die out, / Shall I waste what is left in bemoaning my lot / And prodigal of the time limited by Fate, / Lose it in regretting what is already lost? / If Heaven still reserves for me some spark / Of the fire with which I shone in my first youth / I must use it, sufficiently wise to know / That the finest sunset is neighbour to the night.

⁴If I were wise, Iris, (but that is a privilege / That Nature grants to very few of us), / If I had a mind as well regulated as yours / I would follow your example, at least in something. / To follow it in everything, is too much. One must take / A road from which, without sin, one may wander.

⁵This Iris, Harlay, is the dame / For whom I have two temples made / One in my heart, the other in my book.

⁶I kept a temple for you in my verse / That would have ended with the Universe / . . . In the inner shrine would be her lovely image: / Her features, and her smile gracious and gay / Her art of pleasing all unconsciously / Her charms to which everyone pays homage / . . . I would have made, although imperfectly, / The treasures of her soul shine in her eyes; / For this kind heart infinitely tender / For her friends only, and not otherwise, / Because this mind that's born of Heaven, / With manly beauty, womanly grace, / Cannot be fully described as I would like. / O you, Iris, who know how to charm all, / And know supremely how to please, / You whom one cherishes as oneself / Let this be said without suspicion of love / (a word that is banished from your court: / Let it alone then), grant my Muse your leave / Some day this confused project to achieve.

⁷This savante / Whom Roberval esteems and whom Sauveur frequents / How is it that her eye is dim and her complexion dull? / It is, they say, that on the calculation of Cassini, / an astrolabe in her hand, she has in her roof-gutter / Passed the whole night in following Jupiter.

⁸Topics, agreeable intercourse, where chance provides a hundred agreeable matters.

⁹A good fellow, very social, gay but subject to impulses and inexplicable silences, when an agreeable and profound reverie occupies his mind, one speaks to him in vain.

¹⁰To wander in a garden, lose oneself in a wood, / To lie down among

flowers and inhale their sweet breath, / To listen in dreaming to the song of a fountain, / Or that of a stream murmuring over pebbles . . .

[11]I admit that I am, if I must speak thus, / Butterfly of Parnassus, and like the bees, / With whom the good Plato matches our marvels. / I flit from flower to flower, from object to object, / To a great deal of pleasure I add a little glory.

[12]Even beauty no matter how choice / Surfeits and cloys in the end / I would not eat the same bread twice / Diversity is my device. / I have already said this in another way / For it is a good thing to disguise it / According to this saying / Diversity is my device.

[13]I was given a heart little pleased with itself, / Anxious, and fertile in new loves / That likes to plight its troth / But not for ever.

[14]To Idleness. Let yourself be ruled by this enchantress. / Who alone may calm the heart's emotion; / And prefer, believe me, the gifts of Idleness / To the offers of a vain and mad ambition.

[15]I serve an illustrious Mistress, amiable and wise. / Love, you fulfil my wishes. / Why did you leave me, in the flower of my age / Ignorant of her virtues, her grace and her charm?

[16]I have seen the time when Iris (and it was the golden age / For us people of low estate), / I have seen, I tell you, the time when Iris enjoyed, / Not that common flattery with which Parnassus abounds, / Which was always to her importunate and flat, / But delicate praise had for her its price. / Today she treats this art as a frivolous trifle; / It sends her to sleep; and if I may speak frankly / Praise and verse are for her / That which many sermons are for me.

[17]Some music / In the dwelling philosophic.

[18]Not to err is something beyond my power.

[19]God makes me feel more and more that all that is worldly is a complete void, apart from giving oneself to Him. You know that you are for me everything in this world. And I expect no other help than your charity. Solitude alone carries me to God, all the rest being filled with useless distractions, even the best of occupations.

IX

THE ACADEMY AND THE THEATRE

1. The Academy

After the partial retirement of Mme de La Sablière, La Fontaine's friends realising that he must miss the intellectual company of the salon in the rue Neuve-des-Petits-Champs, suggested to him that he should become a candidate for the Academy. This idea pleased him, for there he would have the company of other writers, many of whom were old friends, and moreover, it was all on the path of glory and would place him among the immortals of his time. Whether or not he reasoned thus, it was plainly evident to others that he should do all he could to strengthen his decidedly precarious financial position.

The *Académie française* had been founded in 1635 by Richelieu, and was limited to forty members. It corresponded at the time to a new tendency towards order and intellectual authority, and was under the supreme sovereignty of the Crown. Outside the King's favour and the applause of the Court there was little worldly prosperity for men of letters: pensions, glory, or a chair in the Academy, all depended on royal approval; and Louis himself relied, at least to some extent, on the support of writers to enhance his prestige. In consequence the royal circle was said to be the most enlightened in Europe.

The death of Colbert in September 1683, seemed to offer La Fontaine an opportunity of becoming an academician, in providing a vacancy and at the same time removing one of his chief opponents. In spite of the passage of time, the Fouquet affair had remained a barrier between minister and poet. But now it seemed the way was clear. However, there was another candidate for the vacancy, namely Boileau, who was in high favour with the King. This put La Fontaine in a difficult position, for he knew that Louis was probably backing his rival. So, with his usual candid simplicity, he went to Boileau and asked him not to stand for election. To this Boileau replied that he would take no steps to forward his own candidature, but if the Academy nominated him, he could not refuse this honour. Both candidates were proposed and in the hope of gaining the King's favour La Fontaine promised not to write any more scandalous *Contes*.

The meeting for the election of Colbert's successor was a stormy one. An elderly member, 'le vieux Rose,' shouted to La Fontaine's supporters, 'I see clearly that what you want is a *Marot*' – a play on the name of the poet and the word 'maraud' meaning a rascal. At this Benserade shouted 'and you a *marotte*' – a fools-cap, comparing the King's secretary to a court-jester. Of the twenty-three members who voted in the first round, thirteen were for La Fontaine, and in the final round he was elected by sixteen votes. It was said that seven academicians had voted for Boileau.

The next day Doujat, director of the Academy, went to ask Louis for authorisation to ratify the election. But the King said he had heard that there had been 'noise and intrigue in the Academy' and he dismissed Doujat, remarking that for the moment he was not quite sure and that he would let the Academy know his intentions, and in a reserved manner gave vague promises for the future.

A few months later, in January 1684, La Fontaine published a *Ballade au Roi* in the *Mercure galant*, praising and flattering the monarch and congratulating him on his military victories. In the Envoi the poet eloquently begs Louis *Console un peu mes Muses inquiètes* and he cleverly uses the refrain to support his request:

'L'événement ne peut m'être qu'heureux.'[1]

La Fontaine asked Mme de Thianges to give the *Ballade* to the King.

In the following March another chair became vacant by the death of Bazin de Bazons, and on the 17th April the Academy met to elect his successor. In order to please the King, the Academicians voted unanimously for Boileau. When the abbé Testu came to announce this result, Louis, much flattered, charged him to tell the Academy to take steps at once to complete La Fontaine's election which till then had been suspended, adding *il a promis d'être sage*. A week later the election of La Fontaine was confirmed by royal consent.

On May 2nd 1684 La Fontaine took his seat in the Academy. Charles Perrault, present on this occasion, reported:

'His speech seemed to me very witty and greatly pleased me, although he read it rather badly and at a speed inappropriate to an oration. After Monsieur l'abbé de la Chambre had replied to him with gravity and dignity, La Fontaine read a piece of verse in form of an Epistle addressed to Mme de La Sablière, in which he gave a description of his life and behaviour, in a word a general confession extremely unaffected which was very well received and made a good impression after what had happened about his reception...'

Strangely enough La Fontaine's speech was not printed in the records of the Academy, as was usual. The director only printed his own reply, and when asked why he had done so, he gave 'such strong reasons that the company accepted them.' Was it fear of the unconventional style, or of the disapproval of their monarch, that allowed this blatant injustice to pass?

In the *Discours à Madame de La Sablière*, to which I have already referred, the poet feeling that she has taken the better way, accuses himself for not having followed her example, and confesses:

Des solides plaisirs je n'ai suivi que l'ombre:
J'ai toujours abusé du plus cher de nos biens;
Les pensers amusants, les vagues entretiens,
Vains enfants du loisir, délices chimériques,
Les romans, et le jeu, peste des républiques,
Par qui sont dévoyés les esprits les plus droits,
Ridicule fureur qui se moque des lois,
Cent autres passions, des sages condamnées,
Ont pris comme à l'envie la fleur de mes années.

And regretting the hours wasted, he addresses himself reproachfully:

Douze lustres et plus ont roulé sur ta vie:
De soixante soleils la course entresuivie
Ne t'a pas vu goûter un moment de repos.
Quelque part que tu sois, on voit à tous propos
L'inconstance d'une âme en ses plaisirs légère,
Inquiète, et partout hôtesse passagère.
Ta conduite et tes vers, chez toi tout s'en ressent,
On te veut là-dessus dire un mot en passant.
Tu changes tous les jours de manière et de style;
Tu cours en un moment de Térence à Virgile;
Ainsi rien de parfait n'est sorti de tes mains.[2]

In lamenting that his work has been so varied, he almost appears to regret his Fables, for he asks:

Que me servent ces vers avec soin composés?
N'en attends-je autre fruit que de les voir prisés?

C'est peu que leurs conseils, si je ne sais les suivre,
Et qu'au moins vers ma fin je ne commence à vivre;
Car je n'ai pas vécu; j'ai servi deux tyrans:
Un vain bruit et l'amour ont partagé mes ans. . .

Iris, he concludes, could teach him in what real living consists, and she would say:

C'est jouir des vrais biens avec tranquillité;
Faire usage du temps et de l'oisiveté;
S'acquitter des honneurs dus à l'Être suprême;
Renoncer aux Philis en faveur de soi-même;
Bannir le fol amour et les vœux impuissants,
Comme hydres dans nos cœurs sans cesse renaissants.[3]

This ends his honest and powerful *Discours*, a meditation that must have pleased Iris, and gratified the most solemn of the academicians.

After his election, the Academy became to a great extent his centre of interest, where he spent much of his time, though he said that he always took the longest way when going there, and when, as often happened, he arrived too late to receive his *jeton de présence*, he was always good-tempered about it. Very soon he began to take part in the discussions and dissensions that arose. About a year later, in 1685, the academicians voted for the expulsion of Antoine Furetière, one of La Fontaine's oldest friends, guilty of having obtained a privilege – that is the right to publish a dictionary he had compiled without their consent. La Fontaine was among those who voted for this measure. Some days before the session at which Furetière was to appear before the president and five delegates from the Academy, the assembly allowed Racine, La Fontaine and Boileau, to go and see the culprit and in the name of them all to beg him to give signs of submission. They found him 'inaccessible to reason.' The cause of this upheaval was that the dictionary on which the Academy was working was shortly to appear and was considered as the only sure authority. In voting against Furetière, La Fontaine was openly on the side of his new confrères, many of whom were also friends of long-standing. This led Furetière to hit back fiercely at La Fontaine, Charles Perrault, Quinault, Benserade and others; and on his exclusion from the Academy he attacked these members in a series of pamphlets known as *Factums*. In the second of these he savagely accused La Fontaine of having failed in the theatre, saying of him that 'when he wanted to put on a play, the actors did not dare to give a second performance for fear of being stoned; that he was incapable of writing an opera, (allusion to Daphné), and that he had written licentious *Contes*, 'so that one might call him *Aretin mitigé!*' But this was not all, he was also accused of being a too complaisant husband and of exalting *le cocuage volontaire* in his *Contes*.

But the most interesting of these spiteful backbitings was the accusation that at the sessions devoted to the Academy dictionary, he 'took the defence of *termes libres* usual in the ancient tongue, and that all his reading consisted in Rabelais, Petronius, Ariosto and Boccacio and suchlike authors.' This accusation may well be considered as a compliment, for it shows how anxiously La Fontaine guarded the natural, simple forms of language which the *Précieux* had done much to destroy. In this quarrel Boileau secretly took the part of Furetière. Many cruel, and sometimes ridiculous verses were exchanged, La Fontaine replying to the *Factums* with spirit, till growing tired of this distraction, he shrugged his shoulders saying of his adversary, '*qu'il fallait qu'il fût ladre.*'

In 1687 a special meeting was held by the Academy to celebrate the King's recovery from an operation. On this occasion a poem by Charles Perrault, *Le Siècle de Louis le Grand*, was read to the assembly by the abbé Lavau. This reading was punctuated by groans from Boileau who finally got up and declared that it was a disgrace that the great men of antiquity should be condemned. Whereupon M. Huet, bishop of Soissons, stood up and ordered Boileau to be silent, saying that if it were a question of taking the part of the ancients, he himself would be a more suitable person to do so, as he had a far greater knowledge of the subject, but that they were there only to listen and not to interrupt.

The reading of Perrault's poem stirred up the old quarrel of ancients versus moderns, and incited La Fontaine to write a poem justifying his devotion to the classics. But the Furetière affair had taught him to be diplomatic and not to stir up the enmity of old friends. So now he carefully approached Huet, whom he hardly knew, but who was an intimate friend of Perrault and a personal enemy of Boileau. La Fontaine also took precautions vis-a-vis to the King in first addressing his own flatteries to Louis (in an *Épitre à Bonrepaux*), which put him in a position to disapprove of Perrault's compliments.

In his *Épitre à Monseigneur L'Évêque De Soissons, En Lui Donnant Un Quintilien De La Traduction D'Oratio Toscanella*, La Fontaine shows an admirable critical judgement, and also justifies his own methods:

Mon imitation n'est point un esclavage:
Je ne prends que l'idée, et les tours, et les lois,

> Que nos maîtres suivaient eux-mêmes autrefois.
> Si d'ailleurs quelque endroit plein chez eux d'excellence
> Peut entrer dans mes vers sans nulle violence,
> Je l'y transporte, et veux qu'il n'ait rien d'affecté,
> Tâchant de rendre mien cet air d'antiquité. . .[4]

This epistle should be studied as a statement of the poet's tastes and theories, it ends in a learned prose passage and is too long to quote here. It appeared first in a pamphlet together with the verses *A Monsieur de Bonrepaux*, a month after the reading of Perrault's poem. We find a further reference to the same quarrel in a letter from La Fontaine to Racine, where taking from *les Femmes savantes*, the theme, *un sot plein de savoir est plus sot qu'un autre homme*,[5] as a pretext to attack Ronsard, he comments on the respect of past generations for antiquity, and adds, things have now changed:

> Des éruditions la cour est ennemie;
> Même on les voit assez souvent
> Rebuter par l'Académie.[6]

The quarrel between ancient and modern, closely allied with the question of tradition and experiment, assumed proportions unimagined by La Fontaine, when Fontenelle enlarged its significance by attacking the Oracles of antiquity in more ways than one. The problem lies at the root of the romantic movement, making possible a return to a more universal poetry.

2. The Theatre

At different periods of his life La Fontaine turned his attention to writing for the stage. This at first seems surprising in one whose talent lay so decidedly in the direction of short narrative poems: but when we consider the triumph of the theatre over all other forms of poetry, we understand his temptation. For the stage, through the genius of Corneille Molière and Racine had become the royal theatre, a truly royal art and the greatest form of poetic expression, as well as the most generally popular, and also, in spite of all hazards, the most remunerative.

I have already spoken of La Fontaine's early comedy *L'Eunuque*, the first of his printed works, which had appeared as early as 1654, when he was aged thirty-three. There is no evidence that it was ever played, and it is certainly an exaggeration to say, as some critics have done, that it indicated a reaction against the Cornellian system, or that it foretold the poetry of Racine. A more personal early work was the comedy *Clymène*, founded on an adventure of the poet's youth and dating from the time of Fouquet, probably written about 1658; its chief interest lies in the poet's reflections of that period. It was not published till 1671 when it appeared in the *Contes et Nouvelles*. In a note concerning this piece, the author said: 'there is no distribution of the scenes, and the thing is not made for representation.'

La Fontaine's next theatrical venture was a ballet, *Les Rieurs du Beau-Richard*. The amateur actors who played in it, whose names have come down to us, were all inhabitants of Château-Thierry. The piece consists of simple quatrains recounting an incident, that took place at Château-Thierry, and was also used in the *Contes et Nouvelles en vers* of 1665.

Since 1674 La Fontaine had belonged to the *Cabale du Sublime*, a coterie that gravitated round the King's mistress Mme de Montespan and her spirited sister Mme de Thianges. The poet had been introduced to them by Saint-Réal, as the writer of the *Contes*. Mme de Thianges, who treated Louis as an honest brother-in-law, was the most intelligent of the three Mortemart sisters; her daughter, the duchesse de Sforza, was said by Saint-Simon to have such an aquiline nose and such red lips that she resembled a parakeet eating a cherry. Mme de Montespan and her sisters were considered the most beautiful women of their time, and all three had intelligence and wit; their brother the duc de Varenne was also a man of wit, and the '*esprit Mortemart*' was commented on a generation later by Voltaire.

When the little duc de Maine, eldest son of Mme de Montespan and the King, was five years old, Mme de Thianges gave him a model of a gilt room called the *chambre du Sublime*. Inside were beautifully modelled wax figures representing the duc de Maine, La Rochefoucauld, Bossuet, Mme de Thianges and Mme de La Fayette. Outside the balustrade, Boileau with a pitchfork prevented seven or eight bad poets from entering, while Racine beside him beckoned to La Fontaine, who stood a little way off. This joke was characteristic of Mme de Thianges and was aimed at La Fontaine's timidity.

It was in January 1674 that the musician Lulli gave the first perform-ance of the opera *Alceste* with the libretto by the well known dramatic poet Quinault. Fragments played at the Court had already met with considerable success, but when it was put on in Paris, a cabal, instigated by Boileau, compromised its expected triumph. At once Mme de

Montespan and Mme de Thianges, who were always plotting some mischief, begged Lulli to replace Quinault by La Fontaine in whom, for the moment they felt an interest. Against his better judgement Lulli rather unwillingly consented and commissioned La Fontaine to write words for the opera. The result of this commission was La Fontaine's opera-ballet, *Daphné*, founded on one of the most vivid of Ovid's Metamorphoses, *Daphne in laurum*. In his version La Fontaine shows great skill in versification, developing forms already used in his fables. And there are some delightful little songs such as:

> Tout me semble parler d'amour
> En ces lieux amis du silence:
> Ici les oiseaux nuit et jour
> Célèbrent de ses traits la douce violence.
> Tout me semble parler d'amour
> En ces lieux amis du silence.
> Heureux les habitants de ces ombrages verts,
> S'ils n'avaient que ce mal à craindre!
> Mais nous troublons leur paix par cent moyens divers:
> Humains, cruels humains, tyrans de l'Univers,
> C'est de vous seuls qu'on se doit plaindre.[7]

For four months he worked on it, but evidently Lulli had decided to be difficult, and said that he was not satisfied with La Fontaine's efforts, finally dismissing the piece as 'a pastoral not worthy to be played before the King.' La Fontaine withdrew leaving the field open to Quinault whose *Thésée* was played at Saint-Germain in January of the following year.

Determined to be revenged on Lulli, La Fontaine wrote a cruel satire, *Le Florentin*, but did not dare to publish it, as Mme de Thianges warned him not to, telling him that the King would certainly not tolerate this fierce attack on his favourite musician. In reply the poet wrote to Mme de Thianges an *Epitre* excusing, and at the same time justifying, his resentment, saying:

> J'eusse ainsi raisonné si le Ciel m'eût fait ange,
> Ou Thiange;
> Mais il me fait auteur, je m'excuse par là;
> Auteur, qui pour tout fruit moissonne
> Un peu de gloire. . .[8]

And of Quinault he says: '*il est l'homme de Cour, je suis homme de vers,*'[9] and ends by begging her '*servez ma Muse auprès du Roi;*'[10] for he still hoped to write operas for the Court. Yet although his attack was evidently written when he was feeling angry and wished to insult his adversary, other verses, written about the same time contained genuine criticism of what he considered bad in Lulli's lack of classical purity:

> Ses divertissements ressentent tous la guerre
> Ses concerts d'instruments ont le bruit du tonnerre...
> Il faut vingt clavecins, cent violins pour plaire,
> On ne va plus chercher au fond de quelque bois
> Des amoureux bergers la flute et le hautbois...[11]

Certainly there is nothing pastoral in Lulli's effects, that genre was already decidedly *vieux jeu* and no longer fashionable; and from the point of view of magnificent and spacious orchestration he might be said to have been the Wagner of his time, as he was also founder of the French national opera. He and La Fontaine were poles apart. Had François Couperin, who was not born till 1668, been twenty years older, he would have been the ideal composer for the delicate harmonies of La Fontaine's operettas; as it was he put the *Épitaphe du Paresseux* to music, matching it with a delightful melody in the year 1711, fifteen years after the poet's death:

> Jean s'en alla comme il était venu
> Mangea le fond avec le revenu,
> Tint les trésors chose peu nécessaire,
> Quant à son temps, bien le sut dispenser;
> Deux parts en fit, dont il soulait passer
> L'une à dormir, et l'autre à ne rien faire.[12]

The opera *Daphné* was published in 1682 with the preposterous *Poème du Quinquina* (*Poème du Quinquina et autres ouvrages*) and in the same volume, the unfinished *Galatée* – a ballet of which there are only two acts – beginning with a simple lyric that was put to music by Lambert and became the popular song of the moment. A variation of the first couplet is found in the *Songe de Vaux* (fragment VII), from which one may suppose that it was an early work:

> Brillantes fleurs, naissez,
> Herbe tendre, croissez;
> > Le long de ces rivages;
> > Venez, petits oiseaux,
> > Accordez vos ramages
> > Au doux bruit de leurs eaux.[13]

L'Astrée, a lyrical tragedy in three acts, was written in 1691, when the poet was seventy. Since his childhood he had been familiar with d'Urfé's long novel *Astrée*, and the first two acts follow closely this story. The music was written by Colasse, Lulli's son-in-law, and it was put on at the Opera in November 1692. It ran for six performances and its failure was commented on in numerous epigrams and anecdotes.

A much worked-on tragedy, *Achille*, which was left unfinished probably on the advice of Maucroix, closes the sum of the poet's published work for the stage. The chief interest of *Achille* for us today, is in the autograph manuscript, now in the Bibliothèque Nationale, for it shows us the poet at work: verses are laboriously corrected before being crossed out, and groups of lines are carefully recopied. Only two acts exist, though a possible ending is suggested in a note in the poet's hand-writing.

It is highly probable that La Fontaine collaborated in various plays with the husband of the Champmeslé, who was a prolific playwright specialising in comic and often risky dialogue and effects, such as we find in his *Valet de deux maîtres*, *La Coupe enchantée*, *Je vous prends sans vert*, etc. It is easy to see that La Fontaine's works belonged neither to this kind of popular diversion nor to the theatre destined to entertain the Court and town; for he lacked that sustained structural development characteristic of dramatic authors. Moreover, his operas were completely lacking in passion, and in spite of their fine lyrical qualities they rarely went beyond the amiability and charm of a pastoral play. Where there is the authentic expression of a state of mind, it is inevitably the anxious preoccupation of the amorous shepherd, a condition characteristic of La Fontaine. He himself was well aware of his deficiencies both in his art and his character, and he never grew tired of remarking on that volatility and inconstancy which were so much a part of his nature.

TRANSLATIONS

[1]The result for me can only be happy.

[2]Of solid pleasures I pursued but the shadow / I have always misused the best of our blessings; / Amusing thoughts, vague intercourse, / Vain children of leisure, fanciful delights, / Novels, and gambling, plague of republics, / By which the most honest minds are led astray; / Ridiculous fury that defies the laws, / A hundred other passions, condemned by the wise, have vied with each other for the flower of my years / . . . Sixty years have rolled over your life;

The course of sixty suns following one another / Has not seen you enjoy a moment of repose. / Wherever you are, one sees at every turn / The inconstancy of a mind given to light pleasures, / Anxious, and always a passing guest, / Your behaviour, your verse, everything shows the effect, / One would like in passing to say a word about this: / You change every day your manner and your style; / You fly in a moment from Terence to Virgil, / Thus nothing perfect ever comes from your hands.

³What use to me are those verses composed with such care? / Did I aim at aught else but to hear them praised? / Their advice is worth little, if I do not take it, / If at least towards my end I don't begin to live; / For I have not lived; I have served two tyrants: / Vain pastimes and love have divided my years. . . . It is time to enjoy real blessings in tranquillity / To make good use of one's time and employ one's leisure; / To observe the honours due to the supreme Being: / To renounce light verse in favour of oneself, / To banish foolish love and futile vows, / Like Hydras constantly reborn in our hearts.

⁴My imitation is not slavery; / I only take an idea, and the forms and laws / That our masters themselves followed long ago. / Moreover if some excellent passage in their works, / Can fit into my verse without any violence, / I transport it there, and that it may not seem affected, / I try to make its air of antiquity my own.

⁵A fool with knowledge is more fool than another man.

⁶The court is enemy to learned works; / One even sees them rejected by the Academy.

⁷Everything seems to speak of love / In this place beloved of silence / Here the birds night and day / Celebrate the heart's sweet violence. / Everything seems to speak of love / In this place beloved of silence. / Happy the denizens of these verdant shades / If this alone was all their pain, / But we trouble their peace with our ways diverse: / Humans, cruel humans, tyrants of the Universe / It is of you alone that one should complain.

⁸I would have reasoned thus if I were an angel, / Or Thianges; but I am an author, and that is my excuse; / An author whose only reward is a little glory . . .

⁹He is a courtier, I am a poet.

¹⁰Help my Muse to gain favour with the King.

¹¹All his divertisements are inspired by war / His concerts of instruments have the noise of thunder . . . / There must be twenty harpsichords, a hundred violins to please, / One no longer seeks in the depth of some forest / The flute and the oboe of amorous shepherds.

¹²John left the world as he had come / Ate capital and revenue, / Riches he held of little value, / As for his time, it was his custom / Two parts to make, and in this way, / To sleep or else to dream all day.

¹³Brilliant flowers, spring, / Tender grass, grow / Along banks green and low; / Come little birds atune your song / To the sweet sound of water's flow.

X

FRIENDS IN ENGLAND AND FRANCE

1. Friends in England

It was during his last year in the rue St Honoré, in August 1687, that
La Fontaine received a letter from Bonrepaux giving him news of
mutual friends who were refugees in England. The centre of this group
was Charles de Saint-Évremond. Born in 1610, he had lived in France,
at Court and in the army, till the age of forty-seven and was much
esteemed by his superior officers. After the Treaty of the Pyrennees,
he wrote a malicious and witty letter against Cardinal Mazarin, which
was found in the papers of Mme Duplessis-Bellière at the time of
Fouquet's arrest. This letter so much annoyed the King that he gave
orders for Saint-Évremond's arrest and imprisonment in the Bastille.
Warned in time, Saint-Évremond escaped from France and took
refuge first in Holland and later in England, where he was welcomed
in Court circles. Like La Fontaine, he was a faithful friend to Fouquet
and he said: 'I have become accustomed to my own misfortunes, but I
will never be resigned to Fouquet's, and since I can only offer my sorrow
for his hardships, there never passes a day that I am not sorry for him.'
Although he received permission to return to France in 1688, he preferred to stay in England, finding there, in spite of political upheavals,
a wider horizon and greater liberty than in France, where it seemed to
him that tyranny and intolerance were bringing poverty and discontent,
since the advent of the King's severe mistress Madame de Maintenon.
He considered that the only censorship required was the poet's good
taste, and he always regretted the time of Louis XIII and of the Regency:

> Temps où la ville aussi bien que la Cour
> Ne respiraient que les jeux et l'amour.[1]

Saint-Évremond was a cultivated poet and a sensitive critic, he wrote
an admirable criticism of Plutarch which might well be applied to
his own *Dissertations*. He was an agreeable and cultured Epicurean,

preferring conversation to reading, and he must have been an excellent talker; one might almost say of him that he was more conversational than thoughtful, for his wise and delicate judgement often played round matters which in themselves were trivial enough. In some ways his Voltairean turn of mind resembled La Fontaine's positive conception of life; both were Gassendists and anti-Cartesian, though for different reasons; Saint-Évremond refuting Descartes' proofs of the existence of God, though remaining a Catholic, and he died at the age of ninety-nine with a Crucifix in his hands. Yet he had always allowed himself to think freely and was therefore considered as a libertine, being honest enough with himself to say, 'devotion is the last of our loves.'

Among Saint-Évremond's many qualities was that just balance between heart and head that makes for real and lasting friendship. He corresponded with his old friends in France, such as Ninon de Lenclos and Mme de La Sablière, and his sensible opinion of women deserves to be remembered: 'one finds women who are capable of appreciation and of tenderness even without love, and who can keep secrets and confidences as do the most faithful of men friends. I know some women who have as much wit and discretion as they have beauty and charm.'

Perhaps when he wrote these words, he was thinking of Hortense duchesse de Mazarin for whom he had a secret and silent devotion. Ever since her arrival in England, to escape from her impossible husband, she and Saint-Évremond had been close friends. Speaking of her house in London, he said: One finds there the greatest liberty in the world and at the same time one sees there an equal discretion. Every one feels more at ease than in his own home, and at the same time every one is as respectful as when at Court.' Hortense's salon was the centre of a cosmopolitan society; among her guests we find Paul Barrillon marquis de Branges, French Ambassador at the court of James II from 1672 till 1689. He was an old friend of La Fontaine who dedicated to him *'Le Pouvoir Des Fables'*, which begins with an eloquent appeal for lasting peace between England and France.

One of Saint-Évremond's special friends was the English poet Edmund Waller, who had been an exile in France and had returned to England at the restoration of Charles II. Waller was a great favourite at the court of the Stewarts, and he was one of the circle who entertained the French refugees, for he was well off and had a pleasant property at Beaconsfield. Bonrepaux referred to him and Saint-Évremond as the two Anacreons, for Waller was now eighty-one and was still a good poet who said of old age:

> The seas are quiet when the winds give o'er;
> So calm are we when passions are no more.
> For when we know how vain it was to boast
> Of fleeting things, so certain to be lost,
> Clouds of affection from our younger eyes
> Conceal that emptiness which age descries.
>
> The soul's dark cottage, battered and decayed
> Lets in new light through chinks that Time has made:
> Stronger by weakness, wiser men become
> As they draw near to their eternal home.
> Leaving the old, both worlds at once they view
> That stand upon the threshold of the new.

At the time of Bonrepaux's letter, Waller had only three more months to live, for he died in October of the same year.

Lady Harvey, a great friend of the duchesse de Mazarin, was among the English who were in close contact with the French colony; she was the sister of Ralph Montagu, English ambassador in France and widow of David Harvey, English ambassador in Turkey. She had visited Paris in 1683, and met La Fontaine at the Bouillons' town house. He dedicated his fable *Le Renard anglais* to her, and it is probable that she suggested the subject which she may have read in the English version of the *Roman de Renart*, for it seems that La Fontaine did not know the French origin of this story – though he knew the *Roman de Renart* at least in part. His fable opens with praise of Mme Harvey; '*le bon cœur est chez vous compagnon du bon sens,*' probably a just estimation of her character, and he also shows a shrewd knowledge of her country-men:

> Les Anglais pensent profondément;
> Leur esprit en cela suit leur tempérament.
> Creusant dans les sujets, et forts d'expériences
> Ils étendent partout l'empire des sciences.
> Je ne dis point ceci pour vous faire ma cour.
> Vos gens à pénétrer l'emportent sur les autres;
> Même les chiens de leur séjour
> Ont meilleur nez que n'ont les nôtres.
> Vos renards sont plus fins. Je m'en vais le prouver. . .[2]

The first part of this passage may be taken as a compliment to the Royal Society, founded in 1662 under the patronage of Charles II, it had already established a reputation for experimental science, and had laid the foundations of modern physics.

At the time of La Fontaine's correspondence with England, the duchesse de Bouillon was the latest arrival there, and we find him writing to her in September of 1687. She had been exiled from France for some more than usually flagrant indiscretion and had taken refuge with her sister Hortense. La Fontaine had been uneasy when he heard that she had been ordered to leave France; why was it, he asked himself, that his patronesses were never content to sit still and enjoy the gifts bestowed on them? But in writing to her he disguised his anxiety:

> Vous portez en tous lieux la joie et les plaisirs;
> Allez en des climats inconnus aux Zéphyrs,
> Les champs se vêtiront de roses.
> Mais, comme aucun bonheur n'est constant dans son cours,
> Quelques noirs aquilons troublent de si beaux jours.
> C'est là que vous savez témoigner de courage:
> Vous envoyez aux vents ce fâcheux souvenir;
> Vous avez cent secrets pour combattre l'orage:
> Que n'en aviez-vous un qui le sût prévenir?[3]

Having thus regretted paternally the rashness of her behaviour, he tells her: 'the English have not a great deal of admiration for anything, only I have observed that they know real merit and are touched by it.' And then to divert her he says: 'Your philosopher was astonished when told that Descartes was not the inventor of the system that we call the mecanism of animals, and that a Spaniard had forestalled him. However even if there is no proof of this I shall continue to believe it, for I think that only a Spaniard would be capable of building such castles in the air as that . . .' Then to justify his mention of philosophy he praises the Duchess's understanding and sympathy for

> Anacréon et les gens de sa sorte
> Comme Waller, Saint-Évremond, et moi. . .
> Qui n'admettrait Anacréon chez soi?
> Qui bannirait Waller et La Fontaine?
> Tous deux sont vieux, Saint-Évremond aussi:
> Mais verrez-vous au bord de l'Hippocrène
> Gens moins ridés dans leurs vers que ceux-ci?[4]

And now he plays with the idea of bringing Anacréon back to earth after which Mme de Bouillon and Mme de Mazarin must assembl them all together in England, 'Mr Waller, M. Saint-Évremond an myself,' and he asks: 'do you think Madame, that one could find fou poets better assorted?' . . .

This is the first suggestion of a visit to England, a project taken up again six years later. But it was difficult to make new plans, and the poet was growing old. Yet how agreeable to imagine himself in a new country, where friendly faces would greet him:

> I would have to see five or six Englishmen and as many English women – who, they say, are pleasant to look at. I would remind our Ambassador (Barillon) of the rue Neuve-des-Petits-Champs and of the devotion I have for him. I would beg M. de Bonrepaux to charge me with some commissions. That would be all the business I would do. Though I had planned to convert Mme d' Hervart, Mme de Gouvernet and Mme d'Heland (sic), because they are persons whom I honour; but I am told that they are not yet well disposed to this. Besides I am not much good, any more than Perrin Dandin, at persuading people until they are tired of arguing. And then I would like to see the English king . . .

Thus he dreams, and finishes his letter to continue dreaming of the circle of friends, the country of rivers and woodlands, the park at Windsor where one would walk by the river Thames after devoting a long time to sleep; that life of philosophy, love and wine, which M. de Bonrepaux had evoked in his letter of the early summer of that year.

La Fontaine's letter was answered by Saint-Évremond on behalf of the Duchess, her sister and the Ambassador, who were all pleased by the poet's compliments. No one knew better than Saint-Évremond how to express graceful sentiments, and after praising the two Duchesses he says of La Fontaine:

> Vous possédez tout le bon sens
> Qui sert à consoler des maux de la vieillesse,
> Vous avez plus de feu que n'ont les jeunes gens,
> Eux, moins que vous de goût et de justesse.[5]

And he continues in prose: 'after having spoken of your wit, a word must be said about your morale:'

> S'accomoder aux ordres du destin,
> Aux plus heureux ne porter point d'envie,
> De ce faux air d'esprit que prend un libertin

Connaître avec le temps comme nous la folie,
Et dans les vers, jeu, musique et bon vin
Entretenir son innocente vie,
C'est le moyen d'en reculer la fin.[6]

Since La Fontaine's letter to the Duchess, the poet Waller had died, and Saint-Évremond says: 'Mr Waller, whose loss we feel deeply, had kept his vigour of mind right up to the age of eighty-two. (*sic*)

Et dans la douleur que m'apporte
Ce triste et malheureux trépas,
Je dirais en pleurant que toute muse est morte,
Si la vôtre ne vivait pas.
Ô vous, nouvel Orphée, ô vous, de qui la veine
Peut charmer des enfers la noire souveraine
Et le terrible dieu qu'on appelle Pluton,
Daignez, tout puissant La Fontaine,
Rendre au jour notre Waller au lieu d'Anacréon.[7]

'May you live even longer than did Mr Waller –

Que plus longtemps votre muse agréable
Donne au public ses ouvrages galants!
Que tout chez vous puisse être conte et fable,
Hors le secret de vivre heureux cent ans!'[8]

In replying to this letter in the following December, La Fontaine gives a sad picture of his sufferings from rheumatism:

Ni vos leçons, ni celles des neuf Sœurs,
N'ont su charmer la douleur qui m'accable;
Je souffre un mal qui resiste aux douceurs,
Et ne saurais rien penser d'agréable:
Tout rhumatisme, invention du diable,
Rend impotent et de corps et d'esprit.[9]

For now sleep that he loved so much and that had always been a necessity for his inspiration, had completely forsaken him. It was this that had caused his delay in sending his thanks for Saint-Évremond's amiable letter. 'You praise me and my verses so generously that my morale has difficulty in remaining modest,' he says in returning the compliment, declaring that Saint-Évremond is one of his masters, one of the fine minds from whom he had learnt his art, and he adds that he has also profited by the works of Maître Vincent (Voiture) and Maître Clément (Marot), not forgetting Maître François Rabelais of whom he is still the disciple. This is no empty compliment, for Saint-Évremond's cultured verses – though disparaged by Boileau – had certainly been enjoyed by La Fontaine who knew them well, and they were to appear in a new edition in 1689, and again in 1692.

'I return to what you say about my *morale*,' continues La Fontaine, 'and I am glad that you have this good opinion of me. I am no less an enemy than you are of a false air of wit: I give the palm of ridicule to whomsoever assumes it.' There follows a clear justification of his attitude towards his art, and these fine verses are at the same time an authentic self-portrait.

> Rien ne m'engage à faire un livre;
> Mais la raison m'oblige à vivre
> En sage citoyen de ce vaste Univers;
> Citoyen qui, voyant un monde si divers,
> Rend à son auteur les hommages
> Que méritent de tels ouvrages.
> Ce devoir acquitté, les beaux vers, les doux sons,
> Il est vrai, sont peu nécessaires:
> Mais qui dira qu'ils soient contraires
> A ces éternelles leçons?
> On peut goûter la joie en diverses façons:
> Au sein de ses amis répandre mille choses,
> Et, recherchant de tout les effets et les causes,
> A table, au bord d'un bois, le long d'un clair ruisseau,
> Raisonner avec eux sur le bon, sur le beau,
> Pourvu que ce dernier se traite à la légère,
> Et que la Nymphe ou la bergère
> N'occupe notre esprit et nos yeux qu'en passant:
> Le chemin du cœur est glissant.
> Sage Saint-Évremond, le mieux est de m'en taire. . . .[10]

These thoughtful lines express to perfection the sensitive logic of the poet's inner life, ending on a note of harmonious gravity:

> . . . De bonne heure! est-ce un mot qui me convienne encore,
> A moi qui tant de fois ai vu naître l'aurore,
> Et de qui les soleils se vont précipitant
> Vers le moment fatal que je vois qui m'attend?[11]

The letter closes with a friendly message from Mme de La Sablière, and the poet's hope of Saint-Évremond's continued friendship. '*A Paris ce jour 18 decembre 1687.*'

2. Friends in France

In the first of his letters to England in 1687, La Fontaine had spoken of
Mme d'Hervart who, he said, consoled him a little for the absence of
the ladies of the rue St Honoré. This was the virtuous Françoise de
Bretonvilliers; in 1686 she had married Monsieur Anne d'Hervart
seigneur de Bois-le-Vicomte, *conseiller au Parlement*, who later took La
Fontaine under his protection after Mme de La Sablière's death. Anne
was a son of Barthélémy d'Hervart the German financier whom La
Fontaine had met at Vaux. Anne had been converted to Catholicism
in 1685; he and his sister Esther had always been on friendly terms with
the poet. Esther had remained a zealous Protestant, she married the
marquis de Gouvernet, and after the Revocation of the Edict of Nantes,
she took refuge in England with her mother, leaving her two younger
daughters in the care of her brother Anne; her eldest daughter married
Lord Holland. The young Mme d'Hervart became a devoted friend to
La Fontaine and welcomed him warmly in her luxurious house in the
rue Platrière quite close to the rue St Honoré, or at the Château of
Bois-le-Vicomte fifteen miles from Paris, where he enjoyed the company of his hostess and her two nieces. Mme d'Hervart was said to be as
beautiful as she was amiable, La Fontaine gave her the *nom de Parnasse*
of Sylvie, and said:

> C'est un plaisir de voir Sylvie;
> Mais n'espérez pas que mes vers
> Peignent tant de charmes divers:
> J'en aurais pour toute ma vie. . .[12]

And in prose he described her as *une femme souverainement jolie, com-
plaisante, d'humeur égale, d'un esprit doux.*[13] This is rather impersonal and
conventional, but he was doing his best to express his gratitude at having
found himself appreciated by such a good hostess. Yet she never
replaced his Iris, and although he was sincerely grateful for all her
friendly attentions, I doubt if he ever completely fell under her charm.
Was she not in fact a little dull? So much virtue and so many good
deeds needed some intellectual gifts to sustain the poet's interest,
kindness alone could never fill the blank left by the wit and intelligence
that had animated the rue St. Honoré. And then, he himself was
changing, he had reached the age when apart from a certain dissipation,

Portrait of Boileau, after Rigaud (p. 85)

Versailles, view of the Orangery (1664) (p. 92)

Portrait of Marie-Anne Mancini, duchesse
de Bouillon (p. 103)

La chambre du philosophe: La Fontaine in his library (p. 163)

it was agreeable to be left at ease, alone with one's own thoughts. The gentle advice of even the most devoted of friends was apt to become a bore.

In his letter to Saint-Évremond La Fontaine had complained sadly about his sufferings from rheumatism, but happily his hope of recovery in the spring was realised, and he was able to ride into the country to Bois-le-Vicomte to visit the d'Hervarts and then to fall in love. This he recounts in a letter to the abbé Vergier, who had been tutor to Anne d'Hervart and still remained attached to the household. If only Monsieur d'Hervart had warned him of the beauty of the girl, he would not have stayed to lunch and would not have lost his way going home. The attractions of the young Mlle de Beaulieu, who was sixteen with large eyes and white skin, had quite dazzled him. As it was he rode for miles and miles, mostly in the wrong direction, and did not arrive in Paris till the next day, having been obliged to spend the night in an uncomfortable Inn.

'Mademoiselle made me waste three or four days in reveries,' he wrote, 'and all Paris is speaking about it. You may tell the company the *Iliad (sic)* of my misfortunes if you wish. Not that I want to make you sorry for me, but even if I did, no one is sorry for people of my age who lapse into such errors.

> Ma lettre vous fera rire.
> Je vous entends déjà dire:
> 'Cet homme n'est-il fou
> Dans l'enterprise qu'il tente?
> Il est plus près du Pérou
> Qu'il n'est du cœur d'Amarante.[14]

And I agree that you would be right to speak like that.' There follows a poem of nearly a hundred lines in praise of Amarante, in which he declares himself capable of always loving her as he loves the spring. Finishing the letter in prose, he laughs at himself and invites his friends to do likewise, for *à quoi servent les radoteurs, qu'à faire rire les jeunes filles*. It is reassuring to know that though he was perfectly shameless in boasting of his folly, he could laugh at himself and invite others to laugh with him, for there is a subtle difference between being laughed with and being laughed at.

In his reply the abbé Vergier assures the poet that his letter had greatly amused the company including Mme d'Hervart; they had all laughed and were not surprised that he fell in love nor that he lost his way, and the abbé adds in mocking verse:

> Hé! qui pourrait être surpris
> Lorsque La Fontaine s'égare?
> Tout le cours de ses ans n'est qu'un tissu d'erreurs
> Mais d'erreurs pleines de sagesse.
> Les plaisirs l'y guident sans cesse
> Par des chemins semés de fleurs . . .[15]

'I am only astonished, Sir, that you did not go on and on as long as your horse and the earth could carry you . . . The title of *Odyssey* would suit your adventure better than that of *Iliad* which you give it for the errors of Ulysses have a certain resemblance to yours, with this difference that he braved the seas to return to his wife, but you would do the same to escape from yours . . .' The letter had been read to Mlle de Beaulieu 'whose youth and modesty forbade her to say what she thought of it.'

In the following years La Fontaine spent much of his time with the d'Hervarts either in the rue Platrière or at Blois-le-Vicomte. He wrote several poems, in his usual graceful style to Mme d'Hervart and her nieces, generally to celebrate passing events such as the marriage of Sabine de Gouvernet to the comte de Virville; such works have little poetic significance. During the summer of 1691 when his opera *Astrée* was being rehearsed in Paris, he made his excuses for staying there, for 'it would be impossible to stay quietly in the country while my opera is being rehearsed in Paris, that could not be expected of any author no matter who he might be. I will therefore stay here where I can come and go as I wish, hiding myself when it suits me, in this way I shall avoid the certain danger of being enchanted in a castle by Madame d'Hervart and her nieces . . .' Unfortunately the opera was a complete failure.

It is interesting to note that La Fontaine had not lost his independence, his character had not changed with the years. There is a well observed portrait of him at the age of sixty-nine, found in a letter from Vergier to Mme d'Hervart:

> Je voudrais bien le voir aussi
> Dans ces charmants détours que votre parc enserre
> Parler de paix, parler de guerre
> Parler de vers, de vin et d'amoureux souci;

> Former d'un vain projet le plan imaginaire,
> Changer en cent façons l'ordre de l'Univers,
> Sans douter, proposer mille doutes divers;
> Puis tout seul s'écarter, comme il fait d'ordinaire,
> Non point rêver à vous qui rêvez tant à lui
> Non pour rêver à quelque affaire,
> Mais pour varier son ennui
> Car vous savez, Madame, qu'il s'ennuie partout.[16]

This suggests the poet's need to escape from direct human intercourse in order to enjoy the two constants of his solitude: the fervour of composition, and the happiness of love which was frequently the motif that dominated his dreams; for what better subject for verse could there be than love and admiration that transpose everyday life into poetry? Yet the reference to La Fontaine's boredom may surprise one in this context.

Vergier, who renounced holy orders in 1688, had a gift for writing parodies and erotic verse, and although he professed admiration for La Fontaine's verse, he was jealous of the poet's genius and success, and also of Mme d'Hervart's affection for this new friend. In the same letter in which the above verses occur, Vergier, who then held a post in the navy, reports having received a badly written letter from La Fontaine saying that he was going to spend six weeks with the d'Hervarts at Bois-le-Vicomte.

> 'I greatly envy him,' says Vergier, 'though he himself is not so pleased to be there as you are to have his company, for you will be amused by his regrettable *petites façons* with *jeunes filles* which shock the innocence of Mlle de Beaulieu. . . . But you know that he is bored, even when with you, especially when you try to control his morals or his expenditure . . .

This spiteful insistence on La Fontaine's boredom is in bad taste and shows that jealousy had caused the ex-abbé to throw aside tact and charity with his clerical cassock. Of course it is not impossible that he had been genuinely shocked by La Fontaine's sensuality, that always seems misplaced in one of his age. For it is true that during this time before Mme de La Sablière's death, a thousand attractions confused the poet's sight, disturbing his studious life. Too often his desires refused to be confined within artistic limits; women were the devil and they continued to disturb his peace: his unquiet mind knew no rest; in vain he laughed at himself, knowing that he was no longer young and attractive to women, though they might be flattered by the attentions of a celebrated poet. Unfortunately he had cultivated an increasing desire for illicit pleasures though he knew that they wasted his time, he also knew that time was growing short and he wished to enjoy himself as long as he could. So we see him still pursuing, still attracted not only by the ravishing beauty of Mlle de Beaulieu, but also by Mlle Certain, and the tougher proposition of the notorious Mme Ulrich.

At this time La Fontaine always referred to his room in the lodging provided for him by Mme de La Sablière as *la chambre du philosophe*, and his friend *l'illustre Certain*, who was also a friend of Lambert and of Pierre de Niert, first *valet de chambre* to the king, used to come and sing to him there. She was still young and pretty and he considered her the Chloris of his heart:

> Jolie, et jeune, et sa personne
> Pourrait bien ramener l'amour
> Au philosophique séjour,
> Je l'en avais banni; si Chloris le ramène
> Elle aura chansons pour chansons:
>
> Mes vers exprimeront la douceur de ses sons.
> Qu'elle ait à mon égard le cœur d'une inhumaine,
> Je ne m'en plaindrai point, n'étant bon désormais
> Qu'à chanter les Chloris et les laisser en paix.[17]

A less accommodating friend was Mme Ulrich, who had at one time been attached to the Bouillon household where La Fontaine first met her. She was an orphan without fortune, her father had been one of the King's violinists. Ulrich, a Swede, Maître d'hôtel to the comte d'Auvergne, had educated her in a convent, and as imprudent as Molière's Arnolphe, had later married her. She was completely unscrupulous, and went from one lover to another always with an eye to her own financial advantage. She is remembered as having published La Fontaine's *Oeuvres posthumes* in 1696. At the time when he came under her influence she was still living with Ulrich, who, having to travel with the comte d'Auvergne, asked La Fontaine to keep an eye on her. But no sooner was her husband out of the way than she skipped off to join the marquis de Sablé, who was her lover of the moment. The two letters that La Fontaine wrote to her on this occasion, were published by her in the *Oeuvres posthumes*. In these epistles, the poet begs her to return to Paris before her husband, and he is disappointed that he himself has been forsaken. However, he has to be content with her offers of board and lodging which of course he cannot accept under the circumstances: 'I accept your offer of partridges, wine from Champagne and the fat pullet, with a room in M. le marquis de Sablé's house, provided the room is in Paris. I accept everything that gives pleasure, and you are steeped in it; but I always come up against this devil of a husband, who is nevertheless a most honest man . . . You will pay him with caresses full of charm, but what will I pay him with?'

Almost daily La Fontaine called to enquire if Madame had returned. He would have liked to console himself with her pretty daughter Thérèse but the girl would have none of him, and he decided that she was *une fière petite peste*. In the meantime he received another letter from Mme Ulrich feigning to be deeply attached to him, and this so flattered his vanity that he promised not to trouble her any more till she thought right to return. The whole affair has the flavour of one of his own *Contes*.

This episode shows La Fontaine in relation to the lesser women attached to the great houses where he was entertained, and throws a somewhat lurid light on his weakness for those of easy virtue. To such women he was fair game, as long as they were pretty and willing, a 'Jeanneton' was as good to make love to as a 'Clymène' – *car tout peut aimer en ce monde*, and *les ripailles en basse compagnie* amused him for a moment as well as anything else, for, as he always repeated, diversity was his device. Yet as I have shown, sympathetic friendships with women – apart from banal love affairs – were numerous and lasting throughout La Fontaine's history; not only with his patronesses and great ladies, but also with others who charmed him by their beauty or talent. Of those, one of the most remarkable was La Champmeslé (whose maiden name was Marie Desmares). Two letters to her from La Fontaine at Chaury – Château-Thierry – show that they were very friendly. In the first letter he says that Racine had promised to write to him, and asks why this promise had not been kept, for 'since he loves nothing so much as your charming person, this would have consoled me for not seeing you.' For now neither woods, fields, streams nor nymphs move him, since happiness depends on her presence. As she had foretold, only his return to Paris could cure his melancholy, and boredom had galloped beside him as soon as he was out of sight of the village steeples – that is, of Paris.

At the time of the second letter – that of 1678 – La Champmeslé had taken up with François-Joseph de Clermont comte de Tonnerre, and was said to be *de-Raciné*, choosing her lovers from *les hommes de Cour* instead of from *les hommes de théâtre*, and La Fontaine's tone is slightly more ceremonious. He tells her that she is the best of friends in the world as well as the most agreeable, and that the excessive heat and her absence has thrown them all into an unbearable languor, and from morning to evening they drink water, wine and lemonade, 'light refreshment for any one deprived of seeing you.' And he asks, 'as for you Mademoiselle, I don't need to ask for news of you, I can tell from here that from morning to evening you collect heart after heart. But what are your courtiers doing? Are you charming away the boredom, the bad luck at cards and all the other misfortunes of Monsieur de La Fare? And does Monsieur de Tonnerre still bring home some small earnings?'

One of the most friendly eulogies on La Champmeslé was La Fontaine's dedication to her of his *Belphégor, nouvelle tirée de Machiavel* which begins thus:

> De votre nom j'orne le frontispice
> Des derniers vers que la Muse a polis.
> Puisse le tout, ô charmante Philis,
> Aller si loin que notre los franchisse
> La nuit des temps! nous la saurons dompter,
> Moi par écrire, et vous par réciter.
> Nos noms unis perceront l'ombre noire;
> Vous régnerez longtemps dans la mémoire
> Après avoir régné jusques ici
> Dans les esprits, dans les cœurs même aussi.
> Qui ne connaît l'inimitable actrice
> Représentant ou Phèdre ou Bérénice,
> Chimène en pleurs, ou Camille en fureur?[18]

Then after praising the perfection of her voice, he sums up their relationship with delicate discernment:

> De mes Philis vous seriez la première,
> Vous auriez eu mon âme toute entière,
> Si de mes vœux j'eusse plus présumé:
> Mais en aimant, qui ne veut être aimé?
> Par des transports n'espérant pas vous plaire,

Je me suis dit seulement votre ami,
De ceux qui sont amants plus d'à demi:
Et plût au sort que j'eusse pu mieux faire![19]

La Champmeslé was remarkable for her intelligence and her fine voice. Racine had fallen in love with her when she played Bérénice, and she had her greatest triumph in *Phèdre*. La Fontaine was also on good terms with her husband M. Champmeslé and collaborated with him in several plays, mostly rather poor. The best known pieces by Champmeslé were *le Florentin* and *La Rue Saint-Denis*, the latter had some success as a comedy on the bourgeois manners of the time. That the Church was not always excessively difficult in its relations with the *gens du théâtre*, was shown by the fact that, having asked for two Masses to be said for his wife and his mother, Champmeslé, on being told that he had paid more than was necessary, ordered a third Mass to be said for himself, at which he would be present. While waiting at the church door for friends, he died suddenly without doctor or priest. This was taken as a happy coincidence. But few people got off so lightly. . .

La Fontaine and Racine remained friends even after Racine had left the theatre, made a bourgeois marriage and become, with Boileau, historian to Louis XIV. La Fontaine was often invited to dine with the family in their apartment in the rue du cimetière-Saint-André-des-Arts, or in the rue des Maçons-Sorbonne. On these occasions the five young daughters found him boring because he talked exclusively to their father about the beauties of classical works, asking many questions about Greek authors or speaking of his own translations of Plato – from a Latin text. The little girls thought that the poet was untidy and slovenly in his appearance, an opinion that La Bruyère, who knew him about this time also expressed: 'He appears common, heavy and stupid; he does not know how to converse, nor to describe what he has seen. But if he puts himself to write something it is the perfection of story-telling . . . In his work everything is lightness itself, elegance, natural beauty and delicacy.'

In fairness to La Fontaine we should compare this description of his physical appearance with the striking portrait painted by Rigaud when the poet was over sixty. Here the eyes of a dreamer-awake look on the world with keen penetration and complete disillusion, and the firm yet sensitive mouth gives the impression of ironical amusement.

Louis Racine in the *Mémoires* on his father, recounts that towards the end of La Fontaine's life, Racine took him to church for the service of

Tenebrae, and noticing that he was getting bored and was doubtless falling asleep – gave him a volume of the Bible containing the minor prophets to read. La Fontaine happened to find the prayer of Baruch and the beauty of the language so impressed him, that for the next few days, whenever he met an acquaintance in the street, after the usual greetings he would raise his voice to ask, '*avez-vous lu Baruch? C'était un beau génie.*' At this period La Fontaine was often to be seen going or coming from the Academy. He walked slowly, stopping from time to time as if considering some aspect of the crowded street, but in reality lost in thought. At such moments he would scarcely recognise friends who might accost him.

Damien Mitton, the friend of Pascal and Méré, who had known La Fontaine since his student days, and who was his near neighbour, remarked on his absence of mind, and added: 'if any one says to the good La Fontaine that he is a visionary, he is vexed. But if he is told that his mind is always filled with beautiful ideas, he laughs graciously which shows that one has said the right thing.' This absent mindedness, of which Damien Mitton had spoken, was certainly noticed by Damien's niece after the poor man's death, when La Fontaine, who had attended the funeral, met her in the street some ten days later, and waking from his reverie, asked for the health of her uncle.

TRANSLATIONS

[1]A time when the air of both town and court was filled with amusements and love.

[2]The English think profoundly, / In this they follow their temperament; / Studying their subjects, strong in experiments. / They extend in all fields the empire of science. / I don't say this to flatter you. / Some people go more deep than others do; / Even those famous hounds of yours / Have keener noses than have ours. / Your foxes are more cunning – as I'll prove . . .

[3]Everywhere you bring enjoyment and pleasure; / If you go to climates unknown to soft breezes, / The fields are at once all covered with roses. / But, since no happiness is constant in its course, / Some cruel north winds trouble the finest days, / It is then that you know how to show courage; / You scatter to the winds those vexing memories, / You have many secrets to combat the storm, / Do you not know one that would warn you in time?

[4]Anacréon and people of his sort / Like Waller, Saint-Évremond and me / . . . Who would not receive Anacréon in his house? / Who would banish Waller and La Fontaine? / Both of us are old, Saint-Évremond also / But will

you see by the fountain Hippocrene / People less wrinkled in their work than these?

⁵You possess all the good sense / Which serves to console for the ills of old age, / You have more passion than have the young men, / Who have less taste and precision than you.

⁶To accommodate oneself to the orders of destiny, / Not to be envious of the more fortunate, / Of that false air of wit that a libertine assumes / To know by experience the folly as we do, / And with poetry, play, music and good wine / To occupy one's innocent life, / That is the way to put off the end.

⁷And in the sorrow that I feel / At this sad and unfortunate death, / Weeping, I would say that every muse was dead, / Were your own not still alive. / O you, second Orpheus, O you, whose inspiration / Can charm the black queen of the underworld / And the terrible god whom we call Pluto, / Deign, all-powerful La Fontaine, / To restore to us Waller instead of Anacréon.

⁸That for a longer time your pleasant muse / May give the public her gallant works! / That all with you may be fable and story, / Except the secret of living for a hundred years!

⁹Neither your lessons or those of the Nine Sisters, / Have known how to charm the pain that overwhelms me; / I suffer from an ill that defies all comforts / And I cannot think of anything agreeable: / All rheumatism, invention of the devil, cripples both my body and my mind.

¹⁰Nothing engages me to write a book; / But reason obliges me to live / Like a wise citizen of this vast Universe; / Citizen who, seeing the world so diverse, / Renders to its Author homage due / To such great works. / This task fulfilled, finer verses and sweet tones / Cannot be said to be most necessary: / But who shall say that they are contrary / To those eternal lessons? / We may amuse ourselves in different ways: / Open our hearts to friends on many themes, / And, looking for the effect that each cause brings, / At table, in the woods, or by clear streams, / Reason with them on the good, on the beautiful, / Provided that the latter is treated lightly, / And that the nymph or the shepherdess / Fills our minds and our eyes for a moment or less: / The path of the heart is a slippery dancing-floor: / Wise Saint-Évremond, it is best to say no more.

¹¹Betimes! can this word still apply to me, / I who so often saw the dawn appear, / And for whom the days rush onwards, / Towards the expected moment of my fate.

¹²It is a pleasure to see Sylvie, / But don't expect my song / To paint so many different charms, / This would take my whole life long.

¹³A woman supremely fair, gracious, good-humoured, and sweet-tempered.

¹⁴My letter will make you laugh. / I already hear you say: / Is this man not mad / In the venture he attempts? / He is nearer to Peru / Than to the heart of Amarante.

¹⁵Ah! who would be surprised / When La Fontaine loses his way? / The

whole course of his years is a tissue of errors / But errors full of wisdom. / Pleasures lead him there unceasingly / By paths sown with flowers . . .

[16]I would also very much like to see him / In the charming walks that your park encloses, / Talking of peace, talking of war; / Of poetry, wine and the cares of love; / Forming imaginary plans of some vain project, / Changing in a hundred ways the universe, / Without doubting, suggest a hundred doubts; / Then go off by himself as he likes to do, / Not to dream of you who dream so much of him, / But only to vary his boredom / For you know, Madame, he is bored everywhere.

[17]Young and pretty, and her person / Might well bring back love / To this philosophic dwelling, / I had banished it from here. / If Chloris brings it back / She will have song for song: / My verses will express the sweetness of her voice. / If for me she has no feeling / I will not complain, since henceforth I may / Only sing of all Chloris and leave them in peace.

[18]With your name I adorn the frontispiece / Of the last verses polished by my Muse / May the whole, O charming Philis, Go as far as our praise breaks through / The night of time. / We will know how to conquer it, / I in writing, and you in reciting. / Our united names shall pierce the black shades; / You will reign a long time in men's memory / After having reigned till now in their minds, and also in their hearts. / Who does not know the inimitable actress / Representing Phèdre or Bérénice, / Chimène in tears, or Camille in a fury?

[19]You would be the first of my loves / You would have had my whole Soul / If in my wooing I had been bolder: / But in loving who does not wished to be loved? / Fearing that my raptures would not please you, / I only called myself your friend, / One of those who are more than half lovers; / And would to Heaven that I might have done better.

XI

PRINCES AND PATRONS

La Fontaine was independent by nature and expressed frankly what he
thought, he did not hesitate to censure the great when they committed
what he regarded as injustice, saying of them that *l'univers leur sait gré
du mal qu'ils ne font pas*,[1] and in the Fables he constantly speaks of the
tyranny of 'lions and wolves' who impose their sovereign authority.
Yet like his contemporaries he knew how to flatter those who dis-
pensed favours, for *la louange chatouille et gagne les esprits*,[2] and he kept
in touch with actualities, constantly on the look out for contemporary
events – victories, family festivals, marriages and deaths, as pretext for
writing verse epistles addressed to celebrities whom he knew, and who
were likely to reward him. In these epistles his tone was discreet,
flattering and more or less ceremonious, according to the degree of
intimacy between the author and his subject. These verses were usually
carefully written, until late in life, when, tired of conventional compliments, he sometimes allowed his boredom to seep through the praise,
and the style became loose at the joints, as in parts of his last epistles to
the Vendômes. In all the works addressed to his patrons it is evident
that he was on friendly and even intimate terms with them.

It is probable that the Grand Condé first noticed La Fontaine about
the year 1664, but the poet may not have visited Chantilly till some ten
years later, for a letter reporting to the Prince the affair La Fontaine-
Quinault at the time of *Daphné*, seems to indicate that their relationship was intermittent, and probably grew closer as La Fontaine became
celebrated.

The prince de Condé, the victor of so many battles, the hero who
had charged at the head of his troops, had retired to Chantilly suffering
from gout during the last ten years of his life. Here the most distinguished men of the time came to visit him: generals such as Créqui,
Navailles, Boufflers and Luxembourg, consulted him as an oracle. The

ministers, Pomponne, Colbert and others, were frequent visitors, together with dignitaries of the church, ambassadors and strangers of note. It is proof of Condé's broad-mindedness that he enjoyed seeing all those guests, and he always took a keen interest in political, religious and scientific questions. At Chantilly ancient foes became reconciled; Huguenots and Catholics sat side by side, Cartesians conversed with Jansenists, all quite at their ease in this hospitable and friendly palace. Under the pleasant shade of the *allée des philosophes*, Bossuet chatted with Malebranche or Fénelon; Bourdaloue with Bourdelot; La Bruyère and Sauveur strolled along conversing together. Here Molière, Racine, Boileau and La Fontaine also came, and many other poets of less renown, all it seemed were welcome. Special permanent means of conveyance were organised to bring guests from Paris to the Château. Those who had requested to see the Prince, left Paris in a coach from the Hotel de Condé, and at Louvres found another carriage waiting for them, which brought them to the castle where they were comfortably lodged and looked after in the most generous fashion. Visitors who had not announced their arrival took the public coach from Senlis as far as la Chapelle-en-Serval, and from there a public conveyance to Chantilly where they could find comfortable lodging at *La Grande Barbe*, *Le Grand Serf* or *La Croix Blanche*.

From time to time the Prince received news of La Fontaine's works through the system of messengers who kept him informed of all that took place in Paris. Thus in May 1680 a certain M. Mondion wrote to Condé sending him one of Plato's Dialogues translated by La Fontaine, who wanted to know whether Condé considered it worth finishing. Again at the time of the poet's election to the Academy we find the abbé Michon, known as Bourdelot, reporting the whole affair to the Prince.

As early as 1673, one of Condé's stewards wrote from Chantilly to the Prince then in Paris, telling him that Boileau had sent a request to be allowed to shoot in the forest:

> 'I am afraid, he said, that M. Despréaux will ruin the whole shooting in the country owing to the number of shots he fires. He has already cost me a barrel of powder and a lot of lead, and he has not been able to shoot a single bird.'

When staying at Château-Thierry in the autumn of 1684, La Fontaine wrote to Condé asking to be allowed to hunt in the forest of Monthural. It is probable that he was a better shot than Boileau, for he must have had some experience, and his poems express a certain enjoyment in hunting, such as in the delightful fable dedicated to the duc de La Rochefoucauld:

> A l'heure de l'affût, soit lorsque la lumière
> Précipite ses traits dans l'humide séjour,
> Soit lorsque le soleil rentre dans sa carrière,
> Et que, n'étant plus nuit, il n'est pas encor jour,
> Au bord de quelque bois sur un arbre je grimpe;
> Et nouveau Jupiter, du haut de cet Olympe,
> Je foudroie à discrétion
> Un lapin qui n'y pensait guère.
> Je vois fuir aussitôt toute la nation
> Des lapins qui sur la bruyère
> L'œil éveillé, l'oreille au guet,
> S'égayaient et de thym parfumaient leur banquet.
> Le bruit du coup fait que la bande
> S'en va chercher sa sûreté
> Dans la souterraine cité;
> Mais le danger s'oublie, et cette peur si grande
> S'évanouit bientôt. Je revois les lapins
> Plus gais qu'auparavant revenir sous mes mains.
> Ne reconnait-on pas en cela les humains?[3]

This exact observation is that of a hunter, the details are described by a poet; there is no exaggeration and only the essentials are noted in this perfect picture of woodland life; it is something enjoyed; the sportsman must have been poet, and the poet sportsman, to give us this *acte de théâtre* of the rabbits' hour. Looking for game was an excellent pretext for wandering off by himself in the forest, and he well knew the peace and contentment that such solitude may give, as he says in *Adonis*:

> Enfin pour divertir l'ennui qui le possède
> On lui dit que la chasse est un puissant remède,[4]

and again in *Les Filles de Minée*, he says:

> Voila Céphale en peine:
> Il renonce aux cités, s'en va dans les forêts,
> Conte aux vents, conte aux bois ses déplaisirs secrets
> S'imagine en chassant dissiper son martyre.[5]

La Fontaine had known Condé's nephews the two Conti brothers from their childhood: Louis-Armand born in 1661, and François-Louis born in 1664. The Grand Condé became their guardian after the death of their parents, Armand prince de Conti who died in 1666, and their mother Anne-Marie Martinozzi (niece of Mazarin) who died a few years later. The two boys were brought up with the Dauphin; Condé was very fond of them and supervised their education, and they spent much of their time at Chantilly.

Their cousins the Vendômes were the sons of Louis de Vendôme, a bastard son of Henri IV. Louis had married Laure Mancini and they had two sons, Louis-Joseph, duc de Vendôme born in 1654, and Philippe born a year later who became Grand Prieur de Malte in 1685. From an early age these two brothers were constantly intriguing with their aunt the duchesse de Bouillon, in whose house La Fontaine must have first met them. They were frequently in disgrace with the King, and were extremely dissipated, indulging in all sorts of excesses, their manners were atrocious. La Fontaine dedicated his poem *Philemon et Baucis* to the duc de Vendôme in 1685, and in the exaggerated praise he bestows on the Duke he refers to the woodland shade of Anet, for he had visited them at their country seat.

When Louis-Armand prince de Conti was ten years old, La Fontaine dedicated to him the *Recueil de poésies chrétiennes et diverses* published in 1671. The Conti brothers were well educated and enjoyed reading. François-Louis in particular read for several hours a day, in bed, in the gardens and even during his walks. While still very young they studied Horace and Cicero, the Fathers of the Church, and the historian Froissart was their favourite author. They both spoke Italian fluently and understood German and Spanish.

In the autumn of 1677 the King allowed the two Conti brothers to serve in the campaign of the Spanish-Netherlands. Both princes proved ardent and even rash soldiers, and thoroughly enjoyed the warfare. When the peace of Nimeguen was signed in August 1678 – a victory for France with its supposed truce of twenty years – La Fontaine wrote an *Ode pour la paix* in which he praised the King's moderation in regard to Holland, and promised a happy future for art. Two years later in verses *A Madame de Fontange*, he lavishly praised the King's mistress, and celebrated in two elaborate epithalamia the marriage of the elder Conti with Mlle de Blois daughter of the King and Mme de la Vallière, also the Dauphin's marriage with the Princess of Bavaria. The part dealing with the Dauphin's marriage is very formal and ceremonious, and that for Conti is more intimate:

Couple heureux et parfait
Couple charmant, faites durer vos flammes
Assez longtemps pour nous rendre jaloux:
Soyez amants aussi longtemps qu'époux . . .[6]

At the time of his marriage Louis-Armand was eighteen and his bride was only thirteen years old. She was beautiful as an angel, and her gracious manners pleased every one. She was also a graceful dancer. Ten years later La Fontaine refers to her dancing in *le Songe*

Mille fois plus legère
Que ne dansent au bois la Nymphe et la bergère;
L'herbe l'aurait portée; une fleur n'aurait pas
Reçu l'empreinte de ses pas . . .[7]

This charming description was doubtless suggested by the lines from Virgil that he had translated for his cousin Antoine Pintrel.

When, after a short but stormy career, Louis-Armand prince de Conti died of small-pox in November 1685, La Fontaine sincerely felt his loss, and wrote an *Épitre* in verse to the younger brother who was in disgrace at his château of L'Isle-Adam on the Oise. This is one of the most moving of La Fontaine's poems, for he is not often found in such direct contact with grief. Here there is real condolence and little of formal eloquence to blur his feelings. He seems to meet the Prince as a friend, with a warm grasp of his hand rather than a reverence:

Pleurez-vous aux lieux où vous êtes?
La douleur vous suit-elle au fond de leurs retraites?
Ne pouvez-vous lui résister?
Dois-je enfin, rompant le silence,
Ou la combattre, ou la flatter,
Pour adoucir sa violence?
Le dieu de l'Oise est sur ces bords,
Qui prend part à votre souffrance;
Il voudrait les orner par de nouveaux trésors,
Pour honorer votre présence.
Si j'avais assez d'éloquence,
Je dirais qu'aujourd'hui tout y doit rire aux yeux,
Je ne le dirais pas: rien ne rit sous les cieux,
Depuis le moment odieux
Qui vous ravit un frère aimé d'amour extrême.
Ce moment, pour en parler mieux,
Vous ravit dès lors à vous-même . . .[8]

Though the praise that follows, addressed to François-Louis himself, would be considered excessive today, it did not seem so then, so used were patrons and poets to fine compliments. A few years later Saint-Simon writing about the younger Conti said: 'even the defects of his body and of his mind had infinite charm. He was the constant joy of the world, the Court and the army.'

A year earlier, on the request of Louis-Armand, then staying at Chantilly in disgrace, La Fontaine wrote a long epistle in prose comparing the Grand Condé to Alexander the Great and Julius Caesar. Evidently the young Prince had suggested the theme, for La Fontaine begins by saying: 'I would have been to Chantilly to offer my humble devotion to your Serene Highness, but I have been looking at the works of the Ancients and of writers of later date to find subjects for a worthy comparison that would please you.' Of the wise old Frondeur he said: 'He is extremely fond of arguing, and is never so witty as when he is wrong . . . He takes victory and reason by the throat to put them on his side . . .' The whole essay is a strange mixture of hyperbole, intimate observation, liberty of speech and touches of humour, as when he alludes to the great man's gout, saying 'I could have compared him to Achilles, but at present the epithet of "light foot" would make the comparison a bit lame.'

The Grand Condé died in November 1686. We have no record of anything said by La Fontaine at this time. Two years later François-Louis, now prince de Conti, married Mlle de Bourbon – one of Condé's granddaughters. They had known each other since they were children. He was now twenty-two, and without being in love he was fond of the little Marie-Thérèse now aged twenty. She was so small that she seemed like a living doll, and although not pretty had a ready wit. They were married in June and set up house in the Hôtel de Conti in Paris. La Fontaine wrote for them an Epithalamium in which he begged them to remain lovers; '*soyez amants fidèles et constants:*'[9] and tells them:

> S'il faut changer, donnez-vous patience,
> Et ne soyez époux qu'à soixante ans.

Evidently he was fond of them both for there is a note of tenderness in his good advice: which comes from an old and trusted friend.

> O vous, pour qui les dieux ont des soins si pressants
> Conservez l'un pour l'autre une ardeur mutuelle!

Vous possédez tous deux ce qui plaît plus d'un jour,
Les grâces et l'esprit, seuls soutiens de l'amour.
Dans la carrière aux époux assignée,
Prince et Princesse, on trouve deux chemins :
L'un de tiédeur, commun chez les humains :
La passion à l'autre fut donnée.
N'en sortez point; c'est un état bien doux,
Mais peu durable en notre âme inquiète.[10]

Matrimony was again discussed in an epistle to Conti a few months later when he was with the army on the Rhine. After telling at some length the story of an unfortunate Protestant lady Mlle de La Force whose secret marriage with the son of a rich Catholic had been annulled, La Fontaine gives his opinion on marriage in general:

Je soutiens et dis hautement
Que l'hymen est bon seulement
Pour les gens de certaines classes;
Je le souffre en ceux de haut rang,
Lorsque la noblesse du sang,
L'esprit, la douceur et les grâces,
Sont joints au bien; et lit à part.
Il me faut plus à mon égard.
Et quoi? – De l'argent sans affaire;
Ne me voir autre chose à faire,
Depuis le matin jusqu'au soir,
Que de suivre en tout mon vouloir;
Femme de plus assez prudente
Pour me servir de confidente . . .
Et quand j'aurais tout à mon choix,
J'y songerais encor deux fois.[11]

The later epistles to the prince de Conti and to his cousins the Vendômes give us a marvellous picture of the poet as he was during the last epoch of his life. The slightly fictitious ceremony of earlier verses addressed to princes and patrons has worn thin, is no longer necessary. La Fontaine need not disguise those tastes which are shared with the highest in the land, the sons of heroes and the heroes themselves. Yet the tone of his news-letters differs considerably: those to Conti are affectionate and discreet, showing a real preoccupation with the young Prince's fortunes, and never missing a reference that might help to ingratiate him with the King. The epistles to the duc de Vendôme are

less intimate but more free and easy both in form and content. La
Fontaine had become gazetteer to the Duke in 1689, and received a
pension, very irregularly paid. The first letter of the series to Vendôme
dates from that year, when he and Conti were both with the Dauphin's
army on the Rhine; the tone is frank and outspoken and has that
familiar ease so characteristic of the poet's amazing fluency; he was not
ashamed to beg or to appear bawdy; and we are reminded of Villon,
when he frankly asks for gold to pay for his drinks and his loves. But
with his usual art he does not begin with such considerations, his first
duty is to flatter his patron:

> Prince vaillant, humain et sage,
> Avouez-nous que l'assemblage
> De ces trois bonnes qualités
> Vaut mieux que trois principautés.[12]

And he recalls the troubled times when he was still a child, for he says,
in speaking of the Duke's recent victories:

> J'aime mieux les Turcs en campagne
> Que de voir nos vins de Champagne
> Profanés par des Allemands;
> Ces gens ont les hanaps trop grands
> Notre nectar veut d'autres verres.
> En un mot, gardez qu'en nos terres
> Le chemin ne leur soit ouvert . . .[13]

Then with his gift of raising questions likely to interest his patrons,
he asks whether mercy and pity are compatible with great victories,
and refers to the facility with which, according to the official view,
Louis had obtained abjurations after the repeal of the Edict of Nantes.
After amusing gossip about minor events in a style of which, as he says

> Les quolibets que je hasarde
> Sentent un peu le corps de garde;
> Ce style est bon en temps et lieu.
> Une autre fois, moyennant Dieu,
> Votre Altesse me verra mettre
> Du français plus fin dans ma lettre.[14]

and having tactfully brought himself into the foreground, he reminds
Vendôme that the abbé de Chaulieu – who now managed the affairs
of the Duke – has not paid the money which had been promised.

'When I am paid,' says La Fontaine, 'my first necessity will be to meet the bill that I have been obliged to run up at the bistrot, after which,

> Le reste ira, ne vous déplaise,
> En bas-reliefs, *et caetera*,
> Ce mot-ci s'interprétera
> Des Jeannetons, car les Clymènes
> Aux vieilles gens sont inhumaines,
> Je ne vous réponds pas encor
> Je n'emploie un peu de votre or
> A payer la brune et la blonde;
> Car tout peut aimer en ce monde . . .[15]

He was in fact very short of funds at this time, he still had his lodging provided by Mme de La Sablière, but to a great extent he had to provide his own food, and he spent all he earned on gambling and on girls. The letter continues, 'I am growing old, soon you will not have to confess and do penance for giving me money, for I shall be dead . . .' And then he cheers up and tells of the high old time they had been enjoying at the Hôtel du Temple, where the Grand Prieur presided, and great freedom of speech and manners went with feasting and night-long revelry; and such parties were frequent:

> Nous faisons au Temple merveilles.
> L'autre jour on but vingt bouteilles . . .
> La nuit étant sur son déclin,
> Lorsque j'eus vuidé mainte coupe,
> Langeamet, aussi de la troupe,
> Me ramena dans mon manoir.
> Je lui donnai, non le bonsoir,
> Mais le bonjour: la blonde Aurore,
> En quittant le rivage maure,
> Nous avait à table trouvés,
> Nos verres nets et bien lavés,
> Mais nos yeux étant un peu troubles,
> Sans pourtant voir les objets doubles.[16]

In short they had made a night of it, drinking, laughing and disputing, and though the Grand Prieur spoke eloquently, no one hesitated to disagree with him: and, says La Fontaine, 'if this had not been the case, I would leave the kingdom in spite of my great respect for the

Vendômes.' The letter ends with the jovial wish that all three of them, the duc de Vendôme, the Grand Prieur and the poet, may live to be a hundred.

These sumptuous carousals were offered by the Grand Prieur to friends whose company was congenial, chosen for their wit, scepticism, freedom of speech and morals. He was immensely rich, and much disapproved of at Court. Having no particular ambitions outside his military glory, he resigned himself to a life of luxurious extravagance, and he was always surrounded by courtesans and favourites, both men and women. It was not surprising that La Fontaine enjoyed the orgies, at which the duchesse de Bouillon often presided, and where he felt at home among old friends such as Chapelle, Chaulieu, and La Fare who had grown so fat that he was nicknamed La Cochonnière. The abbé de Chaulieu some years later was dismissed from his office with the Duke, by order of the King, as he was robbing his master in connivance with the Grand Prieur.

It would be unfair to reproach La Fontaine for enjoying a certain Anacreonic aspect of growing old, for although shameless and disreputable he always remained true to a kind of natural and honest simplicity, sincere to a principle of conduct, too often overlooked by the virtuous, namely that boredom was to be avoided at all costs as a sin against the greatest of all arts – the art of living. He never lost his gift of being all things to all men, in short, an easy and amiable companion.

Yet he shows a more serious side of his nature in a letter to the prince de Conti, much inspired by Horace, and written about the time of the letters to Vendôme. He speaks of current topics with a light and graceful tone, touching on foreign affairs and commenting with discretion on Court matters. When as sometimes happens, he speaks of private individuals such as Mlle de La Force in a letter I have already quoted, he asks Conti not to show this to others, for 'Mademoiselle de La Force is greatly afflicted and it would be cruel to laugh at any one so unhappy.' He shows insight into foreign affairs in speaking of the troubles between the Pope and Louis, and he gives a bird's eye view of what has been happening in England through his description of 'Halefax, Bentin et Dombi (*sic*) who are George Savile Lord Halifax, disgraced in 1686, Thomas Osborne Earl of Danby and William de Bentinck, a Dutch baron created Earl of Portland; all partisans in the revolution of 1688 which crowned William and Mary.

The last epistle of the Vendôme and Conti series is addressed to the chevalier de Sillery on 5th August 1692; Sillery was now *écuyer* to the prince de Conti, and as colonel of Conti's regiment, he took part in the battle of Steinkirk. After the campaign which this battle ended, the princes and general officers came back to Versailles, where Conti was particularly fêted. La Fontaine rejoices in all this and then goes on to describe a magnificent reception given at Chantilly, after the return of the victorious army, by Henri-Jules de Bourbon, now prince de Condé, who had won glory as General under Monseigneur, and had returned to Chantilly in excellent humour. He had a genius for organising entertainments and took endless trouble to enchant and amuse his guests, thus belying Saint-Simon's accusation of sordid avarice. But then Saint-Simon detested him personally.

On this occasion large sums of money were distributed among the faithful associates and dependents of the house of Condé. La Fontaine, on receiving a purse of a hundred louis, records joyfully: *Moi j'en tiens cent louis: chacun m'en fait la cour*, and referring to the prince de Condé continues:

> Il a déifié ma veine.
> Mes soins en valaient-ils la peine?
> Il ne s'en faut point étonner:
> Que ne lui vit-on pas donner
> Dans le temps qu'il tint cour plénière
> Pour une fête singulière?
> Chantilly fut la scène, endroit délicieux.
> Tous rapportèrent de ces lieux
> De grosses et notables sommes.
> Il a payé comme les dieux
> Ce qu'ils ont fait comme des hommes.[17]

In a prose post-script, running short of ideas, he calls the prince de Conti 'a fit subject for Homer or Virgil,' admitting that he himself is growing old and tired: 'I have no longer any fire and energy to give the Prince his due ... When I say I am without fire it is of the author of the *Fables* and *Contes* that I speak, for otherwise I have as much ardour as I had ten years ago ... But if the Prince continues to win victories, neither myself at the age of twenty-five, nor any one else, would have the head to praise him as he deserves.'

This campaign however was the last in which Conti and Vendôme played any important part, and the last on which La Fontaine made any comment. For now he was to be fully occupied with grave and more personal considerations.

[1]The universe is grateful for the ill they did not do.

[2]Praise flatters and pleases people.

[3]At the stalker's hour, when the light / Plunges its beams into its watery dwelling, / Or when the sun begins its course anew, / And being no longer night it is not yet day, / At the edge of some wood I climb into a tree; / And like a modern Jupiter, from the height of this Olympus, / With my thunder-bolt I strike at my discretion / Some unsuspecting rabbit. / At once I see the whole community fly, / Who there, with watchful eye and ears a-cock / Made merry and with thyme flavoured their banquet. / The noise of the shot made the whole troop / Seek safety / In the subterranean city; / But danger is forgotten, and this great fear / Very soon vanishes. And again I see the rabbits / More gay than ever come within my range. / It not this just how human beings behave?

[4]At last to cure the boredom that possessed him / They told him hunting was a powerful remedy.

[5]There is Cephalus in trouble, / He renounces town life, and goes off in the forests, / Tells the winds, tells the woods his secret distress / Deludes himself that hunting will dispel his martyrdom.

[6]Happy and perfect couple / Charming people, make your love endure / Long enough to make us jealous / Be lovers as long as you are man and wife.

[7]A thousand times more light / Than dance in the wood the Nymph and the Shepherdess; / The grass would have carried her; a flower would not / Have been crushed by her light foot-falls.

[8] Do you weep in the retreat where you are? / Does Sorrow follow you so far? / And can you not resist her? / Should I at last, breaking the silence, / Oppose her or flatter, / To subdue her violence? / The god of the Oise on the river side / Takes part in your suffering / And would adorn his banks with new treasures / To honour your presence; / If I had enough eloquence / I would say today, all things should please the eye / I don't say so; for nothing smiles under the sky / Since that hateful moment / That stole a brother extremely loved / That moment, one might almost say, / Stole you from yourself since then.

[9]Be faithful and constant lovers.

[10]If it is necessary to change do not be in a hurry, / Be lovers until you are sixty years of age. / . . . O you whom the gods look after with such care . . . Keep for each other a mutual passion / You both possess gifts that always give pleasure / Grace and wit, That alone sustain love. / In the course assigned to the married, / Prince and Princess, there are two paths: / One of indifference, common to mankind: / To the other passion was given, / Do not wander from this pleasant state / For it does not last long in our troubled soul.

¹¹I maintain and declare boldly / That marriage is good only: For people of a certain class; / I admit it for those of high rank / When nobleness of race / Wit, gentleness and grace, / To property are added – and let them sleep apart. / In this connection I need more / And what? Money without anxiety / To find myself from dawn to evening / With nothing else to do / Than to follow every wish; / And then a wife prudent enough / To be my faithful confidant / . . . And when I have everything to my liking / I would think it over more than once.

¹²Prince valiant, humane and wise / Admit to us that the combination / Of these three good qualities / Is worth more than three principalities.

¹³I prefer the Turks on campaign / Than to see our wines of Champagne / Profaned by the Germans; / These people have too big tankards / Our nectar is worthy of other glasses, / In a word, keep watch that in our land / The path is not open to them.

¹⁴The jests that I risk / Smell a bit of the guard-room; / This style is good in its right place. / Some other time, god willing, / Your highness will see a better / And finer French put in my letter.

¹⁵The rest will go, by your leave, / On bas-reliefs et cetera, / And let this word be taken for / A serving wench, for ladies fine / Are most inhuman to old men, / I cannot promise you as yet / That I don't employ the gold I get / To pay the brunette and the blonde / For in this world all may be fond.

¹⁶We had at the Temple a high old time; / The other day we drank twenty bottles . . . The night being far through / When I had emptied many glasses, / Langeamet, who was one of the party, / Saw me home to my manor. I said to him, not goodnight / But good morning: the blond Aurora / In leaving the Moorish shore / Had found us still sitting at table / Our glasses clean and well swilled; / Our eyes being a little troubled / Without, however, seeing things doubled.

¹⁷He has made me as happy as a god. / Was my work worth so much? / It is not astonishing / For what did he not give / During the time he held full court / For a most remarkable fête / The stage was Chantilly, a delicious place, / Everyone took home from there / Large and notable sums. / He has paid as the gods / What we have done as men.

XII

THE CONVERSION

'There is little more to expect from your poet, I am exhausted, worn out, without the least fire, I don't know how I managed to drag these last verses from my head,' confided La Fontaine to the chevalier de Sillery, in the summer of 1692. He was old and tired, and the time was approaching when matters of the greatest significance were to be attended to. All his life he had paid his court to princes and now he must make his peace with the greatest and most powerful of all Monarchs, he must pray for the forgiveness of his sins and humbly do penance. For many years he had known that sooner or later it would be necessary to plead his cause with the Almighty:

> Tu pourrais aisément me perdre et te venger.
> Ne le fais point, Seigneur; viens plutôt soulager
> Le faix sous qui je sens que mon âme succombe.[1]

We have seen that as early as 1684, on his entry to the Academy, he had read a general confession in the Epistle addressed to Madame de La Sablière, and he referred frequently to his advancing years and to the swift flight of time:

> Le temps marche toujours; ni force, ni prière,
> Sacrifices ni vœux, n'allongent la carrière;
> Il faudrait menager ce qu'on va nous ravir.[2]

La Fontaine's views on religion were extremely simple, and he often insisted that theology was not his strong point. For him Heaven and Hell, even when disguised in classical symbols, were none the less real for being invisible. Like Racine he ignored the current metaphysical and mystical conceptions of God that had existed in Europe since the scholastics of the middle ages, and were actually being expressed in England by the metaphysical poets, Crashaw, Herbert and Vaughan.

Henry Vaughan – the Silurist – was born a year later than La Fontaine, and both died in 1695. Unlike Vaughan, La Fontaine was too directly occupied by his own sensual reactions and the life he saw around him, to 'see Eternity' in any but an objective manner. He was not impious, as even Racine's bigotted son had to admit, but he had banished religious considerations to the horizon on which the sun of his life would set, when the time came he would turn in that direction.

> Malherbe avec Racan, parmi les chœurs des anges,
> Là-haut de l'Éternel célébrant les louanges,
> Ont emporté leur lyre; et j'espère qu'un jour
> J'entendrai leurs concerts au céleste séjour.[3]

He was completely honest when he said that as long as he could enjoy himself, and as long as he could work, he thought it was right to do so.

In the late autumn of 1692 La Fontaine fell ill. He lay in bed surrounded by the terracotta bas-reliefs of his philosophers; on his worktable the play he had just finished was ready to be put in the hands of the comedians for presentation. He had received several of his friends, and he had just dropped off to sleep when Racine and Boileau came to preach repentance. The kindly woman who looked after him was loath to let them disturb her patient. 'He is asleep,' she told them. 'But we have come to exhort him to repent of his sins,' replied Racine; 'he has lived a sinful life,' added Boileau. 'He wicked!' retorted the dame indignantly, 'he is as simple as a child, if he has done wrong it must have been through ignorance for he has no malice. Let him sleep now.' And gently but firmly she closed the door on their disconcerted faces.

Some time later, at the beginning of December, the young Vicar of Saint Roch the abbé Poujet, who was the son of a friend, called to enquire about the poet's health. La Fontaine found the young man sympathetic, and thought it was a good opportunity to speak about a matter that had always troubled him: how was it possible that the *bonté de Dieu* could be reconciled with the torments of the damned? Were not the beauty or the ugliness given to a woman, the intelligence or the stupidity given to a man, original absolutions? Why should not God pardon sinners? The young man listened carefully to the poet's arguments, then patiently he began to discuss the question. La Fontaine became interested in his explanations and asked him to come back the next day.

So every day, and sometimes twice a day, the abbé returned and they became very friendly conversing together. Gradually the question of sin and salvation took a more personal tone, till finally La Fontaine asked the abbé's opinion on his own case, showing him the *Fables*. The young man admired them very much and La Fontaine was extremely pleased, enjoying his new friend's enthusiasm. The next day, encouraged by this success, La Fontaine showed him some *Contes* in manuscript, and after reading them the abbé looked very grave; and later said, 'Monsieur de La Fontaine could not believe that his *Contes* were pernicious. He protested that in writing them, they had never made a bad impression on him, and he could not understand that they could be harmful to those who read them.' The new play was then spoken of, and the poet must needs read it aloud. The young priest was puzzled and rather shocked, but not quite sure of his judgement, for the music of the verse pleased him, though the content seemed suspect. Finally he suggested that they should consult those who were considered authorities on such matters, and several Doctors of the Sorbonne were named, one of whom was the celebrated Jesuit M. Pirot. La Fontaine was at first rather troubled by the idea of submitting his play to such stern judges; others had praised this Comedy, so recently finished, but perhaps it was better to be on the safe side, so he consented. Unfortunately the learned Doctors had no hesitation in condemning the comedy. So without keeping a copy, La Fontaine threw his manuscript into the fire, and watched it burning till the last shrivelled leaf turned to gray ashes or fluttered up the chimney.

The visits of the abbé Poujet continued for ten or twelve days, his religious zeal seemed to have no bounds, and finding himself approved of by his superiors, his authority increased. The good woman, who at this point was really the poet's guardian Angel and more enlightened than any of them, begged the abbé not to worry the poor man who was so easily tired. 'Do not torment him,' she pleaded, 'he is more stupid than wicked, God would never have the courage to damn him.'

Gradually La Fontaine made up his mind; he must make a general confession. Racine had solemnly abjured his past, Mme de La Sablière had steadfastly denied the world for religion, and now the time had come for him to do the same, and he was confirmed in his intention by the news of her death on the 6th January of the new year. Added to this he thought of the death of his old friend Pellisson, who had been converted to Catholicism, and had died suddenly without receiving the last Sacrament, and leaving many debts. 'I must hurry,' thought La Fontaine, 'before it is too late.' His confession had already taken him a month to prepare. So five days later on the 12th February, before a deputation from the Academy, which he had requested, the poet denounced his *Contes* '*infâmes*', declaring his regret at having written and published works which he now considered as infamous, and swore not to publish the new edition that he had prepared for publication. A handful of Academicians attended the ceremony, among them were Racine and Boileau with faces as solemn as the terracotta philosophers who also looked on. After his confession La Fontaine took Communion, and then fell back exhausted on his bed, while priest and audience solemnly trooped out of the room.

There was one redeeming point in this pressure put on the poet, for the same day, thanks to the good offices of Fénelon, the little duc de Bourgogne sent him fifty gold louis, to make up for the profit he would have had from the sale of his book. When this gift arrived in the afternoon from the little Duke, La Fontaine was surprised and greatly delighted, and fell into a contented sleep. The next day he was much better. Now full of religious fervour he began to make projects for new work. He felt a new power, a fresh inspiration, and increased authority. He planned to make a paraphrase of the *Dies Irae* which he would read to the Academy. So cheerfully he got to work; he was not to die yet.

The relief from moral suffering, doubtless combined with the rest imposed by his illness, gave him fresh energy and an eager desire to work. He read his first version of the *Dies Irae* at the Academy in the following June, on the day that La Bruyère and the new abbé Bignon were received. In the first part of this moving discourse, which is a very free translation, we have a fairly exact picture of Heavenly Justice as visualised by the priests and preachers of the time; it is what sinners were told they must expect. The day of Judgement and the book of Judgement were stern realities from which repentance was the only escape. Very sincerely La Fontaine re-states these facts. And then, just as he had tried to persuade Louis to pardon Fouquet, he now addresses a special pleading to Heaven on his own behalf: since he loves God, surely God will save him, since in order to do so He came to earth and pardoned sinners, for

> La prière et l'amour ont un charme suprême;
> Tu m'as fait espérer même grâce pour moi.

And he ends with a touching prayer, a noble forerunner to Verlaine's *Sagesse*.

> Fais qu'on me place à droite, au nombre des brebis;
> Sépare-moi des boucs réprouvés et maudits,
> Tu vois mon cœur contrit et mon humble prière;
> Fais-moi persévérer dans ce juste remords:
> Je te laisse le soin de mon heure dernière;
> Ne m'abandonne pas quand j'irai chez les morts.[4]

In a letter to Maucroix, some months later, La Fontaine sent a copy of this poem from the Latin. 'Do not lose it,' he wrote, 'it is a bit scored out and scribbled on, but you will be able to read it.' Then after commenting on contemporary events, he returned to the consideration of his work in progress, showing great activity and enthusiasm. Here he alluded to works of his that unfortunately have been lost, and also to previous letters that are now unknown. His delight in the learned works which he mentions is proof of his intellectual power in spite of years of doubtful health: 'I will take great care of the *Menagiana*,' he said, referring to the work of the grammarian Gilles Ménage who had recently died. 'But have you not among your papers a copy of the 'prose' of *Lauda Sion salvatorem*? For you once gave me your opinion on this work which I cannot find. I will send you all my Hymns, when I have worked a little more on them. You will compare them with those of the Gentlemen of Port Royal which are printed in the *Heures* under the name of M. du Mont, if this book is not in your country, I will send it to you.' Of La Fontaine's Hymns only the *Dies Irae* has come down to us.

After asking for news of a long list of works edited by Maucroix, La Fontaine recommended his friend to make translations from Livy, and after proposing other authors for translation, he said: 'All this makes a lot of work but that can't be helped. I would die of boredom if I stopped composing. I have a great project with which you could help me; but I won't tell you what it is until I have advanced a bit further.'

In this long and rambling letter, he assures his old friend that he himself is in the best of health, and boasts that he had walked all the way to Bois-le-Vicomte almost without eating – 'it is five good leagues from here.' He also speaks about the crops, wheat and wine still interest him, and he says that he has a strenuous appetite.

Speaking of the death of Pellisson, La Fontaine comments on

Fénelon's reference to him when elected to his seat in the Academy, and also on Bossuet's reference to Pellisson's death. La Fontaine disapproves of their praise, and takes a strong position against all those who, like Pellisson, did not pay their debts. 'It seems that our friend did not torment himself sufficiently,' he insists, advising Maucroix to cut down the notice in which he had expatiated on Pellisson's conversion and praised his qualities.

This indicates a rather ungenerous view, which surprises us in La Fontaine. But perhaps the converted sinner is inclined to be hard on those who get away too easily with what has cost him much pain and torment. Besides which, La Fontaine had always tried to pay up, and had been much concerned many years before this to pay back the sum owed to Maucroix by his father.

The clear-sighted literary comments and advice in his letter to Maucroix, seem to contradict the opinion expressed by Ninon de Lenclos in a letter to Saint-Évremond, about this time, in which she said: 'I know that you wanted to have La Fontaine in England. One scarcely enjoys his company in Paris; his head has become very feeble.' This was written in 1693, after the death of Mme de La Sablière, when Saint-Évremond had invited La Fontaine to go to London where his well-being would have been assured by English friends. However, three months after the loss of Mme de La Sablière, who had provided for him during twenty years, La Fontaine, now recovered from his illness, met Anne d'Hervart who begged him to come and live with them in their house in the rue Plâtrière. La Fontaine replied simply, 'I will do so.' And for the next two years he lived with the Hervarts.

These last years were peaceful and prosperous. The *Fables choisies* appeared in September 1693, the volume contained the fables of book XII of modern editions, to which were added others that had previously been published separately. But unfortunately most of the work of this period has been lost. The inscriptions composed to the glory of the King's victories, to be placed below a series of historical pictures, were commissioned by Du Fresnoy, a friend of the poet, who had planned to fill a gallery at his château. La Fontaine had written fifteen of the descriptions at the time of his death.

While La Fontaine continued to interest himself in pious works, Boileau, for some reason which is not clear, savagely attacked the early conte of *Joconde ou l'infidélité des femmes*, saying of it in his tenth Satire against women:

—Je sais que d'un conte odieux
Vous avez comme moi sali votre mémoire.
Mais laissons là, dis-tu, Joconde et son histoire.[5]

At this time La Fontaine might have agreed with him, though his
respect for Ariosto, from whom his story was fairly closely translated,
had always justified its existence, in spite of the priggish opinions of his
friends. And this explains the fact of his offering a volume of his *Contes*
to an almoner of his parish who came to ask him for money. 'I have no
money,' the poet told him, 'but take this book and sell it.' This sublime
innocence shows more than anything else the innate purity of his mind
where literature was concerned.

As his health declined La Fontaine became absorbed in the idea of
redemption, and this preoccupation remained with him to the end.
The last document that has come down to us, in which we hear his
voice for the last time, is a letter to Maucroix dated 10th February 1695,
two months before his death.

'You are mistaken, my dear friend, if it is true as M. de Soissons told me,
that you think I am more ill in mind than in body. He told me that to
inspire me with courage, but it is not courage that I lack. I assure you that
the best of your friends (myself) cannot count on more than fifteen days
of life. It is two months since I went out, except to go a little to the
Academy to amuse myself. Yesterday on coming back from there, I was
taken in the middle of the rue du Chantre by such an overwhelming
weakness that I thought I was really dying. O my friend, to die is nothing;
but do you realise that I am going to appear before God? You know how
I have lived. Before you receive this note, the gates of Eternity will
perhaps be opened for me.'

Four days later on 14th February, Maucroix, La Fontaine's oldest and
most faithful friend, replied with warm-hearted concern to this
moving letter.

'My dear friend, You may imagine the sorrow that your last letter causes
me. But at the same time I will say that I have consolation in the Christian
disposition in which I see you. My very dear one, the most just have need
of God's pity. Therefore take complete confidence from this and remember
that He has called Himself the Father, and the Pitiful, and the God of all
consolation. Invoke him with all your heart. There is nothing that a
veritable contrition cannot obtain from His infinite bounty. If God does
you the grace of giving you back your health, I hope that you will come
and pass the rest of your life with me, and that we will often talk together
of the mercifulness of God.'

Two months later La Fontaine died in the house of his friends the d'Hervarts. He was buried in the cemetery of the Saints-Innocents. The *cilice* which he had worn till his death was given to Maucroix. He died *avec une constance admirable et toute chrétienne.*[6] Maucroix, who had been his friend for more than sixty years without a quarrel or interruption, and had always loved him, mourned him sincerely and said of him: 'He was the most candid and truthful person I ever knew. He had a very fine mind capable of carrying out all he undertook. His Fables will never die, and will bring him honour for all posterity.'

TRANSLATIONS

[1]Thou mightest easily destroy me and avenge thyself / don't do so, Lord, rather come to lighten / The burden under which I feel my soul succumb.

[2]Time moves on always; neither force nor prayer, / sacrifices or vows, can lengthen life: / We must make the most of what will be taken from us.

[3]Malherbe with Racan, among the angelic choir / Celebrating in Heaven the praises of the Eternal . . . / Have taken their lyre with them; / And I hope that some day / I shall hear their concerts in the celestial dwelling.

[4]Prayer and love have a charm supreme / Thou hast made me hope for the same grace. Have me placed on the right, as one of the sheep; / Separate me from the goats, rejected and accursed, / Thou knowest my contrite heart and my humble prayer; / Make me persevere in this just remorse, / I leave to thee the care of my last hour / Abandon me not when I join the dead.

[5]I know that like me / You have smirched your memory / with an odious tale / But you say, let us leave alone Joconde and his story.

[6]He died with an admirable and altogether Christian constancy.

XIII

THE FABLES

1. *The First Collection*

La Fontaine's *Fables* are one of the finest manifestations of the art of the seventeenth century. To each simple apologue he gives dramatic unity, combining perfect liberty of lyrical expression with the classical qualities of power and clarity. To arrive at this authority and freedom of style, he may be said to have worked his way through accepted classical forms, coming to terms with them and adapting them to a natural order of speech; from this combination of freedom and formal purity, his genius produced the most original and moving poetry.

The Fables were published in two definite Collections with an interval of ten years between them. The first group appeared in 1668, when La Fontaine was forty-seven years old. It contained the first six books, which were later divided into two parts: the first part consisted of books I to III with a dedication to the Dauphin, and the second part was composed of books IV to VI, and the Epilogue. The second Collection was made up of the third and fourth parts published together in 1678, it also contained the *Épitre à Madame de Montespan*. Various fables in these two Collections had been printed separately from time to time in different places.

In the first Collection La Fontaine shows us human vices and virtues through the creatures in whom such attributes appear characteristic. He does not describe men or simple animals, but only their reactions in certain circumstances in which each individual behaves in a typical manner. In this he follows the traditional Greek and Latin fabulists, and his most direct source was doubtless the well known *Mythologia Æsopica* of Nevelet, published in 1610 and re-issued in 1660. This volume contained several hundreds of fables, those in Greek being accompanied by a Latin translation which La Fontaine seems to have generally used, his knowledge of Greek being limited. His chief model was Phaedrus the Latin fabulist who put the prose fables of the legendary Æsop into verse and who said: 'Æsop creator of the fable invented the matter of it, and I have polished the form on the basis of iambic trimeters.' In his preface to book I of the first edition, La Fontaine modestly says that he has neither the elegance nor the brevity of Phaedrus. Nevertheless he does achieve both those qualities, adding to his own version the delicate nuance of his verse and his sensitive observation. But it is difficult to tie him down to any one model or even class of models, for his *Fables* are a work of maturity, the ripe experience of his forty-seven years, nourished by wide reading of both prose and poetry, and a long and penetrating study of poetic technique. Moderns as well as ancients had influenced him, and he delighted in the *Pantagruel* of Rabelais, in the naively conversational style of Marot and also in the frank simplicity of old French in the popular authors who repeated traditional stories.

The accepted authority on fables, at the time of La Fontaine's first Collection, was the advocate Olivier Patru, whom he had known since his student days in Paris. Patru was a member of the Academy, he had translated three fables in prose from Æsop; he maintained that the principle virtue of a fable should be its brevity and simplicity, and that it should be written in prose without any ornament. To this opinion La Fontaine replied in his first edition, begging for indulgence on behalf of his own versions, 'not because one of the masters of our eloquence had disapproved of the idea of putting fables into verse – believing that their chief ornament was to have none, but to persuade him to modify his opinion, and to believe that laconic elegance is not such an enemy to the French Muse that one cannot bring them together.' In the same preface he adds that he has aimed 'at giving amusement and a certain charm to the work of the ancients. For the chief rule in France, and indeed the only one, is to please the reader,' and an '*air agréable* may be given to all sorts of subjects even the most serious.'

La Fontaine beautifully fits the art of verse to his needs, adapting existing forms to his own taste. The stately Alexandrine has its place here, becoming flexible and sinuous when combined with octosyllabic lines, interwoven with those of three or four syllables. In using different metres in this way he creates a pleasant lively style, and varies the place of the caesura to emphasise certain effects, showing a complete mastery of his means. His lines of short *métrage* as in *La Cigale et la Fourmi* speak for themselves:

La cigale, ayant chanté
   Tout l'été,
Se trouva fort dépourvue
Quand la bise fut venue.
Pas un seul petit morceau
De mouche ou de vermisseau.
Elle alla crier famine
Chez la fourmi sa voisine,
La priant de lui prêter
Quelque grain pour subsister
Jusqu'à la saison nouvelle . . .[1]

★

   The language of the Fables is precise yet conversational and as alive as speech. The poet borrows words and phrases, names and personages from Rabelais and others of the preceding century. To each little poem he gives a new dramatic life, the drama is seen in action instead of being reported, and the scenery is generally described in a single figure or with most sensitive detail when landscape is required, and with all the art of extreme brevity, and a sureness of touch that gives life to each apologue. In this consummation of the fable a new genre and a new enchantment are created, and now the organic world of trees and plants shares the same life as men and animals, and the poet tells us:

Jusqu'ici d'un langage nouveau
J'ai fait parler le loup et répondre l'agneau,
J'ai passé plus avant; les arbres et les plantes
Sont devenus chez-moi créatures parlantes.
Qui ne prendrait ceci pour un enchantement?[2]

   This fresh approach to nature seems to me to be one of the most original developments of the poetic art of this classical epoch, in so much as there is an expansion of the then modern movement, that depicts aspects of humanity in the great comedies of Molière and in the music of passion of Racine's tragedies. For now through the more simple means of classical yet free fables, the whole world becomes animated anew; the range of thoughtful action is enlarged to include animals and plants who share universal life and are also ruled by fate. That La Fontaine was aware of this is shown in an important statement of his aims, in *Le Bucheron et Mercure*, addressed to the comte de Brienne:

Je tâche d'y tourner le vice en ridicule . . .
Tantôt je peins en un récit

La sotte vanité jointe avecque l'envie,
Deux pivots sur qui roule aujourd'hui notre vie.
    Tel est ce chétif animal
Qui voulut en grosseur au bœuf se rendre égal.
J'oppose quelquefois, par une double image,
Le vice à la vertu, la sottise au bon sens,
Les agneaux aux loups ravissants,
La mouche à la fourmi, faisant de cet ouvrage
Une ample comédie à cent actes divers,
    Et dont la scène est l'univers.
Hommes, dieux, animaux, tout y fait quelque rôle:
    Jupiter comme un autre . . .³

(the italics are mine).

Although the first published edition came closer than the second collection to the accepted idea of what a fable should be, La Fontaine had already abandoned certain conventional moralities, justifying himself by the opinion of Horace that the man who wishes to succeed must leave alone things outside his competence: 'I have done this,' says La Fontaine, 'in regard to certain moralities with which I could not hope to succeed . . .' Often moral reflections are replaced by a sort of simple logic. No sentimental adage, no improbable triumph of virtue, ever intrude on the realism of events; and when he does point a moral it is 'with the intention of painting the manners and morals of the time,' and such reflections become part of the action in so far as they are generally made by one of the personages, which adds life to the story, as in *Le Corbeau et le Renard*, and *Les Deux Mulets*.

As his friend and contemporary Charles Perrault said:

'On a beau vanter le sel attique . . . mais celui de Monsieur de La Fontaine est d'une espèce toute nouvelle, il y entre une naiveté, une surprise et une plaisanterie d'un caractère qui lui est particulier, *qui charme, qui émeut, et qui frappe tout d'une autre manière.*'⁴

This is very true and well deserved. Yet it would be unfair to La Fontaine to ignore his debt on other grounds to the ancients, for he frequently said that he owed much to them, preferring them above all other writers. In particular Virgil, Horace, and Terence, were his masters; and he very often took directly from them some description of a universal phenomenon, such as spring-time, death, etc, '*constants*' which have belonged to poetry from all time. Sometimes too, he is very close to Lucretius; and many maxims found in the *Fables* had their origin in the works of Plato and Plutarch, both of whom he had carefully annotated. But he rightly said that his imitations were not slavish copies, for he followed the same laws as his masters but re-created their ideas giving them new life in his own very personal poetics or science of poetry, working to obtain the effects he wanted and as he said, *'fabriquant ses vers à force de temps.'* [5]

Taine at the end of last century wrote an admirable though too wordy panegyric on La Fontaine, insisting on his *'esprit gaulois'* and calling him the French Homer. This exaggeration might pass, but when Taine pretends to find in the Fables a definitely historical purpose – such as that of Saint-Simon – he is wrong, for La Fontaine had no intention of portraying special individuals, but only vices and virtues common to all men. The nearer one gets to the author and his text, the more difficult it becomes to agree with Taine's judgements, and his eloquence tends to come between us and the poet. Happily the *papillon du Parnasse* refuses to be caught in the net of critical verbiage.

It is not my intention to analyse the *Fables* in an academic sense, as was the fashion at the end of the last century; such analysis has been done and even over-done by such critics as Saint-Marc Girardin, Taine and many others. It would be useless to repeat what has been already said: and besides, it is evident that the point of view of each generation must necessarily change, impelling criticism to take a new line of approach, in considering the poet's individual vision and that fusion of personality and theme which is the life of all great art. It is sometimes useful to divide literature into categories – and how often such laws have been repeated! Yet in spite of the volumes that have been written round the terms 'classical' and 'romantic', we may well ask ourselves what is more divinely romantic than the greatest classical poetry, or more classical than the most musical of the finest romantic lyrics?

*

In the clear expression of every inflexion of his thought, La Fontaine speaks to each attentive reader; and I shall only point out special examples which illustrate the general trend of his stimulating genius. In all his character sketches he shows a striking knowledge of the type he wishes to draw, such as *L'Homme et son Image*, with its pleasing reference to the *Maximes* of La Rochefoucauld; and in his moving picture of the wood-cutter whom he must often have met when on his rounds as *maître des eaux et forêts*. Crawling along beneath a load of faggots towards his smoky cottage, the aged man lays down his burden and laments his misery:

> Point de pain, quelquefois, et jamais de repos,
> Sa femme, ses enfants, les soldats, les impôts,
>   Le créancier et la corvée,
> Lui font d'un malheureux la peinture achevée . . .[6]

La Fontaine greatly disapproves of pedants and often speaks of them; in *L'Enfant et le Maître d'école* he says of school-masters:

> En toute affaire ils ne font que songer
> Aux moyens d'exercer leur langue . . .[7]

And he also dislikes children, saying of them: '*cet âge sans pitié*' and again speaking of pedants and their pupils:

> Je ne sais bête au monde pire
> Que l'écolier, si ce n'est le pedant
> Le meilleur de ces deux pour voisin, à vrai dire
> Ne me plairait aucunement.[8]

After pedants, misers are the people whom most often he stigmatises and he finds that old age in general is selfish and cruel.

Throughout all his works he shows his sympathy for animals: he is completely at ease with them, and putting aside the human masks of the theoretical beasts of traditional fabliau, he often shows us the real creatures in their native haunts, with all their awareness, their hopes and fears. He is particularly sensitive to the finer instincts of birds, whose unselfish devotion to their young and capacity for friendship had impressed him. All that so marvellously exists in the tiny head of a swallow or a lark, awakes in the poet tender feelings towards nature and inspires him with poetic themes; and all the knowledge he had unconsciously acquired in his childhood at Château-Thierry is revealed, as when he speaks of –

> Une hirondelle en ses voyages
> Avait beaucoup appris. Quiconque a beaucoup vu
> Peut avoir beaucoup retenu.
> Celle-ci prévoyait jusqu'aux moindres orages,
> Et devant qu'ils fussent éclos
> Les annonçait aux matelots . . .[9]

which wakes the image of swallows flying low over the river-boats on the Marne as they do before a storm. This fable, in which the swallow gives good advice to the small non-migrant birds, contains the vivid image of the Sower's hand as seen by birds:

> Voyez-vous cette main qui par les airs chemine?[10]

– a line on which the poet spent much care as existing alternate readings show.

One of the rare instances of the happy frame of mind in which wisdom is rewarded and good advice followed, occurs in *L'Alouette et ses petits*, and the tenderness with which the tale is told enhances this charmingly intimate vignette of country life – from which I can only quote one or two images:

> Les alouettes font leur nid
> Dans les blés quand ils sont en herbe,
> C'est-a-dire environ le temps
> Que tout aime, et que tout pullule dans le monde . . .
> Les blés d'alentour mûrs, avant que la nitée
> > Se trouvât assez forte encor
> > Pour voler et prendre l'essor,
> De mille soins divers l'alouette agitée
> S'en va chercher pâture, avertit ses enfants
> D'être toujours au guet et faire sentinelle . . .
>
> 'Rien ne nous presse encor de changer de retraite;
> Mais c'est demain qu'il faut tout de bon écouter.
> Cependant soyez gais; voilà de quoi manger.'
> Eux repus, tout s'endort, les petits et la mère . . .[11]

And when the time came to leave the nest, how well the scene is described:

> Les petits en même temps,
> Voletants, se culbutants,
> Délogèrent tous sans trompette.[12]

Pigeons, *'au col changeant,'*[13] and doves *'au cœur tendre et fidèle,'*[14] are always given the rôle of faithful friendship, as in the remarkable idyll of *Les Deux Pigeons*; they are also charitable neighbours in *La Colombe et la Fourmi*, which begins so delightfully:

> Le long d'un clair ruisseau buvait une colombe . . .

Here the charitable dove and the grateful ant are seen in contrast to *un certain croquant* – who is a human being.

The Peacock is well observed, with his necklace of

> Un arc-en-ciel nué de cent sortes de soies,

and his fan-shaped tail which he flaunts

> Et qui semble à nos yeux
> La boutique d'un lapidaire.[15]

In the second collection we meet the solitary Heron:

> Un jour sur ses longs pieds allait je ne sais où
> Le héron au long bec emmanché d'un long cou.
> Il côtoyait une rivière.
> L'onde était transparente ainsi qu'aux plus beaux jours;
> Ma commère la carpe y faisait mille tours
> Avec le brochet son compère.[16]

But it was not only birds that the poet delighted in, he had also watched the timid hare, whose anxiety is intimately described in *Le Lièvre et les Grenouilles*. This is one of the finest poems in the whole collection, it is so acutely felt that we seem to be reading a passage of the poet's own autobiography, in which the constant anxiety to which he often referred is described:

> Un lièvre en son gîte songeait
> (Car que faire en un gîte, à moins que l'on ne songe?);
> Dans un profond ennui ce lièvre se plongeait:
> Cet animal est triste, et la crainte le ronge.
> 'Les gens de naturel peureux
> Sont,' disait-il, 'bien malheureux;
> Ils ne sauraient manger morceau qui leur profite.
> Jamais un plaisir pur, toujours assauts divers.
> Voilà comme je vis: cette crainte maudite
> M'empêche de dormir, sinon les yeux ouverts.
> Corrigez-vous, dira quelque sage cervelle.
> Et la peur se corrige-t-elle?
> Je crois même qu'en bonne foi
> Les hommes ont peur comme moi' . . .

Here language and thought are so closely knit that we seem to hear the very heart-beats of the reasoning hare:

> Ainsi raisonnait notre lièvre,
> Et cependant faisait le guet,
> Il était douteux, inquiet:
> Un souffle, une ombre, un rien, tout lui donnait la fièvre.[17]

We may compare this exact portrait with La Fontaine's reflections on his own anxious mind:

> De soixante soleils la course entresuivie
> Ne t'a pas vu goûter un moment de repos;
> Quelque part que tu sois, on voit à tous propos
> L'inconstance d'une âme en ses plaisirs légère,
> Inquiète, et partout hôtesse passagère . . .[18]

Animals seen by other animals make an amusing diversion and give greater reality to their adventures: for example the telling portraits of the cat and the cockerel as seen by the young mouse who recounts his adventures to his mother. The cat appears to him to be a desirable friend *benin et gracieux.*

> Il est velouté comme nous,
> Marqueté, longue queue, une humble contenance;
> Un modeste regard, et pourtant l'œil luisant;
> Je le crois fort sympathisant
> Avec messieurs les rats, car il a des oreilles
> En figure aux nôtres pareilles . . .[19]

But the young cock is seen as a terrifying being, '*turbulent, et plein d'inquiétude;*'

> Il a la voix perçante et rude,
> Sur sa tête un morceau de chair.
> Une sorte de bras dont il s'élève en l'air . . .
> Il se battait les flancs avec ses bras,
> Faisant tel bruit et tel fracas. . . .[20]

This amusing poem is a model of what a modern fable should be, for both story and moral are told in dialogue.

Animal pleasure is wonderfully described in *Le Vieillard et l'Ane* when the old man lets his ass loose to graze in a field as they pass by:

> . . . Et le grison se rue
> Au travers de l'herbe menue,
> Se vautrant, grattant, et frottant,
> Gambadant, chantant et broutant,
> Et faisant mainte place nette . . .[21]

Here the accumulative effect of the present participles marvellously reflects the donkey's movements. When the robbers appear he refuses to go off with his master, why should he go, he asks, 'save yourself and leave me to browse;'

> Notre ennemi, c'est notre maître
> Je vous le dis en bon françois.[22]

This conclusion should not be taken in a strictly political sense, for La Fontaine's thought is of general social conditions, as it is in *Le Loup et le Chien*.

In the second collection, that of 1678, we find the same sympathetic contemplation of animals, apart from the fables dealing particularly with their intelligence – to which I shall return. In *Les deux Chèvres* there is a picture of goats, *ces dames*, which rivals the delight in rural life of the Romantics:

> Dès que les chèvres ont brouté,
> Certain esprit de liberté
> Leur fait chercher fortune; elles vont en voyage
> Vers les endroits du pâturage
> Les moins fréquentés des humains.
> Là s'il est quelque lieu sans route et sans chemins,
> Un rocher, quelque mont pendant en précipices,
> C'est où ces dames vont promener leurs caprices;
> Rien ne peut arrêter cet animal grimpant.[23]

The long wandering movement of these lines gives the reader the impression of being a pursuing goat-herd. The pleasing irony of the political satire – *Faute de reculer leur chute fut commune* – should not be missed.

There are many other instances of careful observation, for all the fauna of Champagne are seen in movement, shy, bold, swift or slow, they fill the scene with their personality, as La Fontaine must often have seen them: '*Damoiselle belette, au corps long et fluet; les grenouilles – la gent marécageuse, fort sotte et fort peureuse;*' '*Le peuple vautour, au bec retors, à la tranchante serre;*' and many others who appear in these episodes of country life, both gay and tragic almost in the same breath, where nothing is dwelt on, though the injustice of '*le roi-lion*' is frequently introduced. All is agreeably light, for as the poet says in his Epilogue to the first collection:

Les longs ouvrages me font peur
Loin d'épuiser une matière
On n'en doit prendre que la fleur.[24]

But it is not only animals that serve as material for the Fables. La Fontaine also feels the greatest sympathy for trees and gardens in general. The first book ends with the little master-piece of *Le Chêne et le Roseau*, which is full of significant wisdom and is said to have been the poet's favourite among the fables of the first collection. The landscape is so sensitively felt that there is not a word, and more – not a letter – in the poem that does not add to its significant beauty. The movement is swift and sure, the observation direct, and the whole poem has a classical perfection while the language remains completely natural. Often has the poet seen those lonely wood-land marshes and watched the wind bending the reeds beside the quivering water *Sur les humides bords des royaumes du vent*; and how beautifully he suggests the grandeur of the mighty oak through its own proud words. Lightly and simply he uses classical terms without the least discord in the fine Virgilian image that ends the poem:

Celui de qui la tête au ciel était voisine,
Et dont les pieds touchaient à l'empire des morts.[25]

2. The Second Collection

Ten years after the first collection, the second volume appeared in 1678. A great development had taken place in both manner and matter. Complete master of his art, La Fontaine had no rivals worthy of the name in his particular genre. Sure of himself and modestly triumphant, he was now acknowledged as a major poet by his contemporaries. In his dedication 'A Madame de Montespan,' which begins the seventh book – that is the first book of the second collection, he says:

L'apologue est un don qui vient des immortels ...
C'est proprement un charme: il rend l'âme attentive,
Ou plutôt il la tient captive,
Nous attachant à des récits
Qui menent à son gré les cœurs et les esprits.[26]

It always seems surprising that Maucroix, when asked what difference there was between the first and second collection of the *Fables*, is reported by d'Olivet to have replied: 'For myself I find no difference and I think our friend (La Fontaine) did not sufficiently weigh his words when he said they were different from each other.' If this statement is authentic, it seems to show that, although his friendship for La Fontaine was enduring, Maucroix had lost interest in poetry and had scarcely troubled to read the second volume of the *Fables*. But d'Olivet is known to be an inaccurate reporter of remembered conversations.

In the *Avertissement* which begins this volume La Fontaine himself explained the essential differences:

> This is the second collection of fables that I have given to the public, and I have judged it expedient to make a difference here from the fables of my first collection, because of the divergence of the subjects and also to give greater variety to my work ... Thus the familiar features and simple characteristics of Æsop's fables are used less often here and are replaced by other embellishments that seem to suit the circumstances of these later tales where they are required ...

He has, he tells us, taken the greater part of the subjects of his new work from 'the wise Indian Pilpay' – or Bidpay as the English call him – and although actually only about a fourth of the ninety fables are of strictly Oriental origin, the tone is no longer that of Æsop, but has a sort of universal pantheism of Eastern origin, and often the least detail leads the poet to the most effective digressions. He has acquired a new gravity, a greater liberty and a meditative ease, through which he expresses the convictions of his experience. These personal interventions are of interest in the development of the literature of the period, for we find La Fontaine disdaining the accepted rules of prosody – which however he knew so well how to use when he wanted – to evolve an extremely personal style: recording his own reactions, and speaking in the first person in a graceful conversational manner and with a pleasing authority, referring to topical events with ease and extreme simplicity, yet neither *parlant le langage des halles*, nor falling into what Boileau called the *élégant badinage* of Marot.

This new depth and amplitude place La Fontaine as a significant fore-runner of the romantic movement, and he should be considered as an ancestor of vers libre, in so much as he had shown to poets, such as Jules Laforgue, how to discard what they did not need, and above all had suggested a closer intimacy between the author and his readers.

And yet, no poetry could be more supremely formal than *Les*

Animaux malades de la peste, with which this second collection opens. Dealing with the constantly recurring theme of social injustice, it begins with a dignity and grace worthy of Bossuet and an eloquence equal to that of Virgil:

> Un mal qui répand la terreur,
> Mal que le ciel en sa fureur
> Inventa pour punir les crimes de la terre,
> La peste (puisqu'il faut l'appeler par son nom),
> Capable d'enrichir en un jour l'Achéron,
> Faisait aux animaux la guerre . . .[27]

Rarely has La Fontaine so completely achieved this nobility of language and the sure proportions so much admired by the poets of his generation, which combine with his lyrical ease to give such charm and lightness to his text.

We have seen that it was Bernier who first introduced the poet to Eastern fables, notably those of Bidpay, which provided magnificent material from the *Livre des Lumières*, translated into French by David Sahid of Ispahan, edited and commented on by Gilbert Gaumen. This new influence produced most happy results, and from the seventh to the eleventh book we find a continuous poetic progress: moralities give place to psychological aspects of behaviour in men and animals, and the 'moral', if there is one, becomes secondary to the idea of universal communication between all living things, and this conception is finely expressed in the 'Epilogue' of the eleventh book:

> C'est ainsi que ma muse, aux bords d'une onde pure,
> Traduisait en langue des dieux
> Tout ce que disent sous les cieux
> Tant d'êtres empruntant la voix de la nature.
> Truchement de peuples divers,
> Je les faisais servir d'acteurs en mon ouvrage:
> Car tout parle dans l'univers;
> Il n'est rien qui n'ait son langage.
> Plus éloquents chez eux qu'ils ne sont dans mes vers,
> Si ceux que j'introduis me trouvent peu fidèle,
> Si mon œuvre n'est pas un assez bon modèle,
> J'ai du moins ouvert le chemin:
> D'autres pourront y mettre une dernière main . . .[28]

Bernier's *Abrégé de la philosophie de Gassendi* was also a fruitful source of ideas on the themes of animal intelligence and the soul in all species.

It was through Bernier's writings and conversation that La Fontaine became familiar with these anti-Cartesian theories, found in Gassendi's works, which so exactly suited his views, giving weight to his arguments, and providing a theory of the soul, a matter that greatly preoccupied him at this period. To this difficult problem La Fontaine found different interpretations, according to whether he was satisfied with the credo of Bernier, or followed the ideas of Plato and Lucretius. Being a poet rather than a philosopher he took what he needed wherever he found it without becoming dogmatic.

Thus he readily adopted the Gassendist notion of an inferior 'soul' common to men and animals, men having over and above this a superior soul which we may define as mind, and of which Bernier says:

'The soul appears to be a very tenuous substance – one might say the flower of matter – consequently the soul is like a little flame . . .' And again, 'one may think of the human soul as being composed of two parts; one incorporeal which is peculiar to humanity, and the other which is common to men and animals.'

In his '*Discours À Madame De La Sablière*,' which appeared in the ninth book, La Fontaine used this theory to refute Descartes' doctrine of animal mechanism:

> . . . Ils disent donc
> Que la bête est une machine;
> Qu'en elle tout se fait sans choix et par ressorts:
> Telle est la montre qui chemine,
> A pas toujours égaux, aveugle et sans dessein.
> Ouvrez-la, lisez dans son sein;
> Mainte roue y tient lieu de tout l'esprit du monde;
> La première y meut la seconde
> Une troisième suit, elle sonne à la fin.[29]

He then gives several authentic examples of animal intelligence, such as that of the stag who employs all sorts of stratagems to save his life:

> Dignes des plus grands chefs, dignes d'un meilleur sort!

And the poet adds with fine irony:

> On le déchire après sa mort:
> Ce sont tous ses honneurs suprêmes.[30]

showing by his just indignation how baseless is Giraudoux' thoughtless assertion of cruelty in La Fontaine's works, a statement which has been irrelevantly repeated by others. The next episode in this poem gives a pleasing example of tenderness and knowledge of animals in a description of the mother partridge:

> Quand la perdrix
> Voit ses petits
> En danger, et n'ayant qu'une plume nouvelle,
> Qui ne peut fuir encor par les airs le trépas,
> Elle fait la blessée, et va trainant de l'aile,
> Attirant le chasseur et le chien sur ses pas,
> Détourne le danger, sauve ainsi sa famille,
> Et puis quand le chasseur croit que son chien la pille,
> Elle lui dit adieu, prend sa volée, et rit
> De l'homme, qui confus, des yeux en vain la suit.[31]

In the *Deux Rats, le Renard et l'œuf,* La Fontaine sums up his theory almost in the words of Bernier:

> J'attribuerais à l'animal
> Non point une raison selon notre manière,
> Mais beaucoup plus aussi qu'un aveugle ressort.

and still following Bernier, he describes man's double soul:

> Nous aurions un double trésor;
> L'un cette âme pareille en tous tant que nous sommes,
> Sages, fous, enfants, idiots,
> Hôtes de l'univers sous le nom d'animaux;
> L'autre encore une autre âme, entre nous et les anges
> Commune en un certain degré . . .[32]

Many of La Fontaine's generation had protested indignantly against the theory of animal automatism, among them Descartes' niece who wrote this epitaph for her dog:

> Ci-gît la fameuse Badine
> Qui n'eut ni beauté ni bonté
> Mais dont l'esprit a demonté
> Le système de la machine.[33]

It was in fact a theory that led to many cruelties and injustices inflicted on animals, and to a great extent these abuses still exist. People who ought to have known better made it an excuse for their sadism, such as Malebranche who is said to have savagely beaten his dog on the pretext that its reactions were merely mechanical. But it does not need any theory to make men kill other creatures, not only in isolated cases but in general, such as in the wholesale slaughter of singing birds all the year round, because laws are not enforced by fines, so that with every man's hand against them, birds are becoming increasingly rare in France. There will soon be none left.

An important passage concerning intelligence occurs in *Les Amours de Psyché et Cupidon*, in which the poet says of animals: *Je les tiens sujets à toutes nos passions; il n'y a pour ce point-là de différence entre nous et eux que de plus au moins, et en la manière de s'exprimer.*[34] And we constantly find that La Fontaine's eloquent pleading for all living creatures comes very close to the conceptions of modern scientists, such as the biologist Jean Rostand who says:

> If there is a sentiment with which I cannot agree it is that which explains animals by mechanical causality, and when it is question of man, believes it a duty to bring in other things. Either there is chance everywhere or intention everywhere. If chance is sufficient to produce the snail, it was also competent to elaborate the human brain. And the Christian evolution is no less strange, which gives to men only a veritable soul with a super-natural dimension and immortality . . .

Another modern scientist, Charles Noel-Martin, holds views on the language of animals, which are very similar to those of La Fontaine. In speaking of the human phenomenon of language, he remarks:

> 'For a long time animals appeared to men to lack all intelligence and to be incapable of communicating between themselves in a coherent manner. The knowledge that has been gradually acquired begins to clear away these tenacious absurdities. All species of animals possess their own range of vocal messages, probably very complex. Men have often put themselves in ridiculous situations . . . by assertions that are nothing but ignorance, and by their anthropocentric blindness.

And this eminent scientist suggests that the maxim 'know yourself' might be replaced by the less ego-centric 'know others and above all know the living beings who are different from man and you will know yourself much better.' A precept that would have been most sympathetic to La Fontaine who already followed it.

*

Although the ideas coming from the East and the theories of Gassendi had greatly occupied La Fontaine, he continued to enlarge his knowledge of classical authors. He now read more deeply, mainly the works of Plato; and Lucretius had become one of his favourite masters: we find many echoes of ideas on ambition and human frailties from the *De Natura Rerum*. Even the animism of Gassendi is sometimes replaced by the determinism of Lucretius. For instance in *La Perdrix et les Coqs*, we find:

> Jupiter sur un seul modèle
> N'a pas formé tous les esprits:
> Il est des naturels de coq et de perdrix.[35]

Therefore it is useless to blame cocks for their bad manners, '*c'est de l'homme qu'il faut se plaindre seulement.*'[36]

Throughout the tenth book man is shown as the chief aggressor towards other living beings, since his cruelty is premeditated and organised. The reasoning of the grass-snake, of the cow and the ox and even of the tree, all point to man's cruelty and ingratitude; and in *L'Homme et la Couleuvre*, '*le symbole des ingrats . . . c'est l'homme.*'[37] So too the wolf who devours the lamb is no worse than the shepherd and others who also eat animals:

> Bergers, bergers, le loup n'a tort
> Que quand il n'est pas le plus fort:
> Voulez-vous qu'il vive en ermite?[38]

In the Oriental fable of *La Souris metamorphosée en fille* we again find the influence of Lucretius when La Fontaine refutes the system of metempsychosis which gives to man and mouse souls '*de même trempe,*'[39] and he concludes with his usual good sense:

> Tout débattu, tout bien pesé,
> Les âmes des souris et les âmes des belles
> Sont très différentes entre elles.
> Il en faut revenir toujours à son destin,
> C'est-à-dire à la loi par le Ciel établie.
> Parlez au diable, employez la magie,
> Vous ne détournez nul être de sa fin.[40]

Thus *la raison décide en maîtresse* and in the end fortune and providence are obliged to call in common sense, who decides that the basic problem remains unsolved.

Latin authority is evident in *La Mort et le Mourant* where La Fontaine returns to the theme of death with greater poetic force in the opening lines:

> La mort ne surprend point le sage:
> Il est toujours prêt à partir,
> S'étant su lui-même avertir
> Du temps où l'on se doit résoudre à ce passage.
> Ce temps, hélas! embrasse tous les temps:
> Qu'on le partage en jours, en heures, en moments,
> Il n'en est point qu'il ne comprenne
> Dans le fatal tribut; tous sont de son domaine;
> Et le premier instant où les enfants des rois
> Ouvrent les yeux à la lumière
> Est celui qui vient quelque fois
> Fermer pour toujours leur paupière.
> Défendez-vous par la grandeur,
> Alléguez la beauté, la vertu, la jeunesse,
> La mort ravit tout sans pudeur . . .[41]

It is rare that topical events are introduced, unless as in this case they have a universal application, and here the poet evidently refers to the death of Henriette d'Angleterre who died suddenly in 1670, and to the infant son of Louis XIV who died soon after birth in 1672.

All La Fontaine's different conclusions, taken from various sources, bear witness to his wide reading. Yet though he learnt much from poets and philosophers of antiquity, a great deal came directly from his own experience and his amazingly keen knowledge of men: he had seen for himself the empty vanity and the sheepish stupidity of all classes from courtiers to peasants, and he used his memories to illustrate his themes; the things he had observed, the situations he had known, all entered into the images of his poetry with a direct and penetrating clarity. In the admirable detail of *Le Coche et la Mouche*, there is a vivid recollection of his journey to the Limousin, when going up the steep *chemin creux*, on the road to Bellac, the passengers were obliged to leave the coach and walk, and he noticed the fly who

> Va, vient, fait l'empressée – il semble que ce soit
> Un sergent de bataille allant en chaque endroit
> Faire avancer ses gens, et hâter la victoire . . .

Le Curé et le mort was also founded on an authentic adventure known to

La Fontaine, as Mme de Sévigné tells her daughter in sending her a copy of this fable: 'here is a little fable that La Fontaine made on the adventure of M. de Bouffler's curé, who was instantaneously killed in the carriage beside the corpse.' In *Le Savetier et le Financier* we find echoes of the peaceful time of the *Pension poétique* when La Fontaine had noticed the anxieties of Fouquet. Friendship and affection are the *leit-motiv* of *Les Deux Amis – qu'un ami est une douce chose*. The same sentiment is expressed in that most musical idyll *Les Deux Pigeons* in which the lover cries *l'absence est le pire des maux*; and in the fables of his latter years he often returned to the theme of friendship, notably in the dedication to Mme de La Sablière of *Le Corbeau, la Gazelle, la Tortue et le Rat*.

After the second collection a later publication appeared, containing a single book – the twelfth – with twenty-four fables, ten of which had already been printed at different times. Five poems were added: *Daphnis et Alcimadure*, an imitation of Theocrites dedicated to Mme de La Mésangère, Mme de La Sablière's daughter, to whom La Fontaine referred in his letter to Bonrepaux; *Philemon et Baucis*, from Ovid's *Metamorphoses* which it follows fairly closely, and three other tales which were included in the *Contes*. These classical themes are treated with great art and characteristic simplicity, yet nothing lacks in their telling; irony, satire and humour, make them amusing reading for all ages.

The last fable in the collection: *Le Juge arbitre, l'Hospitalier et le Solitaire*, has been called La Fontaine's spiritual testament: here he returns to his sacred grove of solitude, that profound source of his genius, of which he had said in *Le Songe d'un Habitant du Mongol*,

> J'inspirerais ici l'amour de la retraite:
> Elle offre à ses amants des biens sans embarras,
> Biens purs, présents du Ciel, qui naissent sous les pas.
> Solitude où je trouve une douceur secrète,
> Lieux que j'aimai toujours, ne pourrai-je jamais,
> Loin du monde et du bruit goûter l'ombre et le frais?[42]

And now in his last fable his message is that each one can only know himself in solitude for:

> Apprendre à se connaître est le premier des soins . . .
> L'on ne le peut qu'aux lieux pleins de tranquillité . . .
> Cette leçon sera le fin de ces ouvrages:

Puisse-t-elle être utile aux siècles à venir!
Je la présente aux rois, je la propose aux sages:
Par où saurais-je mieux finir?[43]

Thus harmony is imposed on the diversity of his poetic genius, for in the end is not Choice the Mercury of Fate, and are not all the Gods the servants of Destiny?

TRANSLATIONS

[1]The Cicada, having sung her song / All summer long / Found herself all forlorn / When the north wind blew strong / not a crumb of worm or fly / Had she put by. / Now she went to complain / to the Ant neighbour / Begging her to do the favour / Of lending just a little grain / Until the spring should come again . . .

[2]Up to the present in a new language / I have made the wolf speak and the lamb reply, / Now I have gone further; the trees and the plants / Have become in my works talking creatures. / Who would not take this for an enchantement?

[3]I try to hold up vice to ridicule / . . . Sometimes I show in a story / Foolish vanity together with envy, / Two pivots on which our life turns today. / Such is this puny animal / Who wished to equal in size an ox. / Sometimes in a double image, I oppose / Vice to virtue, stupidity to good sense / Lambs to ravening wolves, / The fly to the ant / Making of this work / An ample comedy of a hundred different acts, / Of which the stage is the whole universe. / Men, gods and animals all play their parts; / Jupiter like another.

[4]In vain one praises Attic wit . . . that of Monsieur de La Fontaine is of a kind quite new, there is in it simplicity, surprise and jest of a character particular to him, which charms us in quite a different manner.

[5]Building up his verses through force of time.

[6]Sometimes no bread, and never any rest, / His wife, his children, soldiers and taxes / The creditor and forced labour, / Make of him the complete picture of misery.

[7]In every case they only look / For ways to exercise their tongue.

[8]I know no animal on earth / Worse than the school boy, except the dominie / As a neighbour the best of the two / Would not in the least please me.

[9]A swallow on her travels / Had learned a lot / Who ever sees a lot / May have remembered much. / This one, the slightest storm foreknew, / And warned the sailors 'er it blew . . .

[10]Look at that hand that travels through the air.

[11]Larks make their nests / In the corn when it is still green, / That is to say about the time / When all things in the world make love and breed . . . / The corn around was ripe before the nestlings / Were strong enough to fly / And take their flight towards the sky, / The anxious mother going in search of food/

Portrait of Madame de La Sablière, by Mignard (p. 124)

Portrait of Gassendi, engraved by Nanteuil (p. 126)

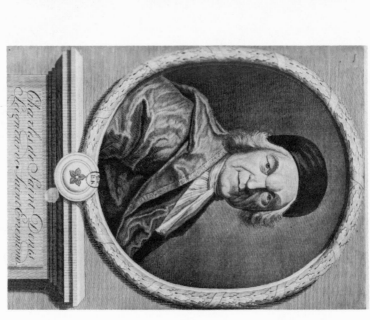

Portrait of Saint-Evremond, by Parmentier (p. 153)

Racine's House at La Ferté-Milon

The long ride from Bois-le-Vicomte (landscape by Watteau) (p. 161)

Portrait of the Grand Condé (Louis de Bourbon) (p. 171)

Château de Chantilly (p. 171)

First gave instructions to her brood, / To keep a careful watch . . ./ There is no hurry yet to change our home, / Tomorrow you must listen when they come / Be happy now, eat well and do not bother: All being well fed, all slept, the children and their mother.

¹²At the same time the baby birds / Tumbling and fluttering, / All stole away.

¹³Pigeons, with changing collars.

¹⁴Faithful and tender hearted.

¹⁵A rain-bow in a hundred shades of silk. / And which seems to our eyes / A jeweller's shop.

¹⁶Going I don't know where, on his long legs, / The heron one day, with his long beak hafted on his long neck / Skirted a river. / The water was clear as it is on the finest days; / My gossip the carp played about / With the pike her compeer.

¹⁷A hare in his form sat musing / (For in a lair what can one do but muse?) / In a profound gloom this hare was plunged: / This animal is sad and consumed with fear. / People of timorous nature / Are he thought, exceedingly unhappy; / They cannot profit from a thing they eat. / Never a pure pleasure, always different assaults. / That is my life: this cursed fear / Prevents me sleeping, except with open eyes / Control yourself, the sage will say. / But can fear be controlled? / I even think, in all sincerity / That men are afraid like me / . . . Thus reasoned our hare / And nevertheless was on the watch, / He was suspicious and anxious: / A breath, a shadow, a trifle, / Everything gave him fever.

¹⁸The course of sixty suns following one another / Has not seen you enjoy a moment of repose / Where ever you are, one sees at every turn / The inconstancy of a soul fickle in its amusements, / Anxious, and every where a passing guest . . .

¹⁹He is velvety like us, / Speckled, long tailed, with a humble bearing, / A modest look, and yet a shining eye; / I think he is much in sympathy / With these gentlemen the rats, / For he has ears of the same cut as ours . . .

²⁰He has an uncouth and piercing voice / On his head a bit of flesh, / A sort of arm that raised him in the air . . . He was beating his thighs with his arms / Making such a noise and such a din.

²¹And the donkey hurled himself / Through the fine grass, / Rolling scratching and rubbing, / Braying and grazing / And leaving many places bare . . .

²²Our master is our enemy / I tell you so in plain French.

²³As soon as goats have browsed their fill / A certain spirit of self-will / Makes them go to seek their fortune; / So they wander off to find / the wildest green and grassy slopes / least frequented by mankind. / Where there is no path nor track, / Some crag or cliff that falls in precipices, / To this those dames are led by their caprices / For nothing stops this climbing animal.

²⁴Long works always frighten me / Far from exhausting any matter / One should only take the flower.

²⁵He whose head was neighbour to the heavens, / And whose feet touched the empire of the dead.

²⁶The fable is a gift from the immortals / ... Truly it is a charm: that makes the mind attentive. / Or rather, holds it captive / Attaching us to stories / Which lead our hearts and spirits where they will.

²⁷A malady that spread terror, / A malady that Heaven in fury / Invented to punish the crimes of the Earth, / The plague (since one must call it by its name), / Capable of enriching in a day Acheron, / Made war on all the animals.

²⁸It is thus that my muse, beside a clear stream / Conveys in the language of the gods / All that is said beneath the skies / By so many beings borrowing the voice of Nature. / Interpreter of diverse peoples, / I make them serve as actors in my work, / For all things speak in the universe; / There nothing is that has not its own tongue. / More eloquent themselves than is my verse, / If those whom I address find me unfaithful, / I have at least shown the way / Others will be able to give the final touch ...

²⁹They say then, / That the beast is a machine / Devoid of choice, everything done on springs, / As in a wound-up watch. / Pace always equal, blind without a plan. / Open the watch look inside the case; / Many a wheel replaces all the world's spirit; / The first wheel moves the second one / a third then follows suit, and rings the hour.

³⁰Worthy of the greatest chiefs, worthy of a better fate. / They tear him to pieces after his death / That is all the supreme honour given to him.

³¹When the partridge / Sees its little ones / In danger, and being only newly fledged / Who cannot yet fly through the air from death, / She pretends to be wounded, and drags her wing along the ground, / Attracting on her steps the hunter and his hound. / Diverts the danger, and thus saves her family, / And then, when the hunter thinks that his dog has seized her, / she says goodbye to him, takes flight and laughs / at the man ashamed, who in vain follows her with his eyes.

³²I would give to animals / Not at all the power of reasoning such as we have / But all the same far more than a blind spring ... We would have a two-fold treasure; / One the Soul that is common to us all, / Wise men, mad men, children, idiots / Guests of the world under the name of animals; / The other yet another soul, between us and the angels / Common to all in some degree ...

³³Here lies the famous Badine / neither beautiful nor good but whose wits / Reduced to little bits / The system of the machine.

³⁴I consider them subject to all our passions, / on this point there is only a difference of degree between them and us, and in the manner of expressing ourselves.

[35]Jupiter has not formed all spirits / On the same model. There is the / Nature of cocks and that of partridges.

[36]It is of man alone that one must complain.

[37]Man is the symbol of ingratitude.

[38]Shepherds, shepherds, the wolf is wrong / Only when he is not the most strong. / Do you wish him to live like a hermit?

[39]Of the same quality.

[40]Everything discussed and well considered / The souls of mice and the souls of the fair / Are very different from each other. / One has always to come back to one's destiny, / That is to say to the law established by Heaven. / You may converse with the devil or employ magic, / You will never turn any being from its end.

[41]Death never surprises the wise man / He is always ready to depart. / For he has taught himself to know / The time when he must be resigned to go. / That time alas! comprises all times; / Whether we divide it in days, in hours, in minutes, / Each one of us the fatal tribute pays. / All are in death's domain. / And the first instant when the sons of Kings' / Open their eyes to the light, / Is that which sometimes brings upon their eyes for ever eternal night. / With grandeur you defend yourself in vain / Plead beauty, virtue, youth, it is all the same, / Death snatches all, without shame . . .

[42]I would like to inspire here love of retirement: / It offers to its votaries riches without encumbrance, / Pure benefits, gifts from Heaven that spring up beneath our feet. / Solitude where I find a secret happiness, / Scenes that I always loved, can I never far from the noisy world enjoy your cool shade.

[43]To learn to know oneself is the first task / . . . (Imposed on all mortals by the Supreme Majesty). Only in tranquillity may this be done. . . . This lesson will serve as conclusion to these works / May it be useful for centuries to come, / I present it to kings, I propose it to the wise: / Where could I find a better ending?

BIBLIOGRAPHY

Works by La Fontaine, published during his lifetime
(Arranged chronologically)

An important part of La Fontaine's work – and certainly the best known – consists of his *Fables* and his *Contes*, which appeared progressively throughout his life; some had been circulated before publication, and a few were printed separately which appeared later in collections.

1. *Fables*

1668   *Fables choisies*, mises en vers par M. de La Fontaine, chez Claude Barbin, 1 vol. in-4°; 2nd ed. 2 vols. 12°, Paris.

1671   *Fables nouvelles*, et autres poésies, chez Claude Barbin, 12°, Paris.

1678   *Fables choisies*, revues, corrigées et augmentées, chez Denys Thierry et Claude Barbin, 4 vols. 12°, Paris.

1685   *Ouvrages de prose et de poésie*, (vide supra), containing 12 unpublished fables.

1694   *Fables choisies*, chez Claude Barbin, 12°, Paris.

2. *Contes*

1665   *Contes et Nouvelles* en vers, première partie, chez Claude Barbin, 12°, Paris.

1666   *Contes et Nouvelles* en vers, deuxième partie, chez Claude Barbin, 12°, Paris.

1671   *Contes et Nouvelles* en vers, troisième partie, chez Claude Barbin, 12°, Paris.

1674   *Nouveaux Contes*, chez Gaspard Mignon, in-8°, Mons (quatrième partie).

3. *Works by La Fontaine other than Fables and Contes*

1654   *L'Eunuque*, comedy in verse, in five acts. (The work was not signed, and La Fontaine's name only appeared in the *Privilège*.)

1658   *Adonis*, Poem offered to Fouquet in 1654.

1659   *Le Songe de Vaux*.

1660   *Les Rieurs de Beau Richard*, Ballet.

1662   *Aux Nymphes de Vaux*.

1662   *Ode au roi* (in defence of Fouquet.)

1663   *Le Voyage en Limousin* (Letters to Mme. de La Fontaine.)

1667   *Poème du Quinquina*.

1669   *Les Amours de Psyche et de Cupidon*.

217

1671   The following poems were published in the collection *Fables nouvelles et autres poésies* (q.v.).
       Le Songe de Vaux (three fragments).
       A M. (Fouquet).
       Ode pour Madame.
       Ode pour la paix.
       Ballade pour la reine.
       Pour la reine (suite).
       Lettre à M.D.C.A.D.M.
       Pour Madame de Sévigné.
       A M. (Fouquet).
       A M. (Fouquet) *Je vous l'avoue, et c'est la vérité.*
       Sonnet pour Mlle. C.
       Madrigal, pour la même.
       Pour la même. Une Muse parle.
       Contre la même.
       Epitaphe d'un paresseux.
       Ballade à M. F (ouquet) pour le pont de Château-Thierry.
       Élégie pour M. F (ouquet).
       Ode au roi sur le même sujet.
       Pour Mlle. d'Alençon, sonnet.
       Pour Mlle. de Poussay, sonnet.
       Pour Mignon, chien de Madame douairière d'Orléans.
       A Mme. la Princesse de Bavière.
       Pour le cardinal de Bouillon.
       Élégie première, deuxième, troisième et quatrième.
       Adonis.
1672   *Daphné*, Opéra in three acts.
1673   *Poème de la Captivité de Saint Malc.*
1681   *Épitre* de Sénèque (Prose translation.)
1683   *Galatée.*
1685   *Ouvrages de prose et de poésie*, des sieurs de Maucroix et de La Fontaine, chez Claude Barbin, 2 vols. 12°, Paris. Vol. 1 by La Fontaine, Vol. 2 by Maucroix. Besides a number of ballades, madrigaux and dixains, some already published, vol. 1 included – A Mgr le Procureur général du Parlement (Achille Harlay). Discours à Madame de La Sablière.
1691   *Astrée*, a lyrical tragedy (founded on d'Urfé's *Astrée*)
1729   Published posthumously – *Le Siège des Augustins*, *Le Chemin de Velours*, *Stances sur le même.*

4. *Collections of the complete works* of La Fontaine, arranged chronologically.

1820–1821 Walckenaer, C. A., ed. *Oeuvres complètes* de La Fontaine, Didot,
           18 vols. in -18°, Paris, 1820–1827.
           Further editions in 1822–23 and 1827.

1872–1876 Moland, Louis, ed. *Oeuvres complètes* de La Fontaine, Garnier,
           7 vols. in-8° Paris.

1883–1893 Regnier, Henri, ed. *Oeuvres* de La Fontaine, Hachette, 11 vols.
           in-8°, Paris.

1932–1942 Pilon, Edmond; Groos and Schiffren, ed. *Fables, Contes, Nouvelles
           et Oeuvres diverses* de La Fontaine. N.R.F. (Bibliothèque de la
           Pléiade) 2 vols. in-16°, Paris.

Books concerning La Fontaine and his Friends and Translations

Académie française, *Dictionnaire* de l', Paris, 1694.

Annales de la Société historique et archéologique de Château-Thierry.

Bailly, Auguste, *La Fontaine*, Fayard, Paris, 1937.

Batterel, *Mémoires domestiques* pour servir à l'histoire de l'Oratoire (rédigés
   avant 1729), published by Ingold et Bonnarder, 3 vols. 8°, Paris, 1902–1905.

Boileau-Despréaux, Nicolas, *Oeuvres*, ed. G. Mongrédien (texte de l'édition
   Gidel, Paris 1870), Paris, 1952.

Bordeaux, Henry, *Marie Mancini*, Les Editions de Paris, 1946.

Brisson, Pierre, *Molière, sa vie et ses oeuvres*, Gallimard, Paris, 1942.

Chaulieu, abbé de, *Oeuvres* (d'après MSS de l'auteur), The Hague and Paris,
   1774.

Chéruel, *Mémoires sur la vie publique et privée de N. Fouquet, surintendant des
   finances*, 2 vols. 12°, Paris, 1862.

Collins, W. L. *La Fontaine and other French Fabulists*, London, 1882.

Deraine, *Mélanges historiques et littéraires*, 4 vols. 8°, Château-Thierry, 1914.

Furetière, Antoine, *Factums*, Amsterdam, 1694.

Giraudoux, Jean, *Les Cinq Tentations de La Fontaine*, Grasset, Paris, 1938.

Huet, Pierre-Daniel (Bp. of Soissons), *Memoirs* (in Latin), Amsterdam, 1718.

Lacroix, Paul, ed. *Oeuvres inédites de Jean de La Fontaine*, 8°, Hachette, Paris,
   1863.

Marsh, Edward, trans, *Forty Fables of La Fontaine*, and *More Fables of La Fontaine*,
   Heinemann, London, 1924 and 1925.

Maucroix, F. de, *Oeuvres posthumes* (incl. letters to Boileau and La Fontaine etc.),
   Paris, 1710.

Maucroix, François de, *Oeuvres diverses*, 2 vols. 12°, Rheims, 1852.

Mauriac, François, *Vie de Jean Racine*, Gallimard, Paris, 1928.

Menjot d'Elbenne, Vte, *Madame de La Sablière*, ses *Pensées chrétiennes* et ses
   Lettres à l'Abbé de Rancé, Plon, Paris, 1923.

Molière, *Oeuvres*, with notes and variants, ed. Alphonse Pauly, Alphonse Lemerre, 8 vols. Paris, s.d.

Moore, Marianne, *Translation of Twenty-four Fables of La Fontaine*, New York, 1954.

Mongrédien, Georges, *L'Affaire Foucquet*, Hachette, Paris, 1956.

Monmerqué, ed. *Six épitres de La Fontaine*, from the La Fontaine papers of Héricart de Thury, Paris, 1820.

Nivelet, ed. *Mythologia Æsopica*, Francfort, 1610.

Nothac, Pierre de, *La Création de Versailles*, fol. Paris, 1901.

Pellisson et d'Olivet, *Histoire de l'Académie française*, ed. Livet, 2 vols. 8°, Paris, 1858.

Perrault, Charles, *Les Hommes illustres du XVII siècle*, 2 vols. fol. Paris, 1696.

Perrault, Claude, *Voyage à Bordeaux*, Paris, 1696.

Racine, Jean, *Oeuvres complètes*, ed. Saint-Marc Girardin and Louis Moland, 8 vols. Paris, 1869–1877.

Racine, Louis, *Vie de Jean Racine*, Geneva, 1747 (see also Racine O. C.).

Regnier, ed. *Oeuvres de La Fontaine*, 11 vols. Paris, 1883–1893.

Risch, Léon, *Avec La Fontaine sur la route d'Orléans*, Paris, 1937.

Roche, L., *Vie de La Fontaine*, Roche, Paris, s.d.

Saint-Amand, *Oeuvres complètes*, ed. Livet, 2 vols. Paris, 1855.

Sainte-Beuve, *Causeries du Lundi*, 12 vols. Garnier, Paris, 1857. Boileau, vol. 6; Chapelle, vol. 11; Chaulieu, abbé de, vol. 1; Fénelon, vol. 10; La Fontaine, vol, 7; Maucroix, vol. 10; Patru, vol. 5; Perrault, vol. 5; Saint-Amand, vol. 12; Scudéry, Mlle de, vol. 4; Voiture, vol. 12.

Saint-Marc Girardin, *La Fontaine et les fabulistes*, Paris, 1885.

Scudéry, Madeleine de, *La Promenade de Versailles*, 8°, Paris, 1669.

Sévigné, Madame de, *Lettres*, ed. Gerard-Gailly, 3 vols. N.R.F. Bib. de la Pléiade, Gallimard, Paris, 1953–1957.

Taine, Hippolyte, *La Fontaine et ses Fables*, 20th ed. Hachette, Paris, 1914.

Tallement des Réaux, Gédéon, *Historiettes* (first published Paris, 1658) New edition, 2 vols. Garnier, Paris, 1834–35.

Walckenaer, *Histoire de la vie et des ouvrages de La Fontaine*, 6 vols. 8°, Paris, 1820, 1822–23, 1827 (first authentic Life and collected edition of La Fontaine).

Wright, E., *Translation of Fables of La Fontaine*, with notes by J. Gibbs, 8°, London, 1892.

INDEX